8th and Rogers
Columbia, MO. 65201
WITHDRAWN

THE PUBLICITY PROCESS
SECOND EDITION

SECOND EDITION   THE

EDITED BY

WITH CHAPTERS BY

1 9 7 5

PUBLICITY PROCESS

DAVID L. LENDT

    EDMUND G. BLINN
    DALE E. BOYD
    C. GENE BRATTON
    RICHARD L. DISNEY
    RODNEY FOX
    KARL H. FRIEDERICH
    CARL HAMILTON
    JOHN HUSEBY
    J. K. HVISTENDAHL
    ROBERT C. JOHNSON
    WILLIAM F. KUNERTH
    DAVID L. LENDT
    M. SUSAN MENNE
    JEROME L. NELSON
    JAMES W. SCHWARTZ
    JACK D. SHELLEY
    LORRAINE WECHSLER

The Iowa State University Press / Ames, Iowa

© 1975, The Iowa State University Press
Ames, Iowa 50010. All rights reserved

Composed and printed by
The Iowa State University Press

First edition, 1966 through five printings

Second edition, 1975

Library of Congress Cataloging in Publication Data
Main entry under title:

The Publicity process.

    First ed. edited by James W. Schwartz.
    Includes bibliographies and index.
    1. Publicity.   I. Lendt, David L.   II. Schwartz,
    James W., ed. The publicity process.
HM263.S38   1975   659.2   75-22293
ISBN 0-8138-1315-8

CONTE

Preface vii

PART 1: THE PUBLICIST AND THE PRESS

1. Publicity and public relations.......................... 3
   David L. Lendt

2. The public relations process 7
   Karl H. Friederich

3. What is news and who decides? 15
   Jerome L. Nelson

4. You should be the expert.............................. 27
   Dale E. Boyd

5. You need to know two news story forms................ 33
   Carl Hamilton

6. Make the most of columns and newsletters 49
   J. K. Hvistendahl

7. Photos and art can help tell your story................. 61
   Robert C. Johnson and John Huseby

8. Advertising: publicity you pay for 85
   C. Gene Bratton

PART 2: SIZING UP THE MASS MEDIA

9. Newspapers: the heavy local coverage medium 105
   William F. Kunerth

10. Magazines: something for everyone.................... 113
    Richard L. Disney

11. **Radio and television: the pervasive media** 121
    Jack D. Shelley

12. **The wire services and syndicates** 133
    Lorraine Wechsler

PART 3: THE CONSUMER AND THE PRESS

13. **Journalism's revolutionary past, present, and future** 141
    Rodney T. Fox

14. **The press and society** 149
    Edmund G. Blinn

15. **Press responsibilities: accuracy and fairness** 159
    James W. Schwartz

16. **Advertising: it helps and it hurts** 171
    M. Susan Menne

    Appendix 181

    Index 185

PREFACE

The Publicity Process, first published in 1966 and edited by James W. Schwartz, Professor and Head of the Department of Journalism and Mass Communication at Iowa State University, has been a popular text and widely adopted. It went through five printings, the most recent in 1973.

In the nearly 10 years since The Publicity Process made its debut, however, nothing has stood still. It is the purpose of this second edition to retain the best of its predecessor, to update it, and to expand it where necessary.

The earlier edition was created through the combined efforts of nine persons, all of whom were then, or had recently been, members of Iowa State's Department of Technical Journalism. The new model reflects some of the changes that have occurred in the department since 1966. Not only has the department's name been changed to better describe its expanded functions, but nine writers not represented in the earlier book have joined seven of its veterans to produce this successor.

Thus, in most respects, the book is a new one. While it clings to the general concepts of the earlier work, it ventures into areas of interest that had not become urgent in 1966. Surging consumerism is an obvious example.

Public uncertainty over the performance of the press, particularly with respect to its coverage of the Vietnam War, the Pentagon Papers case, and the uncovering of the White House conspiracy to subvert the U.S. Constitution, put the press squarely in the limelight where consumers could scarcely avoid evaluating the product they were getting. Although subjected to withering attacks by a later discredited vice-president and other spokesmen of a later discredited administration, the mass media have played an undeniable and carefully designed role in the governance of the nation and, thus, in the lives of its citizens. Understandably, those citizens have taken an increasingly keen and critical view of their newspapers and magazines and of their television and radio newscasts.

This handbook has been subdivided into three general "packages" of information that necessarily overlap on occasion.

Part 1, "The Publicist and the Press," is largely a practical approach to the creation of publicity: how to get it written, how to get it printed, how to get it aired, how to do the most efficient job of helping reporters and editors do their work. It represents a glance at publicity from the inside—from the viewpoint of the publicist.

Part 2, "Sizing Up the Mass Media," includes four chapters of approximately equal interest and value to the would-be publicist and to the consumer of news and information. It is a look at mass media strengths and disadvantages and at the workings of news operations from both the inside and the outside—from the perspective of both the publicist and the consumer.

Part 3, "The Consumer and the Press," treats the traditions of the free press, the moral and legal problems and responsibilities of the mass media, the role of the press as an institution in society, and the lively art of consumer advertising. The philosophical underpinnings of a free press are discussed in the conviction that constructive criticism must be founded on understanding, that the press needs criticism, and that the press receives much criticism that is without value.

The appearance of **The Publicity Process** coincides with several trends apparent in the communications media of the United States. A Roper Organization Report, "What People Think of Television and Other Mass Media," as early as 1973, was prefaced with a statement that spotlighted an important development:

> Just as Roper's interviewers were completing their work for this survey, the last issue of **Life** magazine was published, leaving no national weekly or bi-weekly general-interest magazine. Instead there are the specialty publications; paradoxically, the largest of them, **TV Guide**, owes its existence to the widespread interest in another medium.

Technological innovation, so long the virtually exclusive domain of the transistorized radio and television industry, seems again to have gripped the printers of the nation. More than a decade ago, in a technological flurry, newspapers and magazines were flocking from letterpress to offset reproduction methods. Now, another wave of innovation which is bringing the computer to the news desk, is causing new excitement among the print media.

Educational television, that publicly funded, noncommercial, great bright hope of a decade ago, appears to walk a political tightrope. Governmental controls have threatened its programming autonomy and governmental criticism has been blamed for greater local emphasis on children's shows and less on controversial public affairs programs.

Cable television, gestating 10 years ago and largely relegated to the hinterland of television's fringe reception areas, has made significant inroads into urban centers with promises of free access (for virtually anyone wishing to telecast virtually anything), programming variety, and interference-free reception. Some observers view it as the harbinger of pay television and the end of television as it has existed since its popularity boom in the United States following World War II.

The Publicity Process has been written with these and other significant trends in mind. It has been compiled from a futuristic point of view, with the hope that its specificity will be helpful to persons interested in learning how to make the most of mass media opportunities. Its generality will be equally helpful to persons interested in why the nation's information system is shaped and fueled as it is.

It is a textbook appropriate for college and university students preparing for careers in which they can expect to deal with representatives of the mass media—the retailers of information. It is an equally appropriate text for students eager to know more about the nation's mass information systems in order to be better informed consumers and, therefore, more effective mass media critics.

Its value is not limited to the classroom. **The Publicity Process** has been compiled to serve also as a helpful and timely handbook for the inexperienced person suddenly appointed to take charge of publicity for the church, Red Cross, Anti-Defamation League, Republican Central Committee, YMCA,

PREFACE

or metropolitan Planned Parenthood organization.

It is a helpful primer for anyone who would like to know more about how the nation's mass media operate: how news decisions are made, how information is distributed, how print and electronic media differ and how they are alike, and how ordinary citizens can obtain access to media services.

It is a distillation of many years of experience on the part of the book authors, all of whom have had practical media experience, whether in newspapers, magazines, radio, television, public relations, advertising, or various career combinations. Newsroom jargon, however, has been avoided and footnotes have been used very sparingly. Instead, suggested readings are provided following each chapter for the benefit of those whose thirst outruns the capacity of this volume.

Thanks are due, of course, to the writers whose craftsmanship and cooperation made this book possible. Sincere thanks are in order for two contributors, Karl Friederich and Ed Blinn, who have coordinated Iowa State's publicity methods course and who were instrumental in setting the boundaries for the new edition. Carl Hamilton and Jim Schwartz, who had been through this effort before me, deserve special recognition for their guidance, aid, and comfort.

DAVID L. LENDT

The publicist

1

and the press

The lowly press release is part of the way things are done in a society that values self-government, and when the press release contains news and when it is accurate, it is a lowly thing no longer. Then it is the professional product of professional minds and hands. It is respected on the news desk, it is helpful to the public, and for these reasons it is far more likely to succeed in doing what the publicist hopes it will do.

"BEHIND THE SCENES IN AMERICAN BUSINESS"
— by Reynolds Knight

NEW YORK -- Kid stuff is big business -- a multi-billion-dollar market -- as industry has long known. One of the least-noticed but commercially important aspects of this market is the production of party goods.

Flora Hears, consultant on children's parties to Hallmark Cards in Kansas City, reports that Halloween -- Oct. 31 -- is second only to Christmas as an occasion for children's parties. She tells parents that successful Halloween parties need these ingredients: Dim lighting, everyone in costume, plenty of spooky decorations and a program of games like apple bobbing, treasure hunts and the old-fashioned "pin the blind man's buff -- and a new old one from Hallmark this year called "Pin the Tail on the Devil".

Miss Hears also recommends playing appropriate mood music on a phonograph and providing plenty of kid-oriented goodies: candies, soda and cookies (her firm makes low-cost plastic cookie cutters in the shape of an owl, witch and pumpkin.)

To save clean-up chores afterwards, party expert Hears suggests using paper plates, cups and decorations with a Halloween motif.

Bits O' Business

This year, for the first time, female chemistry and chemical engineering college graduates received higher starting salaries than their male counterparts. "Chemical & Engineering News," the magazine that conducted the survey, didn't report actual salaries but it did say the gals' median starting salary was 5 per cent
...more

1
Publicity and public relations

DAVID L. LENDT

This book is about publicity.

Thus, the first thing to do is explain what we are talking about—what publicity is and, just as important, what it isn't. We might also discuss the role of publicity throughout society; in government, business, education, and charity. Publicity is everywhere. It is important. Modern society could not function well without it.

Let's begin by emphasizing one of the things that publicity is not. It is not public relations, even though many persons improperly use the terms interchangeably. Publicity may be a part of public relations, but it is not and cannot constitute public relations all by itself.

Public relations is everything a government agency, a corporation, a downtown store, or even an individual does to present what is hoped will be an acceptable public image. Public relations may be affected by telephone etiquette or the impression left by a printed letterhead; by the way a person dresses or the kinds of cars the executives drive.

DAVID LENDT is Assistant to the Vice-President for Information and Development and Assistant Professor of Journalism and Mass Communication, Iowa State University. He has edited several weekly newspapers and trade journals and is the author of **Demise of the Democracy: The Copperhead Press in Iowa**.

Virtually every facet of society—every unit of government (whether city, county, state, or national), every store and service establishment, every church and civic organization, every university—is doing something deliberately to create or enhance a certain public image.

The sum of all these deliberate activities is something we call public relations.

Businesses and institutions do a variety of things in public relations because each institution is looked at by many different persons who make up many different groups called publics. (See Chapter 2 for a more detailed discussion of publics.)

Among the many tools used in public relations, one of the most important, and the one with which this book is concerned, is publicity.

What, then, is publicity?

In its simplest terms, publicity is a "news story" or a "publicity release" prepared with the intent and expectation that it will be used by a newspaper, magazine, radio station, or television station.

As such, publicity has a part in the complex system of democratic government provided for in the Constitution of the United States. The framers of the Constitution recognized that the need for a free flow of information in a democratic body politic was as great as a free flow of blood in the human body. When blood ceases to flow freely throughout the entire body, its functions are impaired. A part of society cut off from the full information necessary to make wise decisions will malfunction. It will make unwise decisions. Democracy will be in trouble.

Thus, in the first Article of the Constitution (the framers thought it was that important) are the words: "Congress shall make no law respecting an establishment of religion, or prohibiting the free exercise thereof; or abridging the freedom of speech, or of the press, or of the right of people peaceably to assemble, and to petition the Government for a redress of grievances." (See Chapters 14 and 15 for more detail.)

Unfortunately, things haven't always worked as smoothly as the founding fathers had hoped, although their good sense is still the foundation on which all our efforts and freedoms rest. Ideas, however, do not flow as freely through our democratic system as we would like. Some persons are better publicists than others. (One aim of this book, after all, is to make you a better publicist.) Some groups and organizations and individuals have more talent and more resources and do a better job of publicizing their accomplishments or ideas than others.

Our media, through which must flow the life-sustaining factual ingredients of democracy, do not function perfectly. They represent another facet of free enterprise, but they deal in ideas and information rather than in stockings, stereos, or steers.

When publicity is not flowing freely so that all sides of all questions are openly aired and debated, citizens grow alarmed. Well they might, for the first thing a dictator does is throttle the mass media and bring about an imbalance of information in favor of the dictator's point of view.

So, the subject of this book is extremely important. Ideally, training in publicity will help you to do the best possible job of presenting ideas and causes in a professional fashion and in the best tradition of an open, democratic exchange of information and opinion. It should also help you to communicate more effectively, to read and listen more critically, to understand the media more fully, and, thus, to operate more effectively in the whole democratic process.

Having said those things, the importance of which cannot be overstressed, we return to our original statement that publicity is a press release or news story or publicity release (the names are interchangeable) written with the intent that it will be printed or broadcast in some manner.

THE LOWLY PRESS RELEASE

Because press releases are inexpensive and because they do not require a huge staff to produce them and send them out to the mass media outlets, it should not be surprising to find that press releases are being circulated by thousands of foundations, corporations, public service organizations, politicians, government agencies, and softball teams. Everyone, it seems, is in the press release act. When a publicist sends his or her prize release to the local newspaper, it will probably be delivered to an "In" box already cluttered with scores of other press releases from local sources as varied as the Heart Fund, the League of Women Voters, and the County Republican Central Committee. Those releases may be joined with others from such far-flung sources as the American Soybean Association, United Airlines, General Foods, and the Presbyterian Church in the U.S.A. Each press release is one of many competing for valuable time or space.

The job of a press release is to provide information through a medium to its listening or reading audience. A professionally written press release will do precisely that and nothing more. It will provide only information of substance and interest to the media and will not waste the time of editors with insignificant tidbits of interest only to the author of the press release and perhaps the author's mother.

The persons who act as "gatekeepers" for the mass media—editors of newspapers and magazines and the news directors of radio and television stations who have to make decisions concerning what will be used, what will be altered, and what will be thrown out—are generally well-trained individuals who pride themselves on recognizing news when they see it. As a group, they object to being "used" by press release writers with axes to grind and no news to add to the hopper. (For a detailed discussion of the role of the gatekeeper and how the gatekeeper defines news, see Chapter 3.)

If a press release isn't news to the editors, it won't get their time or attention—except for the time and attention required to pitch the release into the nearest wastebasket.

The newsroom gatekeepers are like the rest of us in at least one respect: they appreciate it when someone is willing to help them do their job well. If information in a release has some news value, if it is accurately and grammatically written, and if the release avoids adjectives that try too hard to sell a point of view, it will stand head and shoulders above most press releases received in most newsrooms. Unfortunately, there are flacks and hacks and otherwise unprincipled persons in the press release business just as there are professionals who take pride in their literacy, accuracy, and objectivity.

Thus, two inviolable rules apply to the writing of a professional press release:

1. It must be news.
2. It must be right.

The information contained in a press release must be scrupulously accurate. An editor may find that a release is newsworthy and may use it on that basis. If, however, the release is inaccurate, the editor is made to look incompetent, his or her paper or broadcast is made to look unprofessional, and, worst of all, the public is misled.

Professional publicists take their responsibility to the public at large just as seriously as professional editors do. With the freedom accorded the press go several responsibilities, one of which is an uncompromising respect for the truth, insofar as the truth can be determined. A publicist who has been careless with the truth in a press release used by a trusting editor will likely get a cold response the next time around. The publicist will have made the editor understandably gun-shy. Editors try to be objective, but an experience like that can bring on a cold sweat every time that publicist's letterhead hits the editor's desk.

Most editors are busy. They live with continual deadlines and their work is made available for public scrutiny day in and day out. The professional publicist, in attempting to gain exposure for certain events or for certain data, attempts to help the editor meet those demanding deadlines.

Most editors are responsible. If there is any question concerning the information in a press release, they will check it out with someone in a position to know the facts. However, most editors are also human beings who, in the rush of doing their jobs, must occasionally rely upon the responsibility and intellectual honesty of other persons, including the publicists who provide unsolicited information to their publications or stations.

If, for whatever reason, a publicist is responsible for submitting a press release that is inaccurate, he or she may be in deep difficulty not only with editors but with other publicists and with the public.

An immediate attempt should be made to correct the error, with a phone call, if necessary, to every recipient of the release. If it is too late for that, the publicist should provide a "correction" notice to each recipient apologizing for the error in fact and including corrected information, for whatever use the editors may wish to make of it.

Factual accuracy is the most important part of making a press release "right," but there is more to it than that. Most editors have a high regard for language. For that reason, and others, press releases should reflect mechanical and grammatical accuracy.

In most advertising, public relations, and publicity offices, drafts of written materials are regularly circulated among several persons. The writers generally seek advice concerning expression or emphasis, rather than corrections of spelling or grammar, but even the professionals make occasional errors. It is a good idea to run press release copy by at least one other person before submitting it for possible publication.

So, the "lowly" press release is an important part of the way things are done in a society that values self-government. It is the simplest way for organizations and individuals with widely divergent interests, goals, and ideas to gain access to the marketplace of ideas on a massive (mass media) scale. If the press release is to accomplish what it is written to accomplish, it must be valuable as news and it must be precise and accurate.

When the press release is news and when it is correct, it is regarded not as a lowly thing but as the professional product of professional minds and hands. It is respected on the news desk, it is helpful to the public, and for these reasons it is far more likely to succeed in doing what the publicist hopes it will do.

SUGGESTED READING

Doig, Ivan, and Doig, Carol. **News: A Consumer's Guide.** Englewood Cliffs, N.J.: Prentice-Hall, 1972.

Emery, Michael C., and Smythe, Ted Curtis, eds. **Readings in Mass Communication: Concepts and Issues in the Mass Media,** 2nd ed. Dubuque: Wm. C. Brown Co., 1974.

Hiebert, Ray Eldon, Ungurait, Donald F., and Bohn, Thomas W. **Mass Media: An Introduction to Modern Communication.** New York: David McKay Co., 1974.

Hohenberg, John. **Free Press, Free People: The Best Cause.** New York: Free Press, 1973.

Rutland, Robert A. **The Newsmongers: Journalism in the Life of the Nation, 1690-1972.** New York: Dial Press, 1973.

2
The public relations process

KARL H. FRIEDERICH

No matter who we are or what we do, from the time we first realize that others appraise us and our performance, we practice some form of public relations. We are less concerned at this point, however, with personal public relations than with public relations efforts in behalf of the institutions—business, industry, schools, government, nonprofit organizations—that are part of our social, political, and economic fabric.

MANAGEMENT'S ROLE IN PUBLIC RELATIONS

For a public relations practitioner to use the professional skills necessary to communicate truth effectively to concerned publics, there must be full recognition by management of the function and philosophy of public relations. Far too many managements still make decisions which may affect many publics without consulting available public relations experts. Company executives, heads of governmental agencies, even presidents of the United States have been obliged to alter plans announced without full consideration of the public's reactions. As a general rule, management does not have the public relations skills necessary to identify relevant publics and communicate with them. Consequently, much vital information about the human factors involved is often missing from management decisions. Modern management and public relations philosophy call for public relations professionals to be part of the

KARL FRIEDERICH is Associate Professor of Journalism and Mass Communication, Iowa State University, a former Fulbright Lecturer, and former editor of newspapers in Nebraska, California, and South Dakota.

management team so that such factors can be taken into account before decisions are made final and binding. Otherwise, the role of the public relations practitioner is turned into that of a publicity hack who grinds out news releases, peddles them to various news media, arranges for open houses, and engages in other such peripheral activities. The public relations practitioner then becomes a member of the "boast and bucket brigade." The boasting consists of extolling the virtues of the institution. On the bucket brigade side, a practitioner spends much time putting out brush fires in the form of community unrest or misunderstanding because management acted, without the advice of public relations counsel.

Rather than having to spend so much time on such remedial public relations, a publicist can contribute much more if he or she can function in a preventive role. This can happen only with management's proper recognition that a public relations philosophy must permeate an entire organization, from the top executive to the most recent recruit.

No institution can long exist in the present-day climate of public interest and opinion unless its performance squares with the realities perceived by the public. This fundamental principle can be expressed in a simple formula:

X (Deed or Performance)
+ Y (Interpretation of Deed or
   Performance) =
Public Attitudes

Implicit in this formula is the fact that we are often more influenced by the way we interpret an event than by the event itself. Thus, depending on our orientation, we can interpret a general price increase by a manufacturer either as a move to take advantage of the consumer or as a necessary step to provide adequate capital for the development of additional goods and services.

THE PUBLIC RELATIONS PROCESS MODEL

The four phases of the Public Relations Process Model are:

I. **Fact-Finding and Research**—Analysis of the priority audiences or publics of an institution and an understanding of their attitudes and degrees of their understanding and support.

II. **Policy Establishment and Program Planning**—Planning a two-way communication program with the priority publics in order to deal effectively with what is important to them and the institution, rather than dealing only with what is urgent.

III. **Communication**—The listening and telling of the institution's story in terms compatible with the mix of the publics.

IV. **Evaluation**—Evaluating and assessing the effectivenss of all public relations activities of the institution.

Phase I, Fact-Finding and Research

As part of Phase I, we are concerned with carrying out an inventory of our own organization. Such an inventory should take into account manpower deployment, physical assets, past and present performance, and the kinds of programs and activities our institution has engaged in over time. We should examine those that have been successful and those that have failed, and attempt to isolate the reasons for each.

Our fact-finding activities also lead us to define the constituent groups, or publics, with which our institution has to deal. For example, let us use a public school system to illustrate the variety of

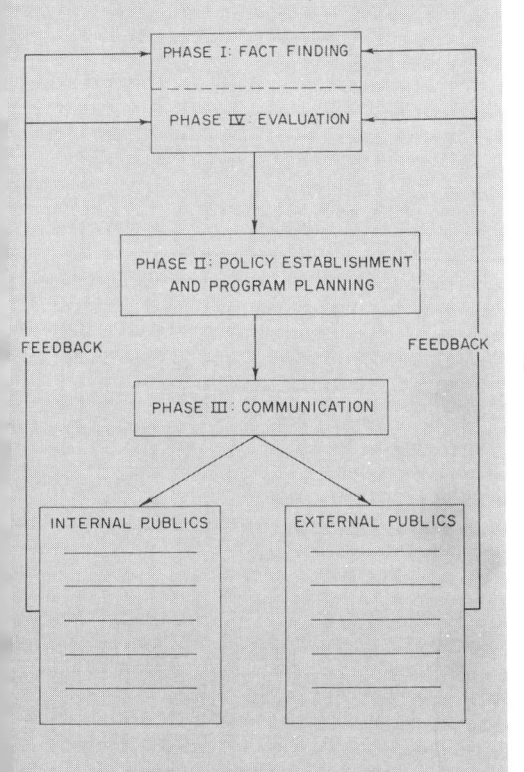

FIG. 2.1. The public relations process.

publics a public relations practitioner might have to deal with.

The internal publics are those groups of individuals who reside or work within the institutional structure, or who are directly associated with the institution. External publics are those groups of individuals who are outside the institution but who have direct relationships with it.

For our school system illustration, the following are considered internal publics:

Students
Administrators
Members of the board of education
Teachers
Counselors
Teacher associates and other paraprofessionals
Student teachers
Student and adult volunteers
Secretaries and clerks
Grounds and custodial staffs
Other plant and transportation employees
Food service employees
School nurses

The following groups are part of the school system's external publics:

Parents of children in the school system
Parents of children not attending public schools
Senior citizens
Other childless citizens
Athletic boosters
Churches
Civic groups
City, county, and state government officials
State and national legislators
Professional groups within the community
Business executives within the community
Labor unions
Suppliers and distributors of school-purchased services and goods
School officials and board members in other communities
PTA or other parental organizations
Social and civic agencies
Chamber of commerce
Patriotic groups
School visitors
Taxpayer groups
Local and regional mass media

The task of defining the school system's publics, their composition, and their attitudes goes beyond this simple classification scheme. We must be aware that members of a given public are constantly shifting and that any one person may be a "member" of several publics at the same time. The public relations practitioner must communicate with a passing parade, not a standing army.

The methods used to determine attitudes within various publics necessarily vary from informal to sophisticated. One of the oldest informal methods is the practice of listening. This can be accomplished by keeping track of personal or telephone contacts, for example. However, reliance should not be placed solely on unsolicited contacts; some attempts should be made to initiate contacts and to use persons as sounding boards. A formal version of this method is the advisory committee or panel. Periodic analysis of an organization's incoming mail can also provide valuable information.

If the organization has field representatives, soliciting and evaluating their opinions about pending or past programs can provide valuable insights into the perceptions persons have about the organization.

Monitoring the output of the mass media can also indicate what others are saying—or whether others are saying much of anything—about the organization. Press clippings and radio-television monitor reports are available from commercial outlets.

Conferences with those involved in a particular situation can reveal attitudes in an informal manner. Careful analysis of opinion polls can further assist in gaining insights into public opinion on a broader level. Similarly, opinion polls carried out in other communities for similar organizations can alert the public relations practitioner to trends and possible problem areas.

The speeches and writings of recognized opinion leaders in the community and region can reveal concerns and problems with which an organization may have to deal.

These informal methods can be helpful to a public relations practitioner engaging in fact-finding for an organization, but all such informal methods lack the representativeness and objectivity necessary for sound attitude and opinion research.

The formal methods that can be used to tap public attitudes and opinions are cross-section surveys, survey panels, depth interviews, content analyses, and mail questionnaires. Ideally, a public relations practitioner should be able to sit down with members of relevant publics and discuss, face-to-face, their views on particular problems and issues. This approach could work with some publics, such as employees; for others, however, it is impractical.

For this reason, the public relations practitioner may use scientifically designed sample surveys, administered in person or by telephone, of representative groups in each of the publics relevant to the institution's program. (For a related discussion, see Chapter 4.)

The idea behind using survey panels as a method of tapping attitudes and opinions is to find out what happens to the randomly chosen panel members under varying conditions and the passage of time.

Whereas the well-administered cross-section survey will yield good quantitative information, the depth interview offers opportunities for probing the attitudes that underlie expressed opinions.

Analyzing the content of the mass media can tell an organization what is being said about it, whether critical or laudatory. Such information can be codified and, thereby, quantified for various purposes.

Finally, the public relations practitioner who has to operate with a limited research budget can use the mail questionnaire to survey attitudes among relevant publics. The major drawback of this method is the often low rate of return of completed questionnaires. This destroys, or at least impairs, the representative quality of the original sample. The questionnaire generally yields adequate information when administered to largely homogeneous groups whose divergences of opinion are dramatic.

Phase II, Policy Establishment and Program Planning

Assuming that we have taken a close look at the internal setup of our organization and have identified and analyzed the various internal and external publics, we are then ready to move to Phase II of the public relations process—that of establishing policy and planning a program of action.

A public relations program, if it is to succeed, must be based on sound policy and executed by capable personnel. Policy decisions must originate with, or be endorsed by, top management. Policy is often a nebulous or loosely formulated code of action; and there is little point in activating a public relations program for an organization lacking direction.

Returning to the example of the school district, let us assume that the district has the following goals, objectives, and areas of interest:

1. Establishing good rapport with teachers and other school employees, particularly in the area of salary negotiations.
2. Getting voter support for local bond elections for new buildings or operating funds.
3. Establishing or maintaining a favorable image of the schools in the community (through a favorable image of teachers, administrators, and school board members).
4. Maintaining and improving relations with adult and student interest groups.

Our planning must take two general directions. We need to develop long-range programs to achieve the objectives and we need to incorporate short-term plans for specific projects.

In all these activities, the role of the public relations practitioner undergoes a change as the process moves from the fact-finding to the planning-and-programming phase. In Phase I, the practitioner serves generally as an analyst; in Phase II, the practitioner becomes an initiator and adviser. As the program moves toward the action stage, the practitioner becomes an advocate. All these have been traditional roles. The modern public opinion climate suggests another role—that of moderator. Throughout all phases of the public relations process, the practitioner must act as a moderator and arbitrator, bringing together the various publics whose members may hold strong, but divergent, points of view.

This is yet another argument in favor of making the practitioner a party to policy decisions. Otherwise, he or she becomes a glorified errand runner cranking out reams of publicity material, speeches, or annual reports; preparing films or tapes; or putting together educational materials or exhibitions. These are all worthwhile activities, of course, but not when carried on in the vacuum created by excluding the public relations expert from policy planning and decision making.

Phase III, Communication

The word "communication" has its roots in Latin, where it means "common." Our objective in communicating with various publics is to establish commonality between the institution and those for whom we intend our message. The process of communication is perhaps more easily understood if we examine it in incremental steps by referring to David K. Berlo's model in Figure 2.2.

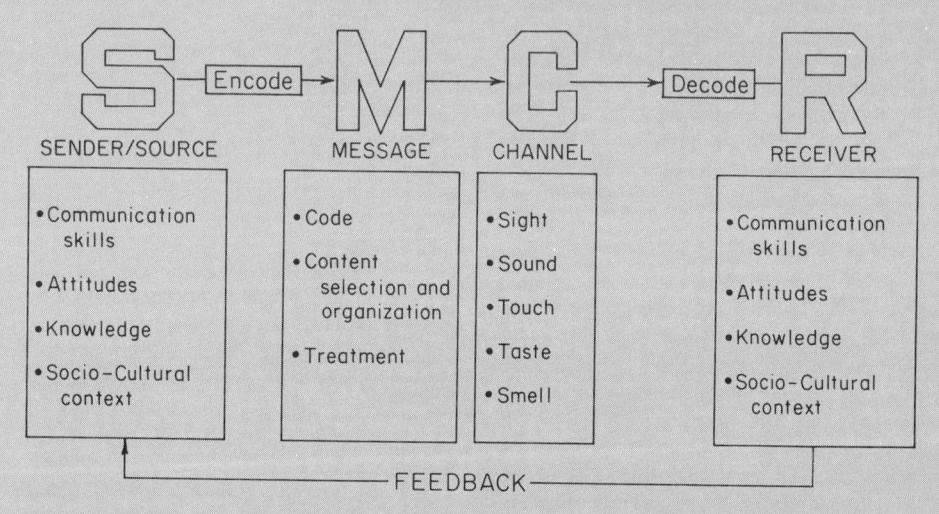

FIG. 2.2. Berlo's S-M-C-R Model.

In referring to communication as a process, we simply mean that it is an ongoing activity or event. As we interact with others, we are communicating. Communication thus becomes the process through which we try to transmit our messages—thoughts, ideas, emotions—to other human beings. The major goal of our communicative efforts is to have the person(s) for whom the message is intended accept the message and behave accordingly.

The illustration shows that within the communication process, we encounter the following elements: Source (or Sender), Message, Channel, Receiver, and Feedback.

All communication must come from somewhere: a **source** or **sender**. The source might be one person, a group of persons, a corporation, a government agency, or any other institution. Several factors determine how a source will operate in the communication process. One is the source's communication skills both for sending and receiving. We also have to consider the source's attitudes about self, about the subject matter of the message, and about the various publics at whom the message may be directed. How a source will operate is also affected by the source's knowledge of the subject and of the publics. (Analysis of the relevant publics, emphasized in the fact-finding phase, can pay dividends here.)

In the Berlo model, the **message** is what the public relations practitioner attempts to transmit to his or her publics. The process of putting the message together is called encoding. Several factors are involved in encoding, including the selection of a code; the message must be written or spoken in some language (set of symbols, such as English). For some kinds of communication, we have to think of code in terms of photography, film, or music; even gestures are possible codes. We need to consider the level of difficulty of the code for various publics. If we are trying to communicate some scientific achievement to publics consisting of scientists and elementary school children, we obviously have to take into account the differences in intellect and education of the two publics.

Once the message has been encoded, it has to be committed to a **channel** for transmission. We can consider channels in several ways. Perhaps the simplest is to utilize the five senses to receive the message. Viewed in this manner, the channels of communication are ways of presenting a message so that it can be seen, heard, touched, smelled, or tasted. In a more practical sense, channels include: Public speech, discussion, and interviews; radio and recording; television and motion pictures; demonstrations and on-the-job training; and newspapers, magazines, and books.

The fourth element in the communication process is the **receiver**—the person or persons on the end of the communication process opposite the source. The factors operating on the source (communication skills, attitudes, knowledge) also operate on the receiver, whose function is decoding the message.

As a sender (source) of messages, the public relations practitioner is interested in determining the effectiveness of his or her message via **feedback**. It is easier to obtain feedback to a message when the communication process takes place in a face-to-face conversation. When the practitioner uses the mass media, however, feedback is not only delayed, but it is usually incomplete. It often must be actively sought.

Some Implications for Success In Communication. The S-M-C-R Model provides us with a good framework within which to consider some of the factors that determine the success or failure of communication. After all, the public relations practitioner often communicates on behalf of client or employer with the intent of bringing about change in the receiver.

Most individuals have had experiences with toy gyroscopes. You spin the wheel within its frame and the gadget seems to take on a life of its own. While the gyroscope is not impervious to outside forces, it is resistive to them. It has its own internal arrangement of energies in equilibrium. There seems to be an aura of magic attached to it when we consider its partial independence from such a basic force as gravity. The operating gyroscope represents a dynamic system in equilibrium.

If we would think of individuals in our various publics as gyroscopic organisms, perhaps we would do a more realistic and effective job of communicating. The gyroscopic "organisms" spin along; absorbing and consuming; resisting and casting off things in an impersonal, self-serving, and preoccupied process that selects from the environment those things that preserve and sustain internal equilibrium.

Why the analogy of human beings with dynamic mechanical gadgets? Because an institutional public relations strategy should assume that individuals are actively preoccupied with their own concerns; that they are, in fact, actively resistant to becoming involved in the concerns of the institution; and that many view institutions, whether large or small, as impersonal, vague, peripheral aspects in their lives.

A public relations message must often penetrate a field of resistance characterized by massive disinterest. The persuasiveness of a public relations message generally must rely exclusively on its appeal to the receiver's self interest.

No message is received in its pure form. Receivers may magnify it, modify it, alter it, misinterpret it, or even ignore it altogether.

Phase IV, Evaluation

The final phase is nothing more than a continuous application of the fact-finding phase. Through evaluation we must ascertain whether we have reached our objectives, as delineated in Phase II.

SUMMARY

Publicity is, thus, one part of the communication phase, which is one part of a four-step public relations process. Professional public relations requires high standards of ethical behavior and consistent efforts to maintain a flow of communication, to adjust messages according to receiver feedback, and to keep in touch with institutional publics.

SUGGESTED READING

Baumel, C. Phillip, Hobbs, Daryl J., and Powers, Ronald C. **The Community Survey: Its Use in Development and Action Programs.** Ames: Coop. Ext. Serv., Iowa State Univ., 1964.

Berelson, Bernard, and Steiner, Gary A. **Human Behavior.** New York: Harcourt, Brace & World, 1964.

Berlo, David K. **The Process of Communication: An Introduction to Theory and Practice.** New York: Holt, Rinehart & Winston, 1960.

Brehm, Jack W., and Cohen, Arthur R. **Explorations in Cognitive Dissonance.** New York: Wiley, 1962.

Crutchfield, Richard S., and Krech, David. **Theory and Problems of Social Psychology.** New York: McGraw-Hill, 1948.

Festinger, Leon. "The Theory of Cognitive Dissonance," in Wilbur Schramm, ed. **The Science of Human Communication.** New York: Basic Books, 1963.

Katz, Daniel. "The Functional Approach to the Study of Attitudes." **Public Opinion Quarterly,** 24 (1960): 170.

Klapper, Joseph T. **The Effects of Mass Communication.** Glencoe, Ill.: Free Press, 1960.

Rokeach, Milton. **Beliefs, Attitudes and Values.** San Francisco: Jossey-Bass, 1969.

Slonim, Morris James. **Sampling.** New York: Simon & Schuster, 1966.

Yarbrough, J. Paul. "A Model for the Analysis of Receiver Responses to Communication." Ph.D. dissertation, Iowa State Univ., 1968.

3
What is news and who decides?

JEROME L. NELSON

If you've played the "rumor" game, you know how different the message at the end can be from the one that started things off. In the game, the first player reads a message, which he or she then whispers to the second player, who whispers it to the third player, and so on. Even with the best intentions, players make subtle changes in the message as it flows along. The more players, the more changes, and, more often than not, the original message gets seriously mangled.

Knowing this, it's surprising that information reaching us by radio, television, newspaper, or magazine is as accurate as it is. News and information flow to us in much the same way the message in the "rumor" game moves from player to player. The message the announcer reads or the reporter writes may be different in treatment—in the way it's written—from the original, but the odds are great that the meaning of the two is essentially the same. One reason for this is that the gatekeepers—the "players" in the news and information game—share a set of values which they use to assess messages coming to them. If you, as a news and information user, know the values the gatekeepers share, you should be able to make more reasoned criticisms of media performance. If you are called upon to be a publicist or other news source, a knowledge of these values should make it easier for you to get your messages into the media.

JEROME NELSON is Assistant Professor of Journalism and Mass Communication, Iowa State University, a former newspaper reporter, editor, and advertising representative in the State of Washington, and is the author of Libel: A Basic Program for Beginning Journalists.

GATEKEEPERS

Imagine news and information as flowing from some source. A gatekeeper is simply **a person who can change or stop the flow of information before it reaches its intended receiver.**

Most often we think of gatekeepers as the professional journalists who work in the news and information network. But, by definition, news and information sources as well as journalists may be gatekeepers. In fact, a newspaper boy or girl who decided not to deliver your paper could be a most important gatekeeper.

The fact is that the news and information network is huge. Thousands of persons are directly involved in seeing to it that you get a daily package of news and information over the air or in your newspaper. Think for a moment about what happens when a story "breaks" in some faraway place—the Middle East, for example.

Going through the Gates

Say an assassination occurs in Tel Aviv. A nonjournalist witnesses the slaying and calls in the information. A reporter follows up and writes the story. An editor checks the reporter's work, perhaps making a few changes. Another editor sends a version of the story by cable or telephone to a U.S. news service office in Europe. Here another editor decides what part, if any, of the story to send along for American readers and listeners. Then the story must go through the editing process again in New York. Some part of the story is sent along to a regional office where more decisions are made about what should go to your hometown newspaper or radio or television station. Finally, in your town, your editor decides what part of the story, if any, will be used.

Simple, right? Like the "rumor" game. Consider: the editors of the **New York Times** receive approximately 2 million words a day from widely scattered sources. One way to think about that is to imagine a 200,000-word novel. So the editors receive and make decisions about 10 such books every day. From among the 2 million words, they select about 180,000 for use—a little less than one of the 10 books. Of that 180,000, approximately 8,000 words end up on the front page. Every day, all year information flow is affected by decisions, decisions, decisions.

Thus, the gates controlling the flow of news and information open and close. Some stories get shut out altogether; some are severely trimmed; some go through virtually unchanged.

Let's look at the process (Fig. 3.1).

For a moment, walk a mile or two in a publicist's shoes and consider gatekeeping at the source. Let's say you're the publicity person for the local garden club which has a message it wants the general public to have. As publicist, you consult with the officers of the club and other members who know a great deal about the particular message that's to be sent. You learn as much as you possibly can about it. You make sure your goals for the message (or for an entire campaign) are precisely and specifically stated. Then you write the story. When it's finished, you take it back to show to the officers and members with whom you've talked. Some changes are suggested; some facts need to be omitted and others need to be included. You do a new story and you check it again with the officers and members. Finally, after editing and arguing, the writing job is done and you can send the story along to the mass media.

Incidentally, you don't have to be

FIG. 3.1. Gatekeeping at the source. At each gate, three decisions are possible: Stop (the message is not forwarded); Edit (the message is changed before being forwarded); Go (the message is forwarded without alteration).

WHAT IS NEWS AND WHO DECIDES?

working with an organization to go through this process. You yourself might be "the officers and members" with whom you check out a first draft. In fact, it's a good idea to let a story "cool off" for a time and then read it over carefully for errors and omissions.

A Matter of Time

An important thing to consider here is the time element. For the publicist at the source, the pressure to turn out a fast story is not usually as great as it is in the newsroom, and literally months can be spent creating the finished product that gets sent to the mass media. The really critical thing is not time, but accuracy. Does the message say exactly what you want it to say? Have you done everything you can to ensure that the editor will "buy" it? Is it consistent with the goals you have set?

If possible, carry your story into the news room and personally hand it to the editor. If you can't do that and if the story is simple enough, telephone it in, but only as a last resort.

In newsrooms, editors get literally hundreds of letters every day containing what the senders would like to think of as "news releases." For most of these letters, the reception process is swift—open, scan, and dump. In seconds an experienced editor generally can judge the value of what has come through the mails. Your time is worth something and postage costs money. Preparing material for the wastebasket is not very gratifying.

More Gates to Clear

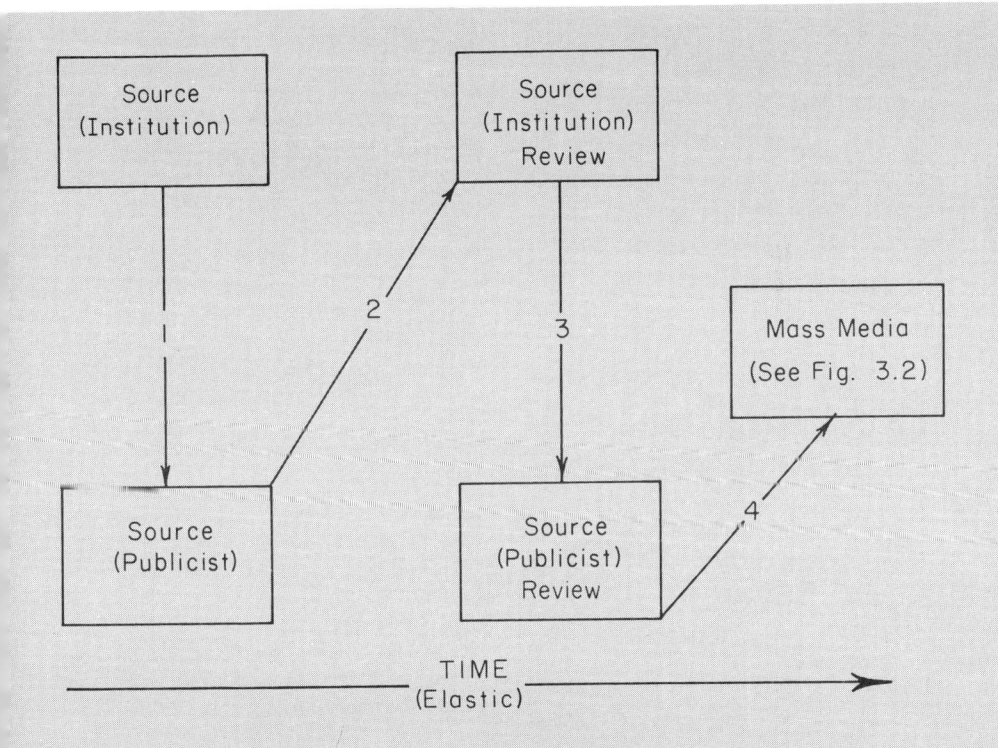

Assume for the moment that the editor finds a story in the mail that may possibly be used. He or she will pass the story along for a rewrite. Sometimes few changes are made; other times the story is cut down or amended in various ways. When this has been done, another editor will examine the story to see if it can be used in that day's paper or in an upcoming newscast. The story could be stopped cold at this point. Assuming it continues, on a newspaper it will be marked for typesetting and a headline will be written for it. Then it will be set into type. Occasionally a makeup editor will discover there is no room for the story and stop it. Or an announcer, glancing at the clock, will find the time has run out and the story doesn't get told.

It's important to consider the time element again. What may have taken months for a source to prepare gets lightning fast reaction in daily newspaper or broadcast newsrooms. There the whole process probably will take less than one eight-hour shift. For weekly newspapers and magazines the process can take longer, but the media response in most cases will be faster than the time spent by the source.

Editors may differ about the wording of messages. More often than not, however, they'll agree on the element within the message that makes it news.

NEWS VALUES

One way to discover what an editor thinks is news or to determine which kinds of messages appeal to him or her is to read the editor's publication or listen to the material the editor airs.

Editors reveal their likes and dislikes in many ways: the way they "play" or place material, select content, or fix length. One editor enjoyed rare place names. If a story reached him and it included a rare place name—such as Medicine Hat, Alberta; Sundance, Wyoming; or Echo, Oregon—it stood a good chance of making the publication.

The advice to read and listen is practical enough, but some values appear to be shared by nearly all professional journalists. Knowing them should help you place your stories or to understand why some stories "make it" and others don't.

A Slippery Situation

News is a slippery concept. Study your daily newspaper. You're bound to see that many different kinds of material are included under the broad heading of "news." Crime, sports, social events, business reports, and many other things appear to be described as news. If you are to be successful, it will help to have a working definition: **News is the report of an event or a situation which has significance or interest or both.**

You'll notice immediately that news is a **report**. It's not the bank robbery itself that's news; it's the report of the bank robbery. The world hunger problem isn't news; a report about the world hunger problem is. The event or the situation is the stuff from which news is made.

A cynic might say that news is what journalists say it is. In a sense the cynic would be right, because, by definition, a journalist has to deal with a problem or an event before it will turn into news. The important thing is that **you,** acting as a source, have the power to make news. All you have to do is convince the journalists that your messages are worthy stories. To do that, consider some of the other concepts in the definition.

One criticism of the American press has been that it is too event oriented. Something has to happen, the critics contend, before the press will act. In the 1960s, it was argued that Watts, the black ghetto in the Los Angeles area, had to explode **before** the press there dealt with problems that many believed were behind the explosion.

The criticism may be valid. It's impossible to say today what might have occurred if the problems of persons living under the pressure of the ghetto had been

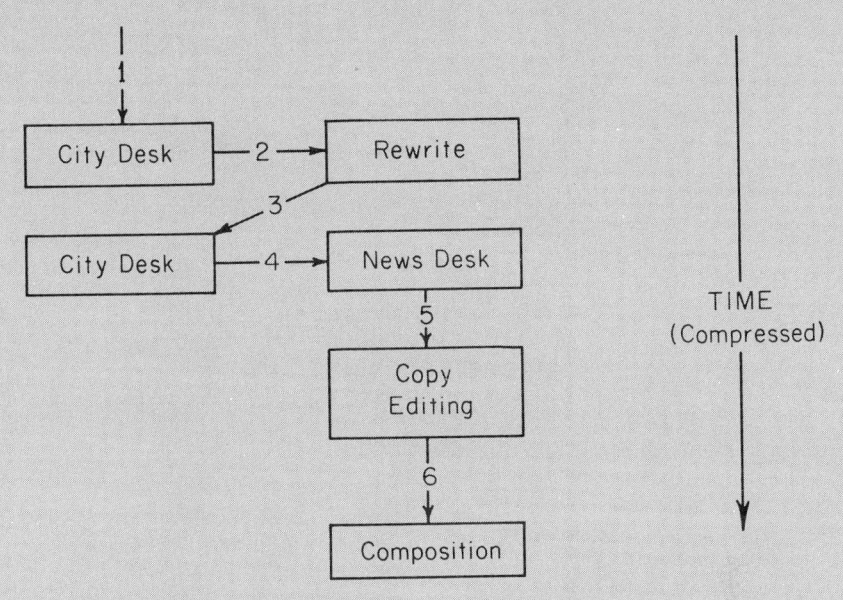

FIG. 3.2. Gatekeeping in a newsroom.

explored by the press. If it had been made aware of the problems, the community might have acted to correct them, thus preventing violent detonation.

An analysis of media content today might suggest that the press has at least begun to deal with problems in the absence of events "to hang them on." For example, more feature stories on consumer difficulties and grievances may be found in the media today. Despite this fact and despite the phrase ". . . or a situation . . ." in the definition above, events are still critically important to editors as they consider a potential package of news.

An Event Is Helpful

If you want to deal with a problem or situation, you can create an event to provide it with a base. The event doesn't have to be earth shaking. Something as simple as a press conference or a speech may be used as an event upon which to base problem- or situation-oriented stories.

But don't ignore a problem or situation simply because you can't think of an event to use for a news peg. By definition, situations can be news. If your problem is significant enough, a journalist may be convinced that it should be dealt with even in the absence of an event "news peg."

What Is Significant?

If "news" is slippery, one of the elements that makes it that way is the eel-like concept of **significance**. If you'll recall some of the propositions inherent in our idea of participatory democracy, however, you may be able to get a grip on it. One of those propositions is that there should be a robust and freewheeling discussion of ideas because, if there is free debate, the truth will emerge. Furthermore, the press in a free society has a duty to provide citizens with information they need to make wise political decisions. So, any event or situation that adds to the continuing debate or provides some needed information is—almost by definition—significant. According to such precepts, virtually any information about any branch of government is significant.

Some critics argue that the media focus too narrowly on these particular precepts, saying for example that the problems of ecology didn't become "news" until such concerns intruded upon public affairs. So, too, critics say, consumer concerns were left largely unreported until advocates like Ralph Nader hurled them into the public arena with congressional testimony and legal action.

Like the criticism that the press concentrates too much on events, these concerns may be valid. If they are, it is up to journalists to define more broadly the area of debate. Clearly, politics and government are not the sole concerns of people today and you can affect the output by letting the journalists know what you think should be covered.

On a day-to-day basis, however, journalists don't think in terms of philosophical premises. They deal in practicalities. To journalists, **significance is the likelihood that an event or situation will have, or has had, some effect upon members of a medium's audience.**

If an event or situation is significant, a story about that event or situation will be significant. Note that this does **not** say that the event or situation or story will be interesting. It simply assumes a similar or parallel quality between the event or situation and the story. Note also that the reporter cannot affect this quality; something is either significant in some degree or it isn't. Reporting about it will make it neither more nor less significant than it already is.

Admittedly, journalists have no really good way of measuring significance. They do measure it in a gross way—by simple head counting. The more members of the audience an event or situation has affected or will affect, the more significant a story is. Therefore, an event that affects all of an audience is more significant than one that affects only part of it. A story about an increase in individual income taxes will generally be more significant than a story about an increase in excise taxes. Odds are that more persons in a given audience pay income taxes than pay excise taxes. If a newspaper attempts to serve an entire state, an event that affected persons throughout the state would be more significant than one that affected only the persons in one city.

Audience a Key. Journalists think constantly about their **audiences.** If an event or situation would not, in the estimation of the journalist, be of significance or interest to his or her audience, the event or situation would go unreported. If you are going to attempt to get a message into the media as news, then you must be sure the message will affect or interest the audience. The larger the audience for your message, the more likely the media will be to use it.

The media generally carry reports of traffic fatalities, such as this radio story lead:

> A Yourtown attorney died early today when the car she was driving slammed headon into a bridge abutment on Nearby Road.

That news lead tells us quite a lot. It answers generally at least the questions: What happened? Where? When? To whom? But, is the story significant?

To answer the last question, you need to determine how many persons in the Yourtown audience the event will affect or has affected. Think about that. Aside from the attorney herself, her family, her friends, her clients, who in the audience will be affected? Many in the audience? Few in the audience?

Here's another news lead:

> Milk prices rose 3c a quart today in all Yourtown grocery stores.

Which of the two news leads is the more significant? It should be obvious that the story about the boost in milk prices is the more significant according to the definition. The odds are that more persons in the audience will be affected by that price increase than by the death of the attorney in a car crash.

It should also be obvious that significance may have little to do with interest.

It may seem surprising that anyone would say that a traffic death was insignificant. Remember that when this concept is employed, it refers either to actual or to potential effects upon members of a medium's audience. Seldom is an individual death significant in these terms. However, it does not follow that all stories about traffic deaths would be insignificant. A story that showed the relationship between auto fatalities and the absence of traffic control at a particular intersection might be very significant. Such a story would go beyond an individual accident to discuss the broader problem of traffic safety for a geographical area. Much the same thing may be said about most stories reporting crimes. An individual story about a person being arrested, tried, and convicted of shoplifting might be interesting. A story about the problem created by shoplifting in a community could be significant.

An individual traffic death or an individual shoplifting conviction can become the "news pegs" upon which a good writer may hang a significant story.

Remember, significance inheres in the event or situation; the writer cannot affect it. A writer can do a great deal about the interest a story will have, however. To put it another way, a good writer can make a significant story interesting, but can't make an interesting story significant.

Many times, all other things being equal, a significant story will be chosen over one that is merely interesting. What this means is that a seemingly routine story out of city hall will "bump" a bright feature about a 10-year-old baton twirler. Editors, of course, try to achieve a balance between what they assume their audiences want and what they believe the audiences should have (accurate information with which to make wise political decisions).

Stories that are both significant and interesting gladden editors' hearts.

What Is Interest?

We might define interest as **the probability that readers or listeners will seek out a story.** Clearly, this is impossible to measure. We can determine if an audience has heard or read a story, but no foolproof method is available to predict whether it will.

Over generations, however, journalists have concluded that certain elements will make a story interesting. The inference is that, if these elements are included, the story will be interesting and readers or listeners will seek it out. The elements most often agreed upon are timeliness, proximity, prominence, unusualness, and human interest.

Timeliness. All news is either timely or current or both.

News is current if it contains a "yesterday," "today," or "tomorrow." It means "now," or at least recently or soon. You may infer the extent to which journalists in your own community value this element by examining the content of the media. How many news stories in your hometown paper contain some clue indicating that the news is current? How many items broadcast by your radio station fail to contain some reference to today, the recent past, or the near future? Consider the following news lead:

> Plans for a new municipal swimming pool were studied last night by the Yourtown city council.

The words "last night" tell us the story is current.

A story is timely if it is appropriate to the time. We seldom read Christmas stories in July or stories about Independence Day in December. Ordinarily we read stories about planting in the spring. When the media carry stories on reaping, harvest time is generally at hand. Consider the following news lead:

> Elementary school teachers whose classes contain more than 25 pupils are probably working too hard and, are therefore, inefficient.

Although the lead does not appear to contain a time cue, it seems safe to say that it is appropriate to this time. Clearly, it is not inappropriate.

Now consider this lead:

> Police today continued their search for two armed men who shot and killed Yourtown Mayor Fred Albion here last week.

The writer appears to be going to great lengths to include a "current" cue in the lead. One would assume that a hunt for killers would continue until it was successful. So, the "today" has apparently been inserted to help maintain interest. The technique is common to "second day" or continuing stories.

If you're attempting to get a story into the media, your odds for success will climb if you're able to make the story current.

Proximity. Proximity simply means that which is nearby.

Imagine a store in your hometown. Now think of a store of similar size in some nearby community. If both these stores burned to the ground the same night, which would you expect to read about in your hometown paper? Well, that's exactly what journalists mean by proximity. All other things being equal, something that occurs close to home is more likely to make it into the media than something that happens far away. In fact, stories that aren't all that equal will often make it if they occur nearby. An American journalist once said, "A dog fight in Brooklyn is worth 10,000 starving Armenians." That's callous and outdated, but the point is well made. If you want to increase the probability that your message makes it, include the element of proximity. The job of a publicist is made infinitely easier if stories can be fashioned with the element of proximity included.

In recent years, nationwide telethons to collect funds to fight various diseases and to help pay the bills of political parties have been held. One story about the Deomocratic party's telethon read, "Twenty-five volunteers worked 21 hours for the Democratic telethon here this weekend." The writer provided a local angle and made a national story proximate and consequently more meaningful for a local audience.

Prominence. Prominence means those who are well known. Although this generally refers only to persons who are well known, some corporations, companies, and landmarks have become prominent, too. Journalists generally assume that stories about prominent persons will be interesting.

If the President of the United States does anything, no matter how mundane, a story about it will show up in the media. Other personalities are also carefully covered. A quick scanning of most newspapers will generally produce at least one story about some show business or sports personality.

Two girls who live in the same dormitory both get the sniffles at the same time. One gets headlines and the other goes unnoticed. One is the governor's daughter.

On the local level, one way to insert prominence into your stories is to consult well-known local personalities such as the mayor, city council members, ministers, priests, rabbis, and teachers. Interview some prominent person about your situation and then include his or her views in your message. For example, "Yourtown Mayor Jim Sittwell today endorsed a Tea Rose Garden Club proposal to plant trees along Main Street." The message, of course, is about trees along Main Street. Prominence enters with the mayor. Do you think it would make any difference if the mayor opposed the proposal?

Unusualness. One problem with unusualness is that everyone has his own definition for it. What constitutes the odd, the out of the ordinary, the strange for you? Still, with some care, the unusual can be made to work for the individual who is trying to make news.

If hail falls, that's not unusual. If baseball-size hail falls, that's newsworthy.

If brothers get together, that's routine. If brothers who haven't seen each other for 15 years get together, that's worth a story. If brothers who haven't seen each other for 15 years meet unexpectedly in the basket of a hot air balloon, the incident will likely get big headlines.

Any story that produces a "Gee whiz!" probably is endowed with the unusual. How many can you recall from the last time you read your newspaper? How many have you listened to on radio or television lately?

Unusualness is an exception to the rule to which a writer can add the elements of interest. The writer can't really make something unusual, but he or she can point out that it is unusual and create interest in the process.

Human Interest. Human interest is another element that seems to vary from person to person. When journalists speak of human interest stories, they refer to those that cause readers to feel emotionally about something. The human interest element is designed to evoke an emotional response such as laughter, tears, or rage. The writer wants the reader to empathize with the persons involved.

A story about a tax increase might make a person angry, even though it included no specific element of human interest. However, if the story were personalized and tried to make the reader understand the pathos of an old man losing his home to confiscatory tax rates, it would contain human interest.

Adventure stories are examples of human interest. Stories and pictures devoted to kids and dogs generally are oozing human interest.

Note, too, that the element of human interest must be obvious. The writer is clearly trying to evoke some emotional response in the following news lead:

> Not since the Barbary pirates threw their captives into the

> dungeons of Tripoli 170 years ago have American sailors known such terror or suffered such torture. . . .

The story goes on to detail what happened to Navy seamen and officers who were taken prisoners by North Korea. Can you decide what emotion the writer was trying to evoke?

Here's another example:

> A Paris hairdresser who used to stroll the boulevards in shoulder-length hair had his locks shorn the other day. Then he put on a big hat stuffed with francs which he proceeded to smuggle into Switzerland. . . .

In this story, human interest and the unusual seem joined.

Here's another human interest lead:

> A former Marine Corps helicopter gunner told congressmen today how he flew more than 100 combat missions in Vietnam "higher than a kite" on hard drugs. . . .

The writer is attempting to create additional interest in hearings on drugs through the use of personalization and human interest.

To use human interest properly requires skill and practice. Some writers describe scenes so vividly that we seem able to experience precisely what they did when they observed the event.

All the devices of fiction are available for use in adding human interest but it is important to remember that news deals with fact, not fiction.

SUMMARY

Gatekeepers all along the news production line, from interested observer or unwilling participant to television news anchorman, affect the information fed to the mass media.

Among professional journalists, however, a fairly standard system has evolved whereby the news value of a situation or an event is judged.

News is the report of an event or situation which has significance or interest or both. Although degrees of significance and interest in a situation or event may be debatable, one or both must be present if a story is to be news.

Interest is usually present in one or more of the following modes: timeliness, proximity, prominence, unusualness, and human interest.

In our judgments of what is news, we must develop a cold, calculating eye for spotting these qualities. Our own press releases are no more newsworthy simply because of the pride we have in their creation. We are understandably prejudiced in our own behalf and on behalf of the events or information we wish to publicize. All too often our disagreements with editors may center on our own inflated sense of the worth of our work rather than the editors' insensitivity or their inability to recognize our "news" when they see it.

SUGGESTED READING

Charnley, Mitchell V. **Reporting,** 3rd ed. New York: Holt, Rinehart & Winston, 1975.
Crowell, Alfred A. **Creative News Editing.** Dubuque: Wm. C. Brown Co. 1969.
Doig, Ivan, and Doig, Carol. **News: A Consumer's Guide.** Englewood Cliffs, N.J.: Prentice-Hall, 1972.
Westley, Bruce H. **News Editing,** 2nd ed. Boston: Houghton Mifflin, 1972.

WHO'S
WHO
IN
1973
OF
PUBLICATIONS
Newspapers
Dailies
Weeklies
Magazines
DELL 6600
THE OFFICIAL
ASSOCIATED PRESS
ALMANAC
1975

4

You should be the expert

DALE E. BOYD

News, by whatever definition, is made up of facts or of statements offered up as facts. For that reason, few activities are of more importance to a newsperson or a publicist than the business of rounding up reliable information. The fact-finding function is a major phase of the public relations process as well.

A cardinal rule for merchandising is to "know the product." A car salesperson couldn't expect to make many sales without knowing about the product. Few prospects would spend much time with the seller if questions about price, gas mileage, engine size, or color choices resulted in vague answers.

The business of knowing the product is frequently referred to by salespersons as "arming yourself with the facts." Attorneys and administrators may call it "doing your homework." Just as the salesperson must know the many features of the car being offered for sale; just as the attorney must be able to cite relevant cases establishing precedence; so must the publicist be something of an expert on the topic or product being promoted.

DALE BOYD is Assistant Professor of Journalism and Mass Communication, Iowa State University, former business adviser to student publications at Iowa State, and former editor, publisher, and major stockholder of an Iowa community newspaper.

Whether your "product" is the good name of the institution you represent, an idea you are personally interested in, an item you are selling, or a fund drive run by your favorite charity, its "sales" success is often directly related to the amount of time and effort you spend learning about the product.

HOW TO BECOME KNOWLEDGEABLE?

How does a person become an expert on the product he or she is promoting? A car salesperson can study price lists, product specifications, and sales brochures made available by the manufacturer. He or she can talk to other sales representatives and to satisfied customers to get armed with answers to anticipated questions. A seller can learn something about the prospective buyer. Attorneys can review similar cases, their dispositions by the courts, and the points upon which the dispositions were made. They can also review the applicable laws and their interpretations.

A publicist also does his or her homework. The publicist becomes an expert on the product being promoted, much as a good news reporter backgrounds each story.

An Example of Backgrounding

You have been named the publicity director for your local Heart Association. Your chairperson asks you to take charge of publicizing the annual campaign banquet. You are told that the banquet speaker will be Dr. Horace Stegman, a famous New York heart specialist.

You have little more to go on so you head for the library to find out more about the speaker. The librarian directs you to **Who's Who in America**, where you find that Dr. Stegman is a graduate of Johns Hopkins University and a recipient of several honorary degrees. You look at **Reader's Guide to Periodical Literature** and discover that the doctor has written a long list of medical journal articles about an innovative treatment for heart patients.

Members of the local medical society are logical sources of additional background material. You call the president and find he was a classmate of Dr. Stegman's at Johns Hopkins. Finally, you phone Dr. Stegman to see if he will make an advance copy of his talk available to the press. He says he has none, but agrees to meet with members of the press before the banquet to answer their questions.

You don't stop there. In your visit with the medical society president, you learn that medicine's best estimate is that one of four Americans suffers from some form of heart ailment. You give the county medical examiner a ring and discover that one of every three deaths in your county last year resulted from heart disease.

You check once more with your chairperson to make sure you have the correct information on the time and place of the banquet, the price of the tickets, where they can be purchased, and the agenda for the banquet program. You learn where Dr. Stegman is staying and arrange for a convenient place for his prebanquet press conference. You learn the seating capacity of the banquet hall, the number of persons expected to attend, the dollar goal of the campaign, the success of last year's drive, the names of key workers, and the related efforts planned or completed for the conduct of this year's drive.

Now, you know your product. You are the resident expert not only on Dr. Stegman but on the kick-off banquet and the campaign itself.

Thus armed with what appears to be a mountain of information about your product, you prepare to "merchandise" it. Other parts of this text are devoted to appropriate merchandising plans, such as preparation of news releases, design and placement of media advertising, direct mail approaches, and others.

What the public finally sees, of course, is the tip of the iceberg. As the publicist-expert of your product, you will have at hand far more information than will be aired or printed. Such a stockpile of data is needed if you are to have the most interesting or significant facts for the consumer. Frequently, the most unlikely source of information will lead you to the most fruitful results.

Background information can be an extra pinch of salt added to an otherwise bland stew. A story about Jigme Singhi Wangchuck assuming the throne as Dragon King of Bhutan holds little interest for most American readers or listeners. But, flavor and expanded interest are added with the information that Wangchuck is only 18 years of age, the world's youngest monarch, and ruler of 1 million citizens in his Himalayan country.

WHERE TO FIND IT

Years ago, it was said that a newspaper editor needed only a dictionary, a wall map, and a copy of **Bartlett's Familiar Quotations** to have all the source material he or she needed. If that was ever true, it was long before the media became so sophisticated in their approach to news and before they took so seriously their responsibilities to their readers, listeners, and viewers.

Here are some publications useful as background information sources:

Unabridged dictionaries—Several are available which offer grammatical usage and syllabication in addition to definitions, spellings, and pronunciations.

Encyclopedias—Several are widely available and most are good general research tools.

Yearbooks and almanacs—These usually include statistics of governments and industries, lists of associations and societies, population figures, and chronologies of important events of the past year.

Maps and atlases—In addition to illustrating the networks of roads, rivers, and geographical boundaries, state maps usually provide location and population figures for cities and towns, lists of parks and recreation areas, and tables revealing distances between selected cities. Atlases furnish precise state and national maps and other information such as area, population, climate, altitude, and economy of the region.

Statistical Abstract of the United States—This useful publication contains a wealth of data collected by agencies of the United States Government and some private sources. Such detailed information as the number of mules on Missouri farms or the value of bank deposits in Alaska can be found here.

Who's Who in America—This is a reasonably complete collection of biographical sketches on prominent living Americans.

Reader's Guide to Periodical Literature—This handy reference features an author and subject index covering general periodicals published in the United States.

Facts on File—This is a digest of world news indexed by subjects and by names of persons compiled from newspapers, magazines, broadcasts, and government reports. A final volume is published annually. Subscribers (libraries and newsrooms) receive weekly updates.

The New York Times Index—This voluminous publication is primarily a subject index, but it is cross-referenced extensively with brief summaries of most major articles that have appeared in the newspaper.

Current Biography—This source contains informal profiles of persons prominent in the news of the day.

N. W. Ayer and Son's Directory of Newspapers and Periodicals and **Standard Rate and Data Service** are described in the Appendix.

This list, of course, is incomplete. The **Congressional Directory** and publications of the U.S. Bureau of the Census are likely additions to the publicist's library. On the local level, publications of the chamber of commerce, city plan commission, the U.S. Post Office, the school district, the telephone company, the street department, railroads, airlines, or auto clubs are valuable sources of information.

DETAILS, DETAILS, DETAILS

Knowing the facts and paying attention to detail are complementary requirements for the publicist. Although it may seem unlikely that you will become a professional publicist for a candidate in a national political race, you may well be involved in local, district, and statewide campaigns, whether political or not. Overlooking a detail in such work can be as dangerous as overlooking a fact

Suppose you had overlooked the detail of arranging a site for Dr. Stegman's prebanquet press conference? Such an oversight could upset your association's effectiveness with the media and would have been unpleasant and embarrassing, at best.

An advance man for one presidential candidate tells of his embarrassment as a result of overlooking a detail during a general election campaign. The crowd that turned out to hear his candidate's highly publicized speech was only about a third of the number expected. One of the largest interstate rivalry football games of the year had been rained out the previous day and had been rescheduled for the day of the political rally. A postponed football game is rare, but it happened; football outdrew politics and the advance man learned to double-check even the smallest detail.

Some Success Stories

A history of the American business community would be replete with large-scale promotional efforts and practices, some of which have been remarkably successful. The coffee break, for example, is not a native tradition. It has become a U.S. institution only since the 1940s, when a Pan-American group flooded the media with testimonials from company executives who said the coffee break increased employee efficiency, improved worker morale, and effected substantial production gains.

The garbage can also owes its wide acceptance to an imaginative promotion. A model ordinance, designed to protect the public from diseases spread by rats, was drawn up and circulated widely by a promotion firm. Adoption of the ordinance by city and town councils across the nation assured heavy sales of the product.

Citrus growers have sought and received endorsements citing their products for warding off colds, and meat packers saw bacon sales jump when they publicized the advice of physicians to "eat a hearty breakfast."

Publicity and public relations are effectively used for purposes other than selling merchandise or services, too. A large insurance company rid itself of its staid Wall Street image by hiring a group of young executives who directed the company's appeal to the college set. A large railroad company's public relations department convinced management to move its main office from the East Coast to the Midwest to help offset what was thought to be a harmful image.

BACKGROUNDING IS RESEARCH

Backgrounding is research. When you look at a highway map to learn that Duluth, Minnesota, is just across the state line from Superior, Wisconsin, or when you consult **N. W. Ayer and Son's Directory** to discover that Iowa has more than 380 community newspapers, you are conducting research. More sophisticated studies, however, are often demanded of the publicist. One auto insurance company recently purchased a **Time** magazine advertisement to expose the fruits of research by its staff. The company's advertisement included a table of comparative automobile insurance charges in 20 representative cities. As might be expected, the sponsor of the advertisement claimed rates generally lower than those of two leading competitors.

In California, a major chain department store was losing money doing business in an antiquated downtown location. Management had all but decided to pull out and consolidate its resources with those of more profitable operations. Faced with the loss of one of its largest advertising accounts, the newspaper in the community conducted a major survey of area shopping habits and trading patterns. The store confirmed the data with research of its own and decided to stay in the market with a new suburban location. As a result, the newspaper retained an account likely to grow even larger.

In a somewhat similar case, downtown merchants of a middle-sized midwestern city had developed an attitude of defeat and had done little in the way of group efforts to offset the crippling effects of a new suburban shopping center. A chamber of commerce survey indicated that shoppers in the area would patronize the downtown establishments if night openings and free parking were available. Downtown merchants took the survey findings seriously, provided the requested conveniences, developed group promotions, and recovered substantial portions of their lost trade.

Occasionally, research uncovers unfavorable results for the publicist and his or her product. Cross-state walks became popular methods for attracting votes and enhancing the images of political candidates after one walking candidate won an upset victory. However, a correlation study indicated that there was "no significant difference" in voter response to the walker and to others on his party's ticket in the areas where he walked. The research suggested that other variables added more to the candidate's election success than did his cross-state walk.

Helpful Statistical Concepts

As a publicist, you may want to leave statistical scientific research to experts. Even so, you should be aware of the following basic concepts:

Sampling—If you are conducting a survey and want to question only a sample of a larger population (or universe, as the statisticians call it), your sample should be representative of that larger population. Collaring the first 10 persons you meet on a street corner will not usually provide a representative sample. Instead, your selection should be handled in such a way that each member of the population has an equal and independent chance for selection.

Statisticians often use a table of random numbers, usually found in statistics books, for drawing samples. Selection of names or numbers from a hat also is accepted as a random selection, as is sampling every nth name in a list such as in a telephone book—provided the first name chosen is randomly selected.

Size of Sample—Obviously, the larger your sample, the less chance for the results to be inaccurate. But, time and cost often limit survey size to a sample of the entire population. The Iowa Poll, for example, uses a scientifically drawn list of 600 households for its surveys and questionnaires.

Mean, Median, and Mode—The mean (average) of some data can sometimes be misleading, as can the median (the midpoint of a group of data). Skeptics are fond of pointing out that a person with his head in a hot oven and his feet encased in ice is comfortable, on the average; or that a millionaire and two bums have an average net worth of more than $333,000. Sometimes the clearest picture of survey results can be given by the mean, sometimes by the median, and sometimes by the mode (the most frequent response).

Correlation and Causation—A common statistical concept is that of correlation or the relationship of one variable to another. Perfect positive correlation is 1.0 and perfect negative correlation is —1.0. Too often, interpreters of data falsely assume that correlation means causation. For example, the fact that persons who take drivers training courses have fewer automobile accidents than those without such training does not mean that drivers training courses cause fewer accidents. Studies show that student dropouts correlate negatively with the number of books in the school's library, but adding books to the library obviously won't eliminate student dropouts. The correlation of variables often has nothing to do with cause and effect.

Variability—Data from populations

tend to cluster centrally and vary from one extreme to the opposite in what is often called a "normal" curve. Measurement of this distribution is accomplished by a formula that produces a "standard deviation unit." About two-thirds of all data in a normal population falls within (plus or minus) one standard deviation from the mean. Percentile is a measurement of variability, as is the range (the spread between the high and low), which is probably the most inadequate measurement of variability.

SUMMARY

Before one merchandises a product, he or she must know as much as possible about it. If this rather brief treatment of backgrounding has served its purpose, it has indelibly noted that: (1) many pounds of data are often distilled into very few ounces of publicity, and (2) the more information a publicist gathers, the more assurance he or she has that the publicity will be adequate.

Good publicity requires a thorough investigation of information sources (some of which are listed in this chapter) and attention to small details. Overlooking a fact or a detail may severely weaken the publicity effort; it may even cause a monumental disaster.

Research is done each time a publicist searches for background information. Research may involve such publicity tools as questionnaires and other sophisticated survey instruments. There is no need to fear such tools, but the publicist should be wary of invalid or unreliable results if such surveys are structured, administered, or interpreted improperly.

Only after the facts are gathered can the publicity be created. Armed with the facts, you can turn confidently to the task of writing your story.

SUGGESTED READING

Borg, Walter R., and Gall, Meredith D. **Educational Research: An Introduction**, 2nd ed. New York: David McKay Co., 1971.

Bruno, Jerry, and Greenfield, Jeff. **The Advance Man.** New York: William Morrow & Co., 1971.

Huff, Darrell. **How to Lie with Statistics.** New York: W. W. Norton and Co., 1954.

Hulteng, John L., and Nelson, Roy Paul. **The Fourth Estate: An Informal Appraisal of the News and Opinion Media.** New York: Harper & Row, 1971.

Read, Hadley. **Communication: Methods for All Media.** Urbana: Univ. of Illinois Press, 1972.

Rivers, William L. **The Mass Media: Reporting, Writing, Editing.** New York: Harper & Row, 1964.

——, **Finding Facts: Interviewing, Observing, Using Reference Sources.** Englewood Cliffs, N.J.: Prentice-Hall, Inc., 1975.

——, Peterson, Theodore, and Jensen, Jay W. **The Mass Media and Modern Society,** 2nd ed. New York: Holt, Rinehart & Winston, 1971.

5
You need to know two news story forms

CARL HAMILTON

Many beginning journalists have the mistaken idea there is something mysterious about the building of a news story. They don't realize that such a story follows a pattern they have been using all their lives. Consider the following breathless announcement by a 14-year-old:

> "Jimmie Elingson got hit by a car this noon. He got a broken leg and a cut on the head. It was at Locust and 16th street. They took him away in an ambulance. The car driver didn't see Jimmie because he jumped out between two cars."

Fourteen-year-old Tom gave this bulletin-like, I-saw-it-with-my-own-eyes report to his fellow students as he rushed into class after lunch. In a manner of speaking, Tom was "writing" a news story, and he was doing a pretty good job of it. He was communicating basic information concisely. He was wasting no words on details or digressions.

Later, with the story "lead" out of the way, Tom would elaborate:

> "You know Jimmie; he's in the seventh grade. He lives over at Gray and School streets. His dad's a lawyer. He's got a little sister and an older brother. The car that hit him was a green Ford with a 77 license. The man driving it was alone. Jimmie yelled some. Both wheels

CARL HAMILTON is Vice-President for Information and Development, Iowa State University, Professor and former Head of the Iowa State Department of Journalism and Mass Communication, former newspaper editor and publisher, and former federal government administrator. He is an Iowa Master Editor-Publisher and author of In No Time At All.

of the car went right over him. A man from the filling station covered him up with a blanket. The police came . . . and then the ambulance. The man that hit Jimmie said his name was Larry Kinney and that he worked for an oil company. He said he just didn't see Jimmie until it was too late. He felt bad. He said he had a little boy, too."

Thus Tom, an eyewitness, "covered" the story adequately. Later—perhaps that evening—his listeners would read the newspaper or listen to radio or television to see what the police had to say, whether charges had been filed, and whether Jimmie might have been hurt more seriously than Tom had known.

YOUR PART IN THE NEWS STORY

If all news were as simple as that event, there would be little need for this chapter on how to write a news story. But it isn't. As the dramatic story of civilization unfolds from day to day and year to year, myriads of both simple and highly complex news situations are identified and reported by the mass media. You are a part of that ongoing story. Wherever you may go or whatever you may do, you will be making news yourself, or serving as a news source, or reporting news, or consuming news, or adapting the basic news story idea to any number of personal assignments.

As you will find, the well-written news story is a model of concise communication that is useful to anyone. The agronomist, the home economist, the scientist, the teacher, the coach, the engineer, the preacher, the doctor, or anyone else who has acquired and polished a skill in news writing all enjoy a distinct advantage over the person who has not. His "story"—whether it involves trying to teach or make a sale or explain a new discovery—will come through faster and more clearly if he has mastered the discipline required of a good reporter. He will get to the point quickly. He will not waste words. When he is through he will stop. And chances are that his audience still will be with him.

Knowing the art of writing a news story, you will both write and speak more effectively in all areas. And learning to write accurately and objectively—as the news reporter must—will give you a new respect for fact, for truth.

JOURNALISM HAS A "STYLE"

Most persons have a background in English composition courses—and perhaps they also harbor an uneasy feeling that "journalism is different." Actually the journalist is as keenly respectful of good usage and clarity of expression as the English instructor; he is equally as pained by spelling errors and bad grammar.

To meet his particular requirements, however, the journalist will adopt some special writing or style characteristics. For example, if you are writing a straight news story—that is, reporting some event that has occurred or is anticipated—you probably will use shorter, less complicated sentences and shorter paragraphs than those you normally use in other writing. You also should be especially aware of the need for objectivity, accuracy, and brevity.

But journalism is not concerned solely with the spot news story. There are the interpretative account that usually carries the writer's name as a by-line, the opinion editorial, the depth report, the feature or color story, and others. One might be written in first person; another might have all the characteristics of the traditional short story except that it will be factual rather than fictional; still another might use the verbatim question-and-answer technique. Each offers its own opportunity for detail, color, and perhaps even suspense.

The point here is that no single mark distinguishes journalism from other forms of writing. You need not approach it as though there were some mystery about it. There isn't. But there are some "rules" and skills that will be emphasized and that will, if remembered and practiced, serve you well in a variety of ways.

YOU'LL USE TWO BASIC STORY FORMS

Although the information you receive from newspapers, magazines, radio, and television is as broad as the thoughts and activities of man himself, two basic story forms will serve for almost any reporting assignment.

1. The **straight** (or spot) news story, reporting events that have occurred or are about to occur.

2. The **feature** story, reporting ideas, discussions, interpretations, background, or human interest matters rather than strictly past or coming events.

READERS RELY ON THE STRAIGHT NEWS STORY

Typically, the straight news story reports political developments, labor and management relations, court actions, accidents, crime and other wrongdoing, deaths, public meetings and events, weather details, and the like. Such information is needed by citizens if they are to form intelligent decisions about their government. They also need facts of this sort in order to conduct business or to carry out their day-to-day affairs.

But the amount of spot news that exists is staggering, and the time a person has is limited. This means that the reader-listener places two conflicting demands upon his newspaper or news broadcaster: He wants to be **fully** informed, at least about certain events, and he also wants to be **concisely** informed. In other words, he wants the greatest possible amount of information in the shortest possible time or space.

A basic story form has developed over the years that attempts to meet that demand. This straight news story structure, called the **inverted pyramid**, tells the most important facts first and the least important ones last. As a result, any person who wants basic facts quickly can get them by absorbing the first paragraph or two, while one who wants more details can read or listen to the entire account.

The Lead Introduces Your Story

The most important element of the straight news story, then, is the beginning, or **lead**. It may be one paragraph long or even longer, but not uncommonly it will be a single sentence that summarizes the entire story. For example:

> A month-long drought was broken in the southwest quarter of the state yesterday when 3 inches of moisture fell during the day-long rain.

Because it sums up the important facts, this is known as a **summary lead**. It answers the primary questions the reader will ask of his news source. That is, it tells him **What** (drought broken), **Where** (in southwest quarter of the state), **When** (yesterday), and **How** (day-long rain). If the questions **Who** and **Why** had been significant to the story, these also would have been answered.

The summary lead does all this in the briefest possible fashion. The information reported in the foregoing example will satisfy many readers. But for a farmer or a grain dealer, this will not be enough. They will want to know what the rain means to crops at this stage of development, whether there were erosion losses, and other related facts. They will read on into the story. On the other hand, a city dweller may be satisfied with little more than passing attention to the lead paragraph, then will turn to some item on which he wants more details. And so it goes with the entire audience. In newspapers and broadcasting you must remember constantly that you are writing for the **general public** whose members have many diverse interests.

The summary lead can introduce any story, no matter how great or relatively insignificant. Without question, the most important American news story of recent years was the resignation of President Richard M. Nixon in 1974. Here was a typical lead on that momentous news event.

> Richard Milhous Nixon, thirty-seventh President of the United States, resigned from office Thursday night. Vice-President Gerald R. Ford, 61-year-old former Michigan congressman, will be sworn in as President at 11 A.M. today in the Oval Office of the White House.

Millions of words were written and spoken in covering that event. Yet, in one sentence, we were told Who and What and When. In a second sentence, we were told Who, What, When, and Where. The Why had consumed more millions of words in the months preceding the resignation, but was treated in the following paragraph of the story as well:

> Mr. Nixon, his presidency irretrievably scarred by scandal and with impeachment and conviction by the Congress all but certain, thus became the first chief executive to resign in the republic's 198-year history.

Although they are direct and simple, there is nothing sacred about one- or two-sentence leads or about any given number of words. What does it take to tell the story—in capsule form—in the briefest space possible? It may even take three sentences. And there is no flashing light at any one point that indicates, "Now, we are through with the lead; this is the body of the story." In most cases, the transition will be apparent.

But, in each case, determine for yourself, as you develop the lead on your story, the 10 (or even 5) words most essential in telling the most important facts of the situation. And decide what is the single most important fact.

Look at the example above:

Because the government was changing hands under circumstances unique in the nation's history, "Richard Nixon resigned" was clearly more important than when, or the fact that Vice-President Ford would be sworn in, or Ford's age. (As time passed, of course, the new President became the focus of mass media accounts.)

You wouldn't, for example, back into your story by saying that "in the Oval Office today, 61-year-old Vice-President Gerald R. Ford, former Michigan congressman, will be sworn in as President of the United States, following the resignation of President Richard M. Nixon."

You may be thinking at this point that the likelihood of being called on to write a news story concerning some great national news event is remote. That may be true. But exactly the same rules apply to your story about the election of club officers, an auto accident at the corner of Fourth and Main, or a report on

Congressman Black's remarks at Monday's Rotary meeting.

Parenthetically, this summarizing skill will serve you equally well in speaking. How many times have you heard someone rise "to make just one more point" and drone on for 10 minutes? Brevity in speaking, as in writing, is a rare and deeply appreciated virtue.

So, as you sort out the facts you intend to use as a beginning for your story, think in terms of the Who, the What, the When, the Where, the Why, and the How. Almost always one or a combination of those elements is clearly the most important or the most significant fact. Frequently it is What happened (or will happen) to Whom under what circumstances? In any case, search for the standout information, use it as a lead beginning, and try to keep your lead as short as possible. You may write a

Who lead: Historian Alex Lightfoot will deliver a memorial lecture here today.
What lead: A new variety of soybeans was released by the state experiment station today.
When lead: Monday, Dec. 6, will be the first day that persons may apply for next year's auto licenses.
Where lead: Lake Pickett will be the site of the Fourth of July picnic sponsored by the local chamber of commerce.
Why lead: Because of sharp increases in university enrollment, a regular schedule of night classes is being introduced.
How lead: Plenty of sleep and an adequate diet were suggested today as the best way of avoiding the flu bug that is plaguing the campus.

Additional examples of summary leads could have been included to illustrate the infinite variety possible within this basic lead style. A more fertile approach, however, is for you to study newspapers or listen to news broadcasts to sharpen your eye and ear by identifying examples on your own.

The main way you will learn to write good, crisp summary leads is to write, and write, and write. Occasionally, that sharp, one-sentence lead will jump right at you. Many experienced reporters, however, will toss out a half-dozen before they find exactly the right combination of words. Most straight news stories begin with summary leads.

Organize Your News Story

The inverted pyramid story structure has advantages not only for the reader but also for the editor and the writer. You already know how convenient it is to find the most important facts packed into the first few paragraphs of a story. These may give the reader all the information he wants. But if he wants more details and has time to read them, they are there, too, in the latter part of the story.

The inverted pyramid also saves editors' time. This is important, for newspapers and news broadcasts are fast-moving operations. Deadlines arrive within hours or minutes. How is time saved? Space (in a newspaper) and time (on radio-television) are at a premium, and to make news fit the available space or time, editors and makeup men frequently must shorten some stories. You know from experience how slow this job can be. When a report follows the inverted pyramid pattern, however, an editor can quickly cut off its final paragraph or paragraphs and feel secure in the knowledge that he is not discarding some essential fact.

The advantage of the inverted pyramid for the writer has to do with ease of story organization, for once the writer has familiarized himself with this story structure, he will find that almost any news event can be told efficiently and effectively with it. It is likewise a form that is easily learned because it represents the natural way to report an important story—the vital facts first, then those of progressively less significance as the account moves on toward its conclusion. If we were to diagram an inverted pyramid story structure, it would look this way:

> SUMMARY LEAD
> ELABORATION OF LEAD
> DETAILS BECOME
> LESS AND LESS
> IMPORTANT
> AS STORY
> UNFOLDS
> •

It should be emphasized that a diagram can represent only an approximation of a typical news story's organization. Once the writer has completed his summary lead, he has to use his own best judgment about what comes next. His goal should be to tell the story as clearly and concisely as he can, moving smoothly from fact to fact in an orderly and logical manner.

That arrangement might be based on chronology (as in a play-by-play account of a football game), on priority (as in a speech report—the speaker's most important remarks may have come last in the speech but are first in the news report), or on sequence (as in any cause-and-effect situation). But however you may shape the body of your story, remember that the story as a whole demands **important facts first**.

Here is an example of a publicity release that begins with a summary lead and is developed in inverted pyramid body style:

From: American Society of
Agricultural Engineers
Saint Joseph, Michigan 49085
The Julian J. Jackson Agency
11 S. LaSalle St.,
Chicago, Ill. 60603

For
immediate release

The agricultural engineer's growing importance in our over-all economy and his broadening interests in a new age in agriculture will be explored at the 59th annual meeting of the American Society of Agricultural Engineers June 26-29 on the campus of the University of Massachusetts, Amherst, Mass.

The world food crisis, housing, water treatment and use, food processing and distribution, and educational specialization will be among the subjects discussed in addition to specific agricultural problems involving engineering.

A panel session on food freeze-drying will deal with the latest research developments in this technique, including applications for meats and Romano cheese. Methods for reducing air-borne contamination in freeze-drying and other food processing operations also will be explored.

In a symposium on water treatment and use, the sanitary hazards of farmstead and rural water system and plumbing connections and the problem of pesticides in farmstead water supplies will be considered.

An innovation at this year's ASAE annual meeting will be a special session on rural family housing. Papers presented at this session will suggest answers to housing problems that also affect other than farm families; for example, housing for the elderly, reduction of sound levels in family houses, economy housing for home and abroad, and home furnishings for gracious living.

More than 200 scientific papers will be presented at the meeting, including many reports on new machinery and techniques to speed full automation of food production on the farm from planting to warehouse or processing plant.

Write As Objectively As Possible

The lead and story styles discussed thus far are so widely used in news reporting that learning how to use them at least passably well should be your first concern. But reporting involves one other less tangible concept. That is the principle of objectivity. Complete objectivity is no more possible in journalism than it is in any other human endeavor. We all tend to see things from our own point of view or in the light of our personal needs and desires. A soaking rain, for example, may appear as a disaster to the contractor who finds his freshly dug basement ruined by cave-ins. But to the farmer the same rain may mean the difference between crop failure and bumper yields. A story reporting this rain would be written differently in the contractor's trade paper than it would in a farm journal because each publication serves a different audience.

Regardless of where a story appears, it should be written as objectively as possible. This means the reporter attempts to be fair and impartial in selecting facts for emphasis and carefully attributes all statements of opinion to some authority or principal involved. Learning to report objectively is important. Learning to detect a lack of objectivity—as a consumer of news—is also important.

Let us take a simple example, using the accident story at the beginning of this chapter. Seventh-grader Jimmie Elingson is hit by a car. A reporter appears on the scene. The boy is crying, obviously in great pain. A broken leg hurts. There is blood on the pavement. The reporter could return to his office and write that "Jimmie Elingson was seriously injured this afternoon when hit by a car at the corner of Locust and 16th street."

But was he "seriously" injured? To Jimmie's mother (and to Jimmie) a broken leg and a cut on the head are no doubt serious. To the doctor, however, the injuries could be pretty routine. If the reporter is to be objective, he should not attempt to interpret the "seriousness" of the matter. He should simply report the broken bone and the cut on the head. If, on checking at the hospital, the reporter found that the injuries were indeed serious and some member of the hospital staff would say so, then the story would go something like this:

> Jimmie Elingson, 13, son of Mr. and Mrs. Bert Elingson, 123 Gray,

> is reported in serious condition at St. Anthony's Hospital as the result of an accident at the corner of Locust and 16th street this afternoon.
> Dr. James McArthur said the boy suffered internal injuries when he stepped from between two cars and was hit by an auto driven by Larry Kinney of 1319 Jefferson St., Moberly, Mo.

The principle observed here is known as **attribution**. The "seriousness" is attributed to some authority, because it is an expression of a judgment or viewpoint. A story saying that "Dr. Jonathan Cluber gave an interesting talk at the West Side PTA meeting on the subject of school dropouts" will cause the alert editor to run his pencil through the word "interesting." The talk may have interested you; it may have been an utter bore to everyone else in the room. (For a further discussion of attribution, see Chapter 15.)

So much for the basic form of the straight news story. Let's now talk of a second basic story form commonly called the **feature story**.

THE FEATURE DEMANDS CAREFUL HANDLING

It is true that journalists use the term **feature** in several ways. They sometimes use it to describe almost anything that goes into the newspaper except the straight news story or news picture. Crossword puzzles, cartoons, and advice-to-the-lovelorn columns, for instance, are features in this sense. In another setting, a news chief may ask a subordinate, "What'll we feature today?" In effect, he is asking, "What can we use for today's main story?"—the story that will go at the top of page one or will take the most important position in a broadcast. The discussion that follows, however, will concern itself with a third meaning—the meaning that a reporter grasps when his chief orders, "Let's do a feature story on the new fire station," or, "Find a feature angle and do something on the state fair."

How does such a **feature story** differ from the **straight news story**? We have learned that a writer, as he works his way through a straight news story, is trying to give a report of important facts, as quickly and efficiently as he can and with a priority order in mind. The writer of a feature story, on the other hand, has something else in view. He may have relatively little concern about how many facts he can jam into a reader's mind—or how fast. Indeed, in contrast to the inverted pyramid story, some feature stories are written so that the most important fact of all—the "punch line," so to speak—comes last.

All of this means that feature stories can seldom be trimmed safely by an editor who arbitrarily strikes away the last sentences or paragraphs, as he would be able to do with the inverted pyramid story. Essential facts may be lost if he does so. The editing of a feature story, therefore, must be a skillful **internal operation** rather than a bit of mechanical surgery that begins with the tip of the story's tail and moves upward through its body.

Feature stories are most commonly found in magazines and in the magazine supplements of Sunday newspapers. But they are regular and important fare as well in daily and weekly newspapers and in broadcasting. The story form is ideally suited for background reports on the news, interpretative pieces, human interest accounts, broadcast documentaries, and opinion and personality interviews. It even adapts well to those bright little oddity stories in newspapers and news broadcasts that oftentimes are based on spot news but really are more a

KNOW TWO NEWS STORY FORMS

commentary on the human condition than they are a straight news report.

Feature Leads Arouse Interest

Like straight news accounts, feature stories must have leads. These come in as many shapes and sizes as there are people to write them, but the best leads tend to be short and to arouse the audience's self-interest or human interest impulses. An example might grow out of the discovery that the governor would be sworn into office on his birthday:

> Hugh Johnson will get a new chair for his forty-sixth birthday. It will be behind the governor's desk at the state capital where he will be sworn in on January 4—46 years to the day following his birth on an Adair County farm.
>
> The governor's mother, reached at her home on the same farm where Gov. Johnson was born, said that this event was "beyond her greatest hopes" and that she couldn't think of a "nicer birthday present for either a son or his mother."

From this point on, the story could be developed into a biographical sketch recounting other important developments that had occurred on the governor's previous birthdays and his age in relation to others who had held the office. The alert reporter might also check the age of the governor's chair to discover whether it was as old as or older than the governor himself.

Obviously, the lead on this story does not attempt to summarize the who, what, when, where, why, and how of gubernatorial ceremonies. Instead, the writer has chosen an unusual human interest angle and attempted to arouse with it the reader's or listener's curiosity and to lead him into the story. The account itself makes no attempt to single out the most important items for early treatment although it may have singled out the most interesting.

Here are additional examples of leads on feature stories:

> They say lightning never strikes twice in the same place, but it does! Lightning kills more than 400 farmers and destroys thousands of farm buildings every year. And most of those deaths and losses can be prevented.

> The young homemaker in America today appears to be a breed of woman unlike any before in history.

> Judi Browne, national baton twirling champion, says learning to twist and twirl at the same time "just comes naturally—if you've got rhythm."

> That old jalopy in Leonard Wood's garage at 1418 West Street is ready to roll again.

> When the Fine Arts Committee opens its first annual Art Fair next Monday, the work of nine Bayville residents will be among the 173 original canvases on display.

And here is an example of a complete feature story:

> They were both blind. Yet, it was "love at first sight."
> At least that was the way Donna Jones and Keith Dumbarton

described the circumstances that led to their marriage yesterday at St. John's-by-the-River Church.

These two totally blind persons found themselves seated side by side at a class for the handicapped at the Montgomery Retraining Center. During a class break, they exchanged a few words and, as Donna described it, "We just seemed to see something special in each other."

From that time on, Donna and Keith managed to be seated side by side in the classes and the romance was not long in developing.

The wedding was conventional. The vows were spoken. The rings were exchanged. The groom kissed the bride. But there were more tears than usual because of the happiness that was so evident on the faces of the couple being joined as husband and wife but who would never see each other—as most persons "see."

That, of course, is a natural for a feature story. It would "write itself," as the saying goes.

The good reporter, however, is the one who takes the ordinary circumstance and, with imagination, comes up with the unusual twist to make a good feature. That takes skill. First, learn to write the simple, straightforward news story. Then try the feature.

Advantages of the Feature

Feature stories normally do not depend upon spot news developments, although they may well be based on news breaks. Therefore they have, relatively speaking, a timeless quality that is not enjoyed by the straight news story. The latter must be published as soon as possible after the event occurs or, in the case of anticipated events, properly timed prior to the incident. Failing this, the news can become stale in a matter of hours, or it may be published so far ahead of the event that it lacks interest for the consumer. Feature stories, on the other hand, often can be held for publication until space or time becomes available—providing, of course, that the subject matter remains relevant.

The self-interest or human interest appeal so typical of feature stories can be of great value to the teacher, the salesman, or anyone who places importance on face-to-face communication. The salesman may use it to capture the client's attention when a straight hard sell might get him pitched out the door. Good speakers frequently use such an appeal to gain quick attention. The scientist may have special need to use the appeal of self-interest or human interest as he attempts to inform laymen about a subject in which their interest is slight. Business uses it in advertising. Teachers use it constantly, or attempt to. Developing the skill to write a dynamic human interest lead should be just as important as learning how to summarize the five W's and an H for the straight news story.

Just as there are no hard and fast rules for developing the straight news story, there likewise are none for organizing the feature story. It can build to a climax, develop in a first-second-third order, take advantage of the way an interview progressed, or assume any one of many other structural forms. As you read your newspaper or listen to your favorite news broadcaster, identify the feature stories and analyze (1) how the leads were written, and (2) how the stories were organized. You will find this a diverting game, and you will be learning at the same time.

The information upon which you base your stories for the media is collected in a variety of ways—from speeches, through interviews, by observation, and through research. Somewhat different approaches are needed by the reporter covering an event like a football game simply by observing it and by the reporter covering a speech for which a text may or may not be available. But by learning the two general reporting forms emphasized here—the straight news story and the feature story—you will be acquiring a basic skill that can be readily adapted to the requirements of the mass media—newspapers, broadcasting, magazines. (Because of the special considerations that must be given to researching, writing, and marketing magazine articles, Chapter 10 is devoted to that subject.)

USING LANGUAGE EFFECTIVELY

Thus far in this chapter we have been talking about leads and story arrangement. Now we should talk about language and how it can be used most effectively. Because this is such a broad subject, we can suggest here only a few relatively simple guidelines.

Know Your Audience

Identifying the audience you intend to reach is the first and most important step in deciding which words to use and how to arrange them (for a discussion of the communication process, see Chapter 2). In a professional journal or specialized magazine reaching an already well-informed and highly educated audience, it is possible to use longer sentences and a more specialized language or jargon than would be wise in the typical news story. But that does not mean that writing a news story is a simple process for simple-minded people. On the contrary, although it is a straightforward task, it is a very exacting one. An enormously wide range of subject matter—the whole spectrum of the day's news—must be presented in a way that will appeal to and be understood by a cross section of the local population.

Choose Words Your Readers Know

Use simple, direct language in ways that will draw the clearest possible picture in the shortest possible space or time. The reporter who is conscious of his audience will use words, phrases, sentences, and concepts that are familiar to his consumers. A word or phrase that is totally suitable on the sports page may not even be understood by readers of the market page or the society page, or vice versa. Too much stress connot be put on knowing your audience. A concert review appropriate for a university newspaper might be totally lost on the audience of a county-seat newspaper.

Do not deliberately "write down" to an audience, but take care not to greatly exceed its level of education in your stories. When a choice is possible, use the simple, rather than the difficult, word. In conversation, people say "buy" more often than they do "purchase." They also will prefer "need" to "requirement." In spite of this, however, the right word, the one that says precisely what you want it to say, is more important than using the simple or easy word. If a "big" word is called for, use it.

Build Active Sentences, Paragraphs

Strive for variety in both sentence length and structure. There is no ideal sentence length, of course, and a series of sentences of equal length is a sure path to monotony. Mix them up. Make some short, some medium in length, and a few on the long side. Generally speaking, average sentence length in news stories tends to be less than the average in most magazines, books, and other written material. Widely read newspapers, news magazines, and other publications have an average sentence length of from 16 to 20 words. Magazines that appeal to a more sophisticated and, presumably, better-educated audience may go substantially above that average. Regardless of audience, however, most writing can be improved by shortening sentences and varying sentence length. That 16- to 20-word average is a good figure to keep in mind.

For vigor and emphasis, you should make most of your sentences declarative in form. Cast them in the active voice rather than the passive. "The dog bit the cat" is a stronger statement than "The cat was bitten by the dog." Not only are direct sentences forceful but they also are less likely to suffer from the burden of vague and needless words.

Don't let your paragraphs get out of hand. The guide for paragraph length is much the same as that for sentences. Build them around a topic sentence and concentrate on only one major idea. Remember, too, that when a paragraph exceeds four typewritten lines, it is getting pretty long for newspaper use or for easy reading by a radio-television announcer.

Quotations Add Interest, Drama

Put "conversation" into your story.

Most people feel that talking is easier than reading. So they feel that "talk" in print is easier reading than other print and are more comfortable with direct quotations and indirect quotations than with straight exposition. Conversation helps in another way, too. Letting your audience know that "this is what the story source said" adds both a human quality and authority. Because the reporter seldom finds it practical to get accurate and extensive direct quotations unless he is getting his information from a printed text or a tape recording, he uses such direct quotations sparingly. He tends to be rather liberal, however, with paraphrases and indirect quotations.

Direct quotations may be handled in several ways. You may use a complete, verbatim quotation:

> "Americans who oppose foreign aid on the ground that it is unpatriotic to spend American dollars on un-American causes are playing with fire," Rep. Carl Smith (R) charged here last night.

You may eliminate irrelevant parts of the speaker's statement, indicating omission:

> "Americans who oppose foreign aid ... are playing with fire," Rep. Carl Smith (R) charged here last night.

You may even choose to quote only a cogent word or phrase and paraphrase the rest of his statement:

> Opponents of foreign aid are "playing with fire," Rep. Carl Smith (R) charged here last night.
>
> Smith also said he was a "possible" candidate for the Republican nomination for governor next year.

"Possible" is quoted to emphasize Smith's status.

If you quote someone and his remarks extend over one paragraph, handle it this way:

> "Every American citizen has a sworn obligation to uphold the foreign policies set by the administration in power," Rep. Carl Smith (R) declared here last night. "That is the first and foremost requirement in today's complex world.

KNOW TWO NEWS STORY FORMS

"To oppose a united front against our Communist enemy is to strike a fatal blow in the midsection of our foreign policy."

Although the attributive phrases appear at the end of sentences in the foregoing examples, they don't have to do so. For the sake of variety and rhythm they can and should appear just as frequently in the middle of quoted or paraphrased sentences or even, at times, at the beginning:

"Debate over foreign policy," Representative Smith asserted, "should end at our shores."

The Congressman emphasized that he was not recommending that free discussion be stifled, only that it is essential that "we speak as one voice abroad."

Although we have emphasized the virtue of quotations as a means of putting "conversation" into your story, too much emphasis cannot be placed on the skill required to do this sort of thing. Many persons speaking either from a platform or in an interview will qualify a simple declarative statement:

"The prospects of a record soybean crop were never better, but it will be at least another 30 days before a crop is finally assured."

Assuming that these remarks were made by the U.S. Secretary of Agriculture, a reporter who put the following lead on his story would be doing sloppy reporting and could anticipate a rebuke from the cabinet officer:

"The Secretary of Agriculture today forecast a record soybean crop."

That makes a nice, sharp lead. But it isn't what the Secretary said. Listen to what the person is saying or trying to say. Many persons use awkward sentences and poor phrases. It is entirely possible for a reporter to use exact quotations—a few words here and a few there—and leave an impression exactly the opposite of what the speaker intended. The words were taken out of context.

An interview or speech story is one of the most difficult to handle. Hundreds and hundreds of words will be spoken. The sharp reporter must capture their essence and give them "life" with a few direct quotes that summarize as accurately as possible the speaker's intent.

And, when your story is finished, be sure that there will be no question in the reader's mind as to the source of the comment. Unless the reader is unmistakably certain that the comment is coming from the speaker, he or she may assume that it is coming from the reporter. That is not the role of the reporter. The reporter reports, and nothing else.

EDITORS LIKE CORRECTLY PREPARED COPY

As you write your publicity story, observing the following suggestions for mechanical presentation will assure a favorable reception when you submit it to the newspapers and broadcasting stations you select as outlets:

1. All news copy—for whatever use—should be double-spaced on one side only of 8½ x 11-inch paper and should begin 2 or 3 inches down from the top of the first page. Set your typewriter

for a 60-space line. Typed copy will have a better chance of being used, and correctly, than will handwritten copy. But if it has to be handwritten follow the same rules.
2. Do not erase on typed copy. Simply XXXX out the section you want deleted and go on. If you misspell a word, XXXX it out and spell it correctly unless the error is simply a transposition of characters. Correct errors of that sort this way: today. Having made these suggestions, however, do not forget that turning in neat copy that needs a minimum of attention from the editor will sometimes get stories published that would otherwise be put aside. There is not much time on the copy desk to rewrite and clean up copy.
3. In the upper left corner of the first page, put your name and telephone number. Just beneath your name include a few words indicating the subject matter covered in the story: Chamber of Commerce Meeting . . . Football practice begins . . . Night school opens Sept. 9. If date of publication is important to the news value of the story, type DO NOT RELEASE BEFORE . . . and the date. Otherwise, type FOR IMMEDIATE RELEASE.
4. If your story runs more than one page, center the word "more" at the bottom of Page 1 and continue your account about 2 inches down from the top of Page 2. In the upper left corner of the second and succeeding pages, write "Page 2—Chamber meeting." At the close of the story, center the word "End" or "-30-" below the final paragraph.
5. Never put more than one story on a sheet of paper, even if the story is only one paragraph long.
6. Do not attempt to write headlines for your news stories. You have no idea of the headline size and style the editor will want, and broadcasters do not normally use headlines. Neither is it wise to demand that a story carry a particular headline or that it appear on a certain page in the newspaper. The editor will do the best he can and his judgment will be better than yours.
7. On stories being prepared for either broadcast or newspaper use, do not try to guess when the material will appear by referring to dates as "tomorrow" or "yesterday" or "Wednesday." Instead, report the event as being held (or to be held) on Wednesday, Dec. 15. The editor or news broadcaster will change that to suit his timing, whereas if you have labeled it "tomorrow"— even though your copy is dated—he still may be uncertain.
8. Rather than telephoning, write and take or send as much of your copy to the newspaper as you possibly can. In the first place, this helps avoid errors. Secondly, the news editor is a very busy person. Expecting him or her to take long items over the phone is expecting too much and it only invites errors. Write it out—and get it in early!
9. You may feel that a picture would help your story or that your news event might well be worth a picture. Call the editor and ask him or her. Perhaps you can take a picture or have one taken that will be suitable. If you ask some member of the news staff to serve as photographer, do this one thing above all else: Say specifically when the picture can be taken and then arrange matters so that it can be taken promptly when the photographer arrives. Making a newsperson wait through an hour-long business meeting, in which there is no news, to take a picture of the newly elected officers will not improve your public relations with the media.
10. Check all names, dates, places, and other vital facts for accuracy.

SUMMARY

Preparation of material according to the suggestions given in this chapter will not automatically guarantee publication, but it will help. Busy editors and broadcasters are always on the lookout for news, but usually don't have time to rewrite badly written copy or check out fuzzy information. If the copy you submit appears technically professional and is dependable, you will find the news media more than willing to cooperate with you and your organization—both now and in the future.

SUGGESTED READING

Alsop, Joseph and Stewart. **The Reporter's Trade.** New York: (Reynal & Co.) Morrow, 1958.

Bush, Chilton Rowlette. **Newswriting and Reporting Public Affairs,** 2nd ed. Philadelphia: Chilton Book Co., 1970.

Charnley, Mitchell V. **Reporting,** 3rd ed. New York: Holt, Rinehart & Winston, 1975.

Read, Hadley. **Communication: Methods for All Media.** Urbana: Univ. of Illinois Press, 1972.

Rivers, William L. **The Mass Media: Reporting, Writing, Editing.** New York: Harper & Row, 1964.

Strunk, William, Jr., and White, E. B. **The Elements of Style.** New York: Macmillan, 1959.

A collage of overlapping newspaper clippings. Only partial text is legible from each piece.

show their fury

By JAMES FLANSBURG

TOWN
Vince Mayberry

...sidents remain with psychiatry, drugs?

By RICHARD WILSON

ON CAPITOL HILL
a commentary

Thousands cheer; our man sneers

O.T. perseveres without a beer

By DONALD KAUL

I knew this was going to be a tough assignment when I took it on but I didn't know it was going to be this tough.

I mean, they don't sell beer at Veterans Memorial Auditorium during the girls basketball tournament.

For who fun and games they will beer at the auditorium but...

Over the coffee

Random Thoughts
By MAXINE DeGARMO

If you missed last week's column, it deals with my vacation in Florida and covered my activities up to the time of arrival in Miami and ended with the promise, or perhaps I should say, the threat, to continue this week.

It is hard to believe that this country is in the midst of a recession or depression when you are in Miami. I might add that other winter travelers to other warm sections of our country also have gained the same impression. Either the great American public is having one last big fling, or we are being brainwashed.

There were no empty hotel rooms in Miami. This didn't bother me as I had accommodations with friends and relatives while on the east coast. On a trip across to Fort Myers and Sanibel Island we found reservations at our fourth hotel contact.

The daily papers reported it was the best tourist season in several years. I would venture it might be the last if those providing services to this industry contributing to this lucrative income, don't learn about courtesy...

To What Extent Should a Columnist Reveal Information About Himself?

By William F. Buckley, jr.
Washington Star Syndicate

IN RECENT WEEKS several correspondents, thoughtfully sending me copies, have triumphantly advised the editors of newspapers in which a feature appears that "Mr. Buckley himself a mem...

...in recent years written critically about Yale on a dozen occasions. So consistently, indeed, that Miss Wyman felt impelled to identify me, at the end of every column I write about Yale, in some such way as: "Mr. Buckley, a graduate of Yale, is, as one would expect, a critic of that university."

I am a Roman Catholic, and have written 20 columns in the last 10 developments which...

federal aid to education, receives a salary from Tufts whose income depends substantially on federal grants.

The Investor's Guide

By Sam Shulsky

Q — I am a widow and in need of more income. I hold E bonds since 1944.

A — You cannot get current income from E bonds any more than you can get blood from a stone. If you need more money currently, or now, you must (1) switch the Es to H bonds, which will get you an interest check every six months; (2) cash in at least 6 percent of your total E bonds every year; (3) redeem all the E bonds, pay the income tax on the interest and reinvest what is left in top quality corporate bonds. Your tax bracket should determine which course is most feasible for you.

E bonds may be converted to H bonds for current income at any time; you need not for the Es to have reason to shares

Q — I would appreciate list of growth...

Sam Shulsky

Thaw me... the quick...

Hints from Heloise
By HELOISE CRUSE

Dear Folks:

Move it over because for a visit and I looked I learned something that I should have told... Why I haven't, I don maybe?

It's about defrosting it's a package of frozen burger, or what.

We usually just put freezer and put it on to defrost and wonder long. Because we JUS drain. That's why.

For years I have all under the package to it so that it will thaw just pick up a grill from burners on my stove, put newspaper on the drain frozen package of and let her dr...

Little thi...

By SYDNEY HARRIS

Coffee was first... as food, and the... wine made from the mented buries ar... pulp.) And later, as... non-alcoholic beverage Its use was suppressed on religious and political grounds by Moslems... The finch is the larg est family of birds in the world including over half the species of birds.

When Alexander Graham Bell, inventor of the telephone, retired to Canada, he stipulated that there be no telephone in his house.

He said it called a...

Bleak outlook for federalism as state, city woes pile up

By DAVID S. BRODER
Washington Post Service

"Uncertainty, frustration, dismay, outrage" — these are the principal moods evoked by the governors in their recent inaugural speeches, budgetary messages and legislative addresses this year.

That was the first sentence in a statement of reports covering the National Governors' Conference mid-winter meeting in Washington last month. It set the tone for as disheartening a prognosis for the future of federalism as has been heard in years.

All through the decade when Presidents Johnson and Nixon were undermining public confidence in government at the national level, there was solace in the fact that local and state governments seemed to be steadily improving their leadership, their capacity and their competence.

Defensive tone

That was not. I am convinced, a myth. The record of the past ten years has been one of renaissance for many of the city halls and state capitols. But the governors' meeting was pretty defensive in tone they hoped that the surgence might carry over into national government and national polities as early as 1976.

There were two meetings of local officials. Some of the governors stayed overnight after their own meeting to join city, county and regional officials at a meeting of the Future of Federalism Commission sponsored by the Advisory Commission on Intergovernmental Relations.

At both sessions, the tone was defensive, not optimistic.

For one thing, the local governments are broke again after a brief flush of affluence. They are uncertain of what...

Credit counseling and tips for jobless periods

By JANE BRYANT QUINN
© 1975 Washington Post

NEW YORK, N.Y. — If you lose your job and can't pay your bills, you should check a non-profit counseling service. They have special programs for the unemployed, designed to tide you over a temporary period of short money. The counselor will make suggestions as to how to live sensibly on your income, when you have one and the emphasis is on some sort of moral... creditors so you pay too many... back to work again...

$400 a month...

MONEY MATTERS
By JANE BRYANT QUINN

looks from...

ne Maahs

of the increase in food used by wider cost margins gate and the consumer's DA economists increase in consumer food percent was due to higher percent was due to higher...

... to read that University of yd has reaffirmed his the boycott of lettuce Cesar Chavez — shou part of individuals are rsity's purchasing encouraging to learn... and that he ated in the ption all other should not the boycott lowest bid duce desired r bidding

item on spation that... you don't...

chikee!" With his t furnish the gas. car supply the unsur if you have an ac...

Back in I persons, such 2:15 percent... By 1964 the percent and times. And by to 7.9 percent $1,043.

In a 20 year period, the tax rate was up 3.5 times and the maximum total tax was almost 10 times...

Forced to Food Sta...
MORE RELUCTANT IOWANS SEEK...

Down on his luck and out of a job, Richard Steve joined the increasing numbers of Iowans who are turning to federal food stamps to help get them through hard times.

Steve, 44, of Indianola, had been laid off four weeks earlier from his job as a serviceman and driver for a Des Moines oil jobber.

Steve, a widower, and his nine-year-old daughter, weren't out of food yet. "But it was to the point where I was getting nervous," he said.

Because more and more Iowans are...

Tribune Report
By Larry Fruhling

daughter was hand-issued by the Warren County Social Services Department the same day he walked in and applied.

Steve got his stamps, which can be used the same as money to buy groceries, for...

U.S. one must understand the history of Mexico's political and economic development. Furthermore, any American should Mexico that any movement is the U.S. take into consideration the realities of our political...

The most significant factor that the President (who has a six year term) runs our country with the almost absolute power that Richard Nixon would have liked had in the U.S. And any given president may have a political philosophy or stance that that is...

an American student in Moscow were pointed out to me a low-lying statue of the Soviet Union where some natural experiments were reported to be going on. The American monkeys habituated to tropical climates were changes outdoors in Moscow's subzero temperatures. Survivors of this ordeal... to have developed the idea an...

The newest report is drawn largely from the investigations of a Canadian psychiatrist, Norman B. Hart, who was former resident on the Menninger Foundation at Topeka, Kan. The chief of psychiatrists and trainer and...

An ener... and a hu...

"At wit's end"
By ERMA BOMBECK

It is a scientific fact that ... es are attracted ... their mothers umbilical cord...

Some ... are attracted to refrigerators only...

a time when... our son the other day he bounced shuffled over to and opened both do stood there for 20...

lp or are you just bre... nothing to eat," he gr...

ccumb...

boot, I how fore it D. I'm but the border was shadows on peaks. Olympian fortunately Eastern Col Nebraska unbearably

As we d every cloud became a ca and every r foothill. Finall unmistakably protrusion on t "Hey," cri passenger.

...happen when we crossed the... Colorado border into Colorado

Country Candor

southern Southe...

Atlanta, "but, damn, we got running out our ears here you going to win the White House on He are those who say Carter, age 50 not going to win the White House anything. Not in 1976. And maybe he know it. Though his campaign has been fast-paced keeping his sights on Georgia this year — he insists on the best launching pad in Atlanta, hardly course. Some observers feel his Pennsylvania thinking is preliminary or exploratory. The president, or cabinet officer. He has his present law from nothing in the really running for vice but unwilling to spend a second term in the may be after all..."

6

Make the most of columns and newsletters

J. K. HVISTENDAHL

Persons whose duties require them to supply information to the public should not overlook the possibilities of columns and newsletters. More persons read "Dear Abby" and "Heloise" each day than read the lead news story, the editorials, the sports pages, or even the comic strips of most American newspapers. The names of the late Drew Pearson and his successor, Jack Anderson, are certainly better known to the public than are the names of most congressmen. Local columnists such as Herb Caen, in San Francisco; Mike Royko, in Chicago; and Donald Kaul, of the Des Moines newspapers, are better known in their areas than are the editors and publishers who pay their salaries. Columns can have wide appeal and can command large audiences.

Newsletters, which have many of the characteristics of the column, have flourished in America since World War II. They differ from columns in that they are mailed separately to specific and well-defined audiences while columns are distributed through the mass media, usually to newspapers and magazines. The newsletter is more flexible than the column; just as in a personal letter, you can stop when you've said all you want to say, and you can add more pages when you have more to say. The newsletter is almost always aimed at a specific audience with a common interest in the subject of the newsletter—sky diving, dairying, hunting and fishing, raising dogs, outdoor cooking, button collecting—or nearly any other common interest. An interesting and informative newsletter has a head start in reader commitment, because the reader has already declared an interest in the subject of the newsletter by virtue of joining a club, taking up a hobby, or by the way he or she earns a living.

The column and the newsletter, however, are alike in most respects and for that reason are treated together in this chapter. Both the column and the newsletter are more informal than the news story. They are less objective, deal with a variety of topics, and appear on a regular basis under a known sponsorship. Both are prime instruments for carrying information to the public in such areas as agriculture and home economics extension, outdoor recreation and wildlife, education, government and social

---

J. K. (Jake) **HVISTENDAHL** is Professor of Journalism and Mass Communication, Iowa State University, a former news editor for papers in Washington and Oregon, and author of **Producing the Duplicated Newspaper**.

security, soil conservation and environment, and religion. In many states, county extension directors and home economists are expected to supply weekly columns to newspapers in their counties as part of their jobs. Columns written by employees of the Soil Conservation Service and state conservation and wildlife agencies are less frequent but are becoming more common. Persons in all these areas have the responsibility of informing and educating the public. And one of the most effective ways of reaching the public in rural areas, along with local radio, has been through a regularly written local column.

With specialization growing in industry and agriculture, the newsletter is being used more and more frequently to reach the specialist. County extension offices in the Midwest are now sending separate newsletters to dairymen, field crop farmers, cattle feeders, sheep raisers, and other specialists. The agricultural column in the local newspaper cannot be quite so selective; it must deal with a more general agricultural audience and, indeed, often includes city dwellers who have problems with lawns and gardens.

THE COLUMN

There are nearly as many types of columns as there are columnists, but the kind used most often to educate and inform the public is the informative column. It is used widely to publicize events, ongoing programs such as soil conservation, new practices and policies in agriculture and home management, and new information from government and private sources that should be communicated to the public.

The news story, as pointed out in Chapter 5, is written formally and objectively in an impersonal manner. The column can be more personal in nature because the writer is identified with his or her "by-line" and often with his or her picture. The writer of the column, unlike the writer of the straight news story, can occasionally write in the first person ("I" or "we") and can urge action. A county extension director may write the following for part of a column:

> I have received five telephone calls this week from persons whose junipers are turning brown. If you're having the same trouble, hold a sheet of paper under the brown area, tap it, and if you have some small green bugs on the paper, chances are you have spider mites. Spider mites are easy to eliminate if you act when they first appear. Call or write the office and we'll send you a bulletin that tells you exactly what to do to put yourself one up on spider mites.

Although the "I" approach may be used occasionally, most of the time it should be avoided, because readers resent the excessive use of "I" in print even more than they do in personal conversation. The use of "I" in the example above, while acceptable, could be eliminated by writing, "Five persons have called the office this week about their junipers turning brown."

The use of "I" is more acceptable in narrative (story-telling) items in which its use is more natural, such as in this example from an outdoor recreation column:

> My son and I tried out the new bicycle trail between Des Moines and Saylorville last week. We started at 8 A.M. from West Des Moines, working on our way

> gradually upstream, stopping (in my case) to catch my breath occasionally and (in his case) to enjoy the view.

Starting a Column

How do you go about establishing a column in a local newspaper? Perhaps the surest approach is to write several sample columns and take them in person to the editor, in the case of a weekly or semiweekly paper, or to the news editor, in the case of a daily. You might suggest a name for the column which is appropriate for the subject matter, and even present a rough sketch of the column heading you'd prefer. The usual arrangement is that you supply the column at no cost to the newspaper, and the newspaper runs the column at no cost to you. The arrangement is mutually advantageous; you receive an invaluable forum for promoting your program and the newspaper receives an interesting feature for its readers. A side benefit for you is that a column increases your visibility to the public you are trying to reach, a fact which will not be lost on your boss and which is bound to enhance your effectiveness on the job. (This arrangement, of course, is generally available only for nonprofit organizations.)

Once you've reached an agreement with the editor to produce a column, you have several obligations. You should deliver the column to the newspaper each week at the specified deadline, often several days before publication. If you agree to one column each week, you should have a column prepared despite out-of-town trips, floods, visiting mothers-in-law, and office emergencies. Many veteran extension columnists have long since learned that it is a good idea to have a spare column "in the drawer" for those inevitable emergencies. During vacations, you can depend on others in the office to take over the column, invite outside guest columnists to write it, or you can prepare several columns in advance.

You are also obligated to write a column of sufficient interest to justify the space it is taking in the newspaper. No paper can afford to run a dull column with a narrow appeal week after week. An uninteresting column ceases to be a public service.

Writing an Interesting Column

Not everyone can be a Sydney Harris, Erma Bombeck, Art Buchwald, or Abigail Van Buren. But almost anyone who has a genuine interest in his or her job and some specialized knowledge and information of use to the public can develop a successful local column. Here are some tips on writing informational columns, gathered from a study of some of the more successful columns written by outdoor recreation specialists, extension directors, home economists, soil conservation specialists, and others:

1. **Keep column items short.** A column that deals with four or five topics appeals to a wider audience than a column that deals with only one topic.
2. **Don't repeat announcements and information that will appear in news stories in the same paper.** Deal instead with topics that have their own news or feature value.
3. **Use a light and informal touch.** Occasionally some humor can be used. The best humor is from local sources. (For example: "The children of Mr. and Mrs. Charles Spotz have raised a runt pig which they say is a good deal smarter than the family dog. They've taught the pig to do three tricks, but they've never been able to teach the

dog any. The question is, how do you get a pig that smart to market?")
4. **Use local names.** The statement that "names make news" is still valid for weekly and small daily papers. Readers are almost always more interested in **persons** than **things**. (Because personalizing and localizing are so important to column writing, they are discussed in more detail later in this chapter.)
5. **Localize items in your column.** As you learned in Chapter 3, readers are more interested in situations and events close to them. What is happening in Washington, D.C., is of some importance to them, but the interest they have in the event can be heightened by showing the effect it's likely to have on the local scene.
6. **Avoid the use of trade names.** Editors consider the use of trade names an infringment upon the advertising function of the newspaper.
7. **Consider writing a column as an all-week, continuous enterprise.** This doesn't mean you have to spend all your time at it, but you should record items as they occur to you by jotting them down in a notebook. Also, keep a file folder in which you drop ideas for column material. That way, you'll have plenty of material to choose from when you write the column.

Sources of Information

For good reason, a columnist has been defined as "one who is often out of ideas but is well stocked with words." You may agree that the column is an excellent way to reach your publics on a regular basis, but you may still have doubts about whether you will find enough interesting material in your area of expertise to develop and hold a reading audience. It is quite possible, even with all the other demands of your job, that you'll soon be able to produce a creditable column with the total investment of no more than one or two hours a week.

Few columnists write solely "out of their heads." Sydney Harris, whose column is syndicated in several hundred newspapers, admits that most of his ideas come from other persons. He also reads a great deal and makes notes about what he reads for future reference.

Semiprofessional columnists—those who write columns as part of their jobs because it helps them do their jobs better—also have many reliable sources for items. Here are a few of the sources that environmentalists, home economists, conservationists, and extension directors have found useful in helping them fill their columns with interesting material:

1. **Contacts with the Public**—If you are a public servant, you will have varied and frequent contacts with the public. Many will yield a column item or a name.
2. **Publications**—Every professional person has access to professional and trade magazines, newsletters, and direct mail from several sources. Often, this material will yield items of local interest or items that can be applied locally.
3. **Office Calls**—One of the primary functions of those in extension offices, Soil Conservation Service offices, and Agricultural Stabilization and Conservation Service offices is to answer questions. If three persons call with the same question, it is generally safe to assume that another 50 will need the same information.
4. **Your Observations**—What you see and hear as you go about your job can produce column items.
5. **Seasonal Topics**—Each new season brings about new problems in agriculture, homemaking, outdoor recreation, and conservation, as well as most other fields. Items, however, should precede the season slightly. An article on winter feeding of cattle, for

example, is more useful before the first blizzard.
6. **New Research**—The professional who is in touch with his or her field should act as a bridge between the scientist and those who can benefit from scientific knowledge. Interpreting new findings to readers in words they can understand is an important function of many public servants.
7. **Coming and Past Events**—A column should not take the place of the office bulletin board, but it is a good place to remind readers of coming events and to report briefly on past events.
8. **Pictures**—Pictures are not ordinarily used in columns, but there is no reason why they can't be, if you have an unusually good one that complements what the column is attempting to say.

The first rule of public speaking is that you have to get and keep the attention of the audience. The first rule of writing a voluntary column is that you not only have to get the attention of the reader, but you have to develop reader loyalty over a period of time. To do this, the column content will have to be something more than a weekly "hard sell" of your program. Unfortunately, you'll find that not everyone will share your enthusiasm for skillful homemaking, conservation of energy and resources, scientific agriculture, or the wise use and enjoyment of wildlife. As one old North Dakota farmer said, "I don't need anybody to tell me how to farm better. I'm already farming a lot worse than I know how."

For him and others, who may need information in spite of themselves, the light touch helps maintain column readership.

Localizing and Personalizing

The process of localizing and personalizing are so important in both column writing and newsletters that the subject deserves separate treatment. You will recall from Chapter 3 that events that occur closest to the reader have the most impact and interest for him or her. A tornado that devastated a town in Florida would have some interest to a resident of Ohio, but it would have more interest if it occurred in Ohio. It would have even greater interest if it occurred in the reader's home county.

Editorial offices of state extension services provide county extension personnel with packets of information. It is their hope that those on the local scene will rewrite the articles from a local perspective for their columns, a surefire way of increasing reader interest. Even so, some extension directors fill their columns with releases from the state office without any effort to add the important local touch.

There are ways, however, that you can localize and personalize copy for a column without much extra effort:

1. **Source Localization**—A local source is used for attribution, rather than using an outside source. (Example: "now is the time to check your fields for corn root worm," advises Millford Jones, area crop specialist.)
2. **Localization through Local Example**—A specific, local example adds interest and relevance for your reader. (Example: "Tama County corn growers are in the fields this week checking on corn root worm. Henry Vandercamp says his fields appear to be clear so far, and he attributes this to the fact that he made an early application of insecticide last year.")
3. **"Easy" Localization**—This amounts to general, rather than specific, localization of a report. (Example: "Story County farmers are in the fields this week checking on corn root worm." Such localization, which may be better than referring to "The nation's corn

farmers," is inferior to more personal localization.)
4. **Localization through Statistics**—Gleaning local data from more general data can add reader interest. (Example: "More than 10,000 acres of corn in Fayette County were badly infested with root worm last year. Perhaps we can reduce loss this year by taking the following steps. . . .")
5. **Develop Local Angles of National Stories**—State and national stories that appear in your newspaper or in broadcast news programs often have local angles that can be developed. (Example: "News out of Washington that rail freight rates are going up could have the effect of costing Woodbury County farmers about three cents a bushel on corn.")

Although each of these methods of localizaing is better than none, undoubtedly the best of them is localizing by use of local persons as examples. Only a minority of persons may be interested in corn root worm, but more of them will be interested if they know it is Henry Vandercamp's problem with corn root worm, or his solution. Readership increases because readers can count on finding something or someone who relates to them in every column. A column on a local farmer who has solved a serious soil erosion problem is likely to have a better chance of convincing his neighbors to consider the same approach than a professionally written, technically accurate research bulletin on the same subject (although technical bulletins obviously have a place in the diffusion of information).

The Column Format

The editor of the newspaper in which a column may be printed has ultimate control over the format (form or arrangement) in which the column is to appear. It is quite in order for the person offering the column to also suggest a format for an appropriate column heading. (See Fig. 6.1.) Ideally, the column heading should have the following items: A catchy head that identifies the column and indicates its content, the byline identifying the columnist, and a headline that indicates the major content for that particular column. Also, the extension service usually advises county extension directors to include their pictures in the column headings so persons in their communities will learn to identify them and feel they know them more personally.

The column in Figure 6.2, written by an extension director in Lewis County, in the State of Washington, is made up of two single columns of type "doubled up" under a two-column heading which remains the same each issue. The column head has the virtue of being immediately distinguishable from other headlines in the paper. This is accomplished by the use of the rules above and below the column title. Typographically, all this column lacks is a headline identifying the specific content of the major item in this particular column. However, the small all-capital-letter subheadings on each paragraph serve the same function; that is, they tell the reader what to expect in the column.

The use of a headline that changes for each column, and which indicates the content for that column, or the use of paragraph headings indicating the content of each paragraph, serve to break up the solid look of the column and make it more inviting and readable. Further, they provide an index for those who skim the paper (as most readers do) for that which interests them. For example, the subheading, "Birds Nip Blossoms," might be expected to attract readers interested in birds as well as those primarily interested in agriculture.

A column must not only be interesting

WILDLIFE NOTES

BY GLENN JONES, WILDLIFE BIOLOGIST
IOWA CONSERVATION COMMISSION

Farmers throughout Iowa were urged today by the Conservation Commission not to burn off valuable life cover which is critically needed for spring nesting of pheasants as well as other types of w Bob Barratt, Superint

FARM TALK

Dave Hessman
Ida County Extension Director

Report from Capitol Hill

By State Representative
Terry Branstad

YAKIMA VALLEY
Fruit Fact

BY BILL HUDSON
Yakima County Extension Age

Outdoors with Les

By Les Licklider

Tornado Talk

By Don Ambroson
Supt. of Schools

FOR YEARS NOW, Americans have been concerned reading skills taught in their schools.

FARM REPORT

by
Joe E. Legg
Extension
director
Jones county

SUPPORT THE FARMER

Monticello has 3,500 residents and each person eats national age quantities, one Jones county cattleman finishing 630 steers lies the cities' beef; one hogman marketing 1,860 hogs supplies ork; one 100-cow dairy herd supplies the milk and a flock of laying hens fills the annual demand for eggs.

Extension Excerpts

by Elsie Mae VanWert

Hancock Cou

Clips and Tips from ips

by HUGO FEDERHART

FIG. 6.1. Several column headings.

but it must look interesting typographically. Column content printed "solid" with no typographic relief such as paragraph heads or white space looks dull and uninteresting. One easy way to break up the solid look is by use of more frequent paragraphs than you are accustomed to using. Small, bold-faced paragraph headings in capital letters are appropriate whenever you change subjects in the column. (See the use of paragraph headings in Figure 6.2.)

Paragraph headings can be typed in as you write the copy, or they can be "edited in" with pencil after the column has been written. If you type them in capital letters and underline the words, it will indicate to the printer that they should be set in boldface type.

Another possibility is the use of boldface "lead-ins." The first few words of each paragraph in which you change subjects are typed in capital letters and underlined to indicate boldface. In the

FIG. 6.2. Paragraph headings.

Following The Furrow
By Ed Minnick
Lewis County Extension Agent

BIRDS NIP BLOSSOMS
Our office has received another report this year about birds nipping off the blossoms of cherry trees. They don't eat them, they just cut them off by pecking which causes the entire blossom to fall. No one seems to know why the birds do this. Maybe it is a habit like some people chewing grass. If anyone knows more about the birds let us know.

FRUIT SET ON TREES
Last week we mentioned that fruit set could be poor this year due to poor bee activity during the blossoming period of fruit trees. Jim Ballard, WSU Extension horticulturist from Yakima, who works on tree fruit problems in that area claims most of the sprays applied to fruit trees have not proven too successful on apples.

Gibberellic acid has been used to set fruit mostly on pears but it won't work on apples. I guess there is no known spray which will substitute for bee activity in causing fruit set.

Ballard informs me that an all-time bumper crop is expected in the Yakima valley this year. So apples should be plentiful.

Our office has had several inquiries regarding a dark, shellac-type film that covers the limbs and trunks of plum and cherry trees. The film is a form of algae that has established itself on trees due to our wet spring. It does not harm the tree and will peel off and disappear when the weather is drier.

RHODODENDRON SHOW
All rhododendron buffs are invited to the 11th Annual Rhododendron Show sponsored by the Olympia chapter this Saturday and Sunday. The show will be held at Tumwater Falls Park in Tumwater.

On Saturday the show will be open from 9 a.m. to 8 p.m. and on Sunday from 9 a.m. to 6 p.m. The show is open to the public. The park contains over 300 rhododendrons and knaphill azaleas planted by club members in 1966.

BEE REGISTRATION
In case you haven't already done so, you should register your bees at the Extension office. The bee inspector will then visit your hives some time to see if the bees are healthy and give you some helpful hints if necessary.

THOUGHT FOR THE DAY
"More doors are opened by please than keys."

absence of other kinds of relief white space can be used between paragraphs, or paragraph separators such as dashes or asterisks can be used. The typography in Figure 6.2, although better than most columns, could be improved by inserting one line of white space above each paragraph subheading.

PRODUCING THE NEWSLETTER

The newsletter has become the most popular and, in many ways, most effective method of direct communication with defined audiences. The newsletter is used by government agencies, churches, clubs, businesses, schools and colleges, and virtually any kind of organization in need of a direct method of communicating with internal or external publics. (Internal and external publics are discussed in Chapter 2.) The extension service advocates the use of separate newsletters for separate specialized areas of agriculture. The newsletters go only to those who have an interest in the subject matter, so the readership is predictably high as is the ratio of cost to effectiveness.

The newsletter is characterized by informality, flexibility, and low cost. A quality newsletter can be produced successfully in almost any modern office. There are several means of producing newsletters appropriate for almost any size organization. The liquid duplicator (Ditto) can be used for very small organizations that do not require more than 80 to 100 copies. The standard mimeograph can provide a higher quality reproduction and perhaps triple the number of copies that can be run off before stencils must be recut. Pictures may be included in mimeographed newsletters by the use of a special process of "screening" the pictures. The cost is low, but the quality of pictures is not as good as in offset methods; head sizes in pictures must be large because detail is lost in the reproduction process.

Office offset (Lithograph, for example) offers the opportunity to produce a professional-looking newsletter with runs of several hundred copies. Pictures may be used if they are prescreened through a special process. Line drawings may be used—if they are distinctly black on white—by pasting them right on the page layouts.

The office offset is clearly the preferred method of producing a newsletter if it is to go to several hundred persons on a regular basis. The cost of the original equipment, however, is several times higher than the cost of a quality mimeograph machine, and it may not be wise in a small office.

Newsletters of large state and national organizations, going to thousands of persons, are usually done by professional printers by the offset method. In such quantities, the work can usually be done at less expense out of the office.

The dry copier, which can be found in nearly every office today, can be perfectly satisfactory as a way of reproducing the newsletter, but the costs per copy are exceedingly high.

The Newsletter Nameplate

The nameplate appears at the top of the newsletter and serves the same purpose as the column head. Like the logotype in a department store ad, it identifies the source. A neatly printed nameplate with commercial type looks more professional than a hand-lettered nameplate. Since it can be used over and over in most processes, the cost of having a nameplate made up by a printer, or through use of "paste-up" type, may be well worth it. The nameplate need not take up more than the top 3 inches of the page; some newsletter editors waste a great deal of valuable paper with nameplates that are too elaborate. (See Jack O'Dwyer's small, but effective, nameplate in Figure 6.3.)

You can introduce color into your newsletter at low cost by having a year's supply of nameplates printed up in advance on the proper paper stock. Or, if your printing equipment permits, you can produce a year's supply on your own machine, eliminating the chore of cleaning up the equipment each issue for each color.

The size and shape of your newsletter is limited only by the capacity of the

FIG. 6.3. Newsletter nameplates.

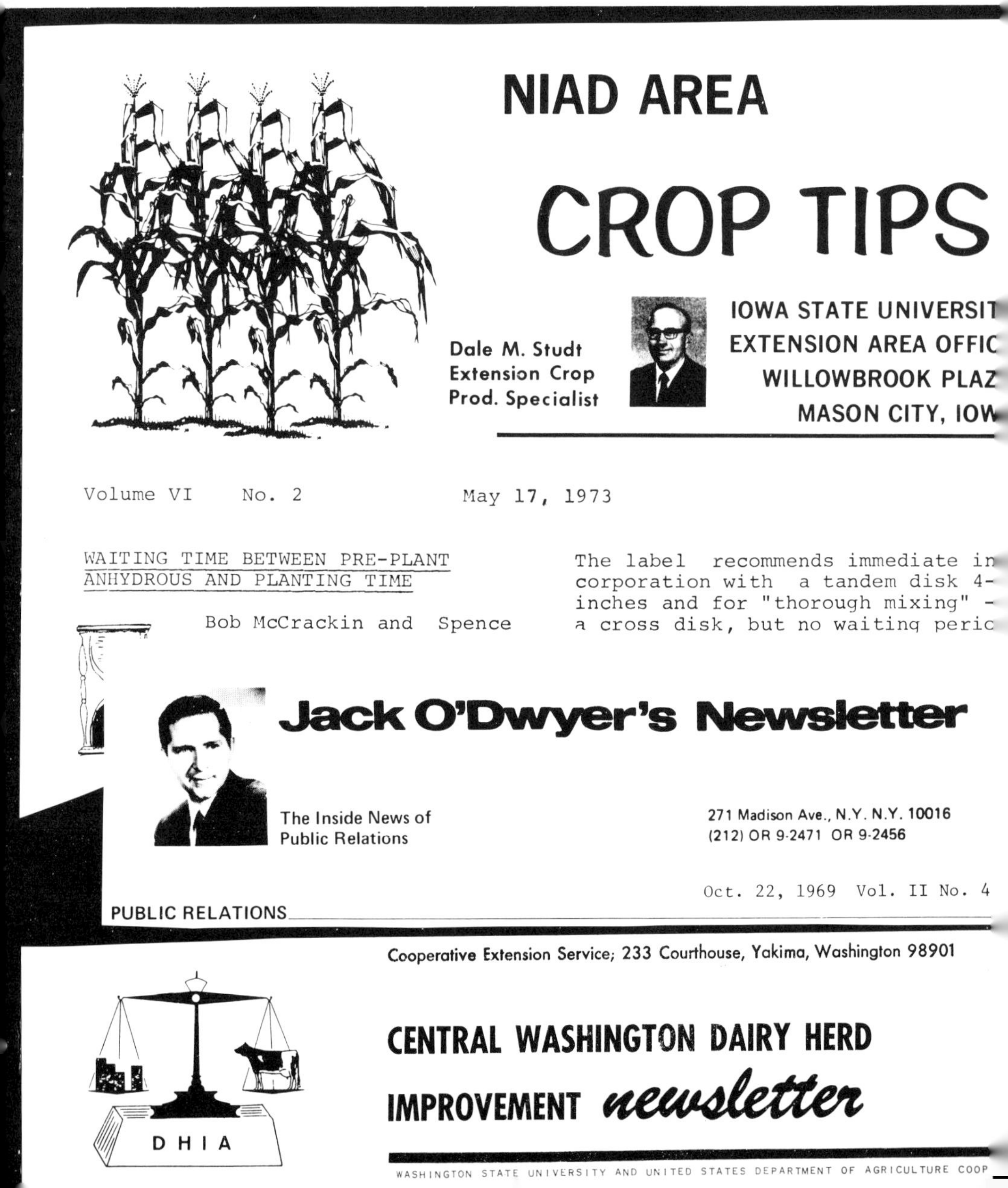

CONGREGATION GETS NEW ALTAR

The new altar arrived this week from St. Paul
and has been installed in time for Sunday
services. Bill Olson and Herman Smith....
                                         Centered headline,
                                         underlined; block paragraphs

The altar was built by the Concordia Church
Supply house and . . . .

NEW COURT HOUSE   New County Court House
OFFICIALS SWORN IN officials were sworn in
                    Tuesday in noon-hour   Inset headline
services. Circuit Court Judge Homer Smith
presided over the ceremonies.

PUBLIC RELATIONS IS IMPORTANT

     Public Relations, when viewed as a
     medium in itself rather than a con-
     tinuous program, can be an important   Flush left headline,
     marketing tool.   indented block paragraphs

FISH FARMING by two Guthrie Center farmers
is creating interest in commercial fish   All-capital lead-ins;
farming in Iowa. It is a profitable sideline.   block paragraphs

LITTLE BUT BIG IMPROVEMENT

Although there have been many major improvements in City Hall, a relatively small one
took place in the Fire Department April 3.   All-capital flush left
A new kitchen has been added to make life   headline; block paragraphs
easier for the fire fighters.

FIG. 6.4. Examples of typewriter typography.

printing equipment you use, but standard paper sizes are 8½ x 11 inches and 8½ x 14 inches. These sizes fold easily into standard envelopes for mailing or may be folded once and stapled with the address imprinted in a box on the final page. Twenty-pound paper permits printing on both sides without the disadvantage of "see through" of ink. Colored paper may be used at additional cost.

Newsletter Typography

Newsletters may take many forms, but perhaps the most economical and effective use of space is the two-column format. (See "Crop Tips" in Fig. 6.3.) The two-column format makes it possible to single-space the type, and it is ideally suited to displaying the short items that should make up the newsletter. By pretyping, the columns may be justified (evened up) on the right margin. If this takes too much time, it is quite satisfactory to use unjustified columns.

Electric typewriters with interchangeable typing heads make it possible to use larger type for headlines, but even with a standard office machine you can achieve considerable variety in typography (Fig. 6.4). Headlines should be separated from copy by one line below and two above each headline.

Cartoons and line drawings, available through office equipment stores, can be used easily in the offset process, less so in the mimeograph process. It is good advice to hold down the size and not use more than two illustrations per page. More illustrations make a cluttered looking page in which the illustrations dominate, rather than accentuate, the message you are trying to deliver.

Newsletter Content

Newsletter content, of course, is dictated by the information you are trying to transmit to your readers. In essence, the approach suggested for columns makes good sense for newsletters: short items, and informal touch, plenty of names, localization, and personalization. Because a newsletter is usually begun to meet a specific communication objective, the content more or less takes care of itself. It is a way of announcing meetings, bringing new information to readers, and promoting your program. The flexibility of the newsletter permits you to adjust the length of your message to the needs of your audience. If you keep the audience in mind, and keep your own objectives in mind, you should be able to produce a newsletter that will make your program more effective and serve your constituents well.

SUMMARY

Columns and newsletters offer unique opportunities to publicists willing and able to devote some of their energy and imagination to planning and writing them.

In return for the advantages they provide, columns and newsletters exact a price.

Although a column, circulated in a mass medium, demands no cash payment, it must be continually produced. The schedule can become rigorous and troublesome in the midst of other responsibilities and the quality of the column can suffer accordingly.

The newsletter's frequency can be controlled by the writer, but it too demands time and thought devoted to its contents. In addition, layout, production, and distribution take their share of resources. The newsletter also demands financial commitments for paper, supplies, printing, and postage.

Newsletters and columns, however, can have long-term effects through their continuity and the loyal readership they can create.

7 Photos and art can help tell your story

PHOTOGRAPHS

ROBERT C. JOHNSON

Pictures are increasing in number and improving in quality in almost all forms of mass communication. Journalists have found that good pictures attract attention, arouse interest, and represent a powerfully effective means of telling a story in a way that words alone cannot.

Television is the medium that perhaps has done more than any other to make twentieth-century America picture conscious. Now that the viewing public can be transported almost instantaneously to the scene of a news event and can watch it unfold, people no longer are satisfied solely with word descriptions of what is going on around them. They want to see what the people and places in the news look like. They expect pictorial reports in virtually all mass media and on all manner of topics.

ROBERT JOHNSON is Associate Professor of Journalism and Mass Communication, Iowa State University, where he specializes in teaching photography.

Recognizing this growing demand for pictorial communication, the professionals who work for newspapers, television stations, and magazines are eager to obtain and use as many pictures as possible. This means there are outlets for your publicity pictures; you have the opportunity to convey a favorable impression of your organization, your project, or your company. But conveying that favorable impression depends, at least to some extent, on how much creative effort you invest in getting a good picture—one that is worth publishing.

TAKING THE PICTURE

Whether you take the picture yourself or have a photographer from the newspaper or television station carry out the assignment for you, you will want that picture to say what you intended. A professional photographer can help you arrange subject matter and adjust lighting. It is his responsibility to expose the picture correctly and produce a satisfactory print. But his work will be eased considerably if you have a clear idea of the picture's purpose and can tell him what it is.

If you must take the picture yourself, it will be up to you to select and arrange subject matter, plan the background and create lighting effects so the picture will carry out its purpose. Any camera you use should have a lens capable of producing an 8 x 10-inch enlargement that is sharp and clear from corner to corner. This generally rules out box cameras with their simple lenses, but almost anything else will work if you use it properly.

When you cannot do the photography yourself, arrange to have the newspaper or television station send a staff photographer. This minimizes cost to you, but you will have to sell the people you contact on the news value of the event and the worth of the picture before they can justify assigning photographers. Wherever possible, you should start working with the media at least a week ahead of the time you want the picture taken so the assignment can be fitted into photographers' schedules.

If the picture is for a newsletter, brochure, magazine, or some publication that does not have a staff photographer, you may be able to hire the newspaper or television station photographer to take the picture on his own time. Still another possibility might be the local portrait or wedding photographer. Even an amateur who has access to a darkroom and produces photographs of good quality can do the work for you. In these cases, you should expect to pay his expenses and up to $5 for the first print of each picture. Additional prints of individual pictures should cost less than the first one.

In general, it is safe to publish news pictures without obtaining releases from persons pictured. If you want to be safe, however, it is wise to obtain a written release from every person whose picture appears in advertising, promotional, or news-editorial pieces. Here is an all-purpose release form recommended by the Photographers' Association of America.

City_____, Date_____

For value received, I hereby consent that the pictures taken of me by _____, proofs of which are hereto attached, or any reproduction of the same, may be used or sold by _____
for the purpose of illustration, advertising, or publication in any manner. I hereby certify and covenant that I am over twenty-one years of age. (A parent or legal guardian must sign for a minor.)

Signature of model or subject

Witness

PHOTOS AND ART

STRIVE FOR TECHNICAL QUALITY

Before a picture can be reproduced with any degree of success in a publication or on television, certain mechanical and technical requirements must be met. Perhaps the most important of these involves picture clarity. The images must be sharp and distinct. If the picture is blurred or fuzzy, one or more of several errors is responsible:

1. **The camera was moved when the shutter was snapped.** Practice releasing your camera shutter gently and slowly, just as the crack marksman squeezes away a rifle shot. The slightest poke or jab at the shutter will jar the camera sufficiently to blur the entire picture, even at relatively fast shutter speeds.
2. **The subject moved at the moment of exposure.** Try to catch your subject during a relaxed moment when sudden or violent movements are unlikely. One way is to have the subject concentrate on a point away from the camera but plausible to the story you want to tell, so that you can take several successive exposures without disturbing the basic composition of the picture.
3. **The camera was not focused properly.** The photographer who persists in prolonging the focusing operation unnecessarily is a trial to everyone, but it is important to focus the camera carefully. On a camera with a ground glass focusing screen, one way is to rack the focusing knob forward and backward through the point of greatest image sharpness, reducing the amount of turn each time until you are right on target. The camera with a rangefinder system seldom presents a focusing problem. Just remember to perform the operation!

One of the reasons technical excellence is so essential is that some quality inevitably is lost whenever a picture is reproduced in newspapers or magazines or on television. For the continuous tone photograph that you carry around in your billfold or purse to be reproduced in any medium, the tones in it would have to be broken into a pattern of dots or lines (look closely at the illustrations in this chapter). In the process both tone and clarity are reduced somewhat.

The photograph that reproduces best is one that has a full contrast range from jet black to clear white, with most of the picture area composed of the various shades of gray between these two extremes. There also should be visible detail in the picture's shadow areas as well as texture in the white areas. If you think about it, you will realize that the shadows cast by objects seldom are completely black and that even pure white shirts or blouses have visible folds and fabric patterns. The technically excellent picture will portray these nuances of tone faithfully.

As you judge a picture for reproduction purposes, look for **tonal separation** between the objects that are important to the photograph's story. If there is only slight contrast, the objects will tend to blend together and become nearly indistinguishable from one another in the reproduction process. It is also likely that the picture that looks muddy or washed out will be unacceptable for publication, as will prints that are full of dust specks and scratches.

PREPARING PICTURES FOR PUBLICATION

Now here are some mechanical considerations you will want to observe as you take, select, or prepare pictures for publication:

1. The white borders around the edge of the print should not be cut off. The editor may want to use this space to indicate the exact area of the picture he wants to reproduce.

FIG. 7.1. A good picture tells its story in an original or unique fashion without distorting the message. Avoid the overworked lineup arrangement and look for a creative way to convey the message.

PERRY STRUSE

2. Don't write on the back of a picture. Almost any mark on the reverse side of a print will leave an impression on the surface and show up in the reproduction process, even though the surface impression may not be visible to the eye.
3. All legends, identifications, or instructions which are to accompany a picture should be typed on a separate piece of paper. Use rubber cement to fasten the upper edge of the paper to the back of the print so the message is visible below the picture. Adhesives other than rubber cement tend to wrinkle the photograph.
4. Avoid bending the picture because surface cracks will show up in reproduction. If you are sending a photograph by mail, sandwich it between two pieces of stiff cardboard and label the envelope "Photograph. Do Not Bend."
5. Most larger newspapers and magazines prefer 8 x 10-inch prints. Many smaller daily and weekly newspapers, however, are not equipped to change the size of a picture in the engraving process. For this reason, you ought to check with the publication to see if you should submit the pictures in the exact sizes they will be when published and what sizes are wanted. Another possibility is to measure the paper's column width and then submit prints that are one, two, and three columns wide, thereby offering the editor a choice.
6. If the picture is to be used on television, a color slide in a horizontal format is best because it conforms quite closely to the rectangular shape of the television picture tube.
7. For print media, matte dried rather than glossy prints will do nicely. The shiny surface of the glossy print causes reflection problems and any unevenness in the gloss will cause engraving problems for newspapers.
8. Television stations can and do use 35

mm. color slides, but magazines and newspapers normally will not accept them because they are not equipped to reproduce them.

The cost of reproducing color pictures in print is extremely high. Before submitting color pictures to a magazine or newspaper, it would be wise to check with the editor. Also, find out what the publication's requirements are as to the type and size of film to use. Generally, magazines want a "transparency" or "color positive" film 2¼ inches square or larger. Newspapers, on the other hand, usually want a color negative and a color print.

FIG. 7.3. When the subjects in a picture are looking at the camera, the reality and natural atmosphere of the photograph are lost. The picture becomes another example of individuals having their pictures taken. One of the most difficult jobs faced by a photographer is keeping the subjects interested in what they are doing and not in what the photographer is doing. The example is extreme, having been taken from behind the persons involved, but it is illustrative. It also demonstrates the effect of carefully choosing the foreground of the picture. (Also see Fig. 7.10.)

FIG. 7.2. Human beings are interested in other human beings. When an editor is faced with a choice between a picture that includes a person and one that does not, the decision is generally an easy one. The human element suggests action and adds a sense of reality. Greenhouse plants may interest members of the garden club, but the addition of a person widens the audience and increases the impact of the picture.

9. The standard motion picture film for television is 16 mm., but because of the expense involved and the rather high level of competence required, it is best to use film only when the station is willing to do the shooting, processing, and editing. Some stations are equipped to use Super 8 color film.

PICTURES MUST TELL A STORY

Although these technical and mechanical considerations are of great importance, observing them will not necessarily guarantee a picture that will interest an audience or convey a message. In the last analysis, it is subject matter—what it is and how it is presented—that determines the communicative worth of a picture. Happily, there are no eternal rules governing how any par-

LAUREL STUDT

ticular subject should be photographed. If there were, all pictures of a given type would come close to being exactly alike. As a matter of fact, that happens all too frequently—even in the absence of such rules. How often, for example, have you seen group shots or award presentations where picture after picture looked the same? Or how many times have you seen the little knot of basketball players with arms stretched upward toward the ball or hoop? When each successive picture begins to look like the previous one, no one can blame the audience for ignoring the photograph or giving it only a passing glance. Those same pictures, however, taken with a little planning, a few props where that is possible, and some imagination can be new, interesting, and informative experiences for the audience.

You don't need to be a veteran photographer to blend these ingredients into the picture taking process, although the more practice you get the better you should become. Just observing two fundamental principles can improve almost anyone's photography in only a matter of hours: (1) Put action into your pictures, and (2) keep them simple.

FIG. 7.4. When the size of an object is important to a picture, it is necessary to compare it with an object of known size. Subjects may be made to appear very large by selecting a very small object for direct comparison. A tiny transistor seems even smaller in a large, muscular hand than in a tiny, delicate hand. It is also possible to make objects look larger by placing them nearer the camera than the object of known size. This is a photographic trick familiar to most fishing enthusiasts.

USE IMAGINATION TO SHOW ACTION

Perhaps the easiest and most useful way of getting action into your pictures is to include people, or animals, or both. If you are photographing a machine, for example, show its operator as well, and have him turning a dial, pushing a button, or engaging in whatever activity he normally would under the circumstances. Even having him wipe the sweat from his brow might be logical. The important considerations really are two: (1) That the action be plausible to the situation, and (2) that the action be of the kind the camera can portray.

In not many circumstances is it plausible or desirable to have persons looking into the camera. That is the sort of action you don't want. If the person is supposed to be driving a tractor, operating a lathe, or removing a cake from the oven, he ought to paying attention to what he is doing and not gazing into the camera lens. Otherwise, all the realism is lost. The person becomes someone having his picture taken rather than a man performing a task.

The second consideration—action the camera can portray—is equally important. Reading, for example, is a mental rather than a physical process. The camera can show a person in the act of reading, but the picture will be more interesting if that person is shown turning a page or frowning in puzzlement over some difficult passage in the book. It is the suggestion of physical action that makes the difference.

It is not always necessary to have the entire person or animal in the picture. In fact, when you are photographing rather small objects, just showing the upper torso of a person, or a face, or even a hand will be enough. For example, if you wanted to photograph a fisherman tying a fly or a homemaker sewing on a button, these rather intricate operations would become almost meaningless in a picture that included the entire person. Instead, try a closeup of the key objects, and include just the face and hands, locating them as strategically as possible. The human element will introduce action, arouse interest, and provide a means of establishing the relative size of the central subject matter—the fly or the button. The world's largest ear of corn will look just like any other ear of corn unless some comparison is made in the picture.

Finally, the reality you are trying to portray in a picture by using living creatures to introduce action can be lost if they are not in a realistic situation. That is, under most circumstances you should not expect a farmer to be feeding hogs in his best suit. Unless he is cautioned against it, however, he might show up wearing a dress suit because he is going to have his picture taken.

CUT CLUTTER FOR IMPACT

The second basic guide to setting up effective pictures—simplicity—is achieved in part by getting the subjects as close together as possible, positioning the camera as close to the subjects as possible, and selecting a camera angle which will eliminate everything that does not contribute to the meaning of the picture.

When an individual looks at a group of persons or objects, they are seen as part of a larger panorama. There can be considerable distance between the objects, but they will appear to be unified because the human eye can cover the surrounding space with great speed and remarkable efficiency. In a photograph, however, this space effect is eliminated. The scene becomes a restricted one and,

PAUL ANCERSON

FIG. 7.5. Simplicity is one of the most important factors in a good picture. When setting up a picture, is is best to avoid clutter in either the foreground or the background.

instead of a reasonably unified group, you are likely to have a series of disunified individuals. The spaces between persons or objects may seem insignificant to the eye, but they stand out in a photograph like the gap left by a missing tooth.

This principle applies to all pictures, not just to those involving groups. If you were photographing a home economist and her prize-winning cake, for example, she normally would hold the cake at about waist level—a pose that looks perfectly natural to the eye. In a photograph, however, her face would be at the top of the picture and the cake at the bottom, leaving too much unused space between the two. The picture would lack unity. In fact, instead of a single picture you have two: one of the head and one of the hands and cake. To achieve unity, you might have the woman hold the cake up to her face—so close that she undoubtedly would protest. This might not look natural to the eye, but it would be effective in the finished picture. Another way of solving the problem would be to raise or lower the camera enough so that very little space existed between the face and the cake, even though there was considerable actual distance between the two objects.

One of the most difficult impulses to overcome in photography is the one that motivates you to make sure that "everything is in the picture." When grandpa decides to take a picture of little Ralph opening presents on Christmas morning, his first move is likely to be a step backwards to make sure that he gets all of little Ralph and his package in the picture. Then he takes another step back to include the Christmas tree, then another step to get Uncle Charlie and Aunt Mabel in the picture. The result may be an interesting picture for the family album, but it would quickly find its way into an editor's wastebasket. What he is more likely to want is a picture characterizing the emotions of a child on Christmas morning. So instead of backing up, move in closer—then move closer still. In our example, all you would need is the expression on the boy's face and a recognizable fragment of the Christmas present. It is the expression that conveys the human interest and the gift that conveys the meaning. Everything else merely serves as a distraction from the main point.

It is easy to move back, but it takes real courage to move in close and

FIG. 7.6. Another way to simplify a picture is to move the camera in close to the subject. An interesting picture can usually be made even more appealing by taking it from the close rather than the distant viewpoint. This method brings out textures and details otherwise overlooked by the casual viewer.

TIM DONOVAN

RUSSEL CAMPBELL

FIG. 7.7. A low camera angle frequently can be used to eliminate background clutter. The low viewpoint will place subjects against the sky rather than against trees, crowds, power poles, or other unrelated objects.

HUGH ZIKE

FIG. 7.8. One of the best ways to eliminate a cluttered background is to shoot the picture from a high camera angle. It may be necessary to take the photo from a chair, a nearby window, or a ladder. It can sometimes be done by holding the camera above the head. In any case, it is often useful in simplifying a picture and in revealing an intriguing perspective.

sacrifice all those things which it might be nice to show in the picture. If you think the editor might want a picture of the family, move them in close to the boy so they form a unified group. Then take a close picture of the group.

Even in a case where it is possible to get a simple picture from some distance away, the picture is likely to be more interesting if taken from a closer viewpoint. This emphasizes detail—detail that people fail to notice in their busy everyday lives. If the picture is of a loaf of bread, a shot taken from 6 feet away will show the bread, but one taken from 3 feet away will show the loaf and the texture of the bread itself.

BEWARE THE BACKGROUND

The background against which a picture is taken is probably the greatest source of confusion in pictures. The human eye is extremely selective. That is, your eyes see only a very small area at a time. Look at an object, even something as small as a pencil. You see the pencil

JACK O'KEEFE

FIG. 7.9. Sometimes the background of a picture can be used to help tell the story. In such instances, the background must be carefully chosen. Anything that does not contribute to the meaning or the character of the subject should be removed or avoided by shifting the camera position.

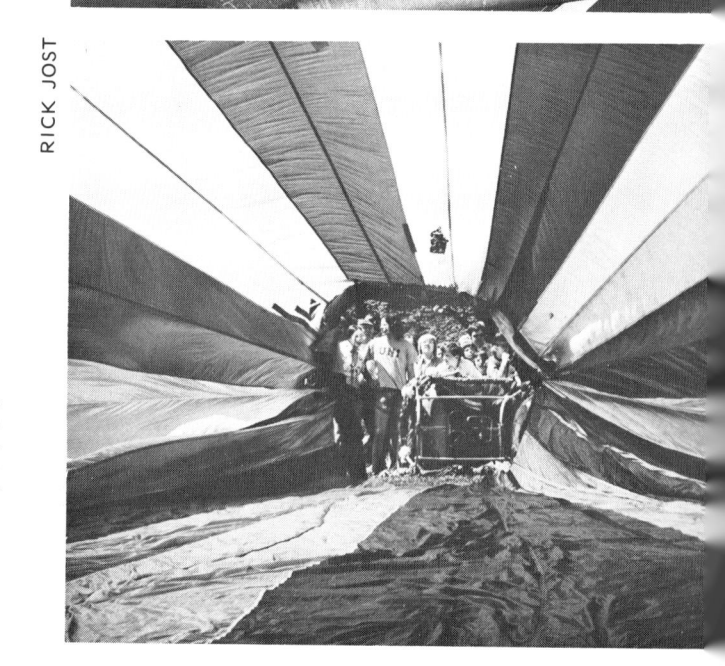

RICK JOST

FIG. 7.10. The foreground of a picture can also be used to effectively tell the story. Initiative and imagination resulted in a photograph with drama and personality rather than a mundane record of the back of a crowd peering into a balloon. (Also see Fig. 7.3.)

after your eyes have moved from end to end and side to side. The eyes examine small parts of the object and the mind puts the image together. This is especially significant for the person setting up a picture because the eye sees only what it is interested in and ignores or screens out the unwanted or the distracting. A camera lens, however, is not nearly as selective as the human eye. If something exists in what is being viewed by the camera lens, the film records it, whether it is related to the subject of the picture or not.

PHOTOS AND ART   71

FIG. 7.11. Lighting is almost as important as subject matter in a good photograph. Strong lighting conditions, such as those found in direct sunlight, lend a feeling of strength and forcefulness to the persons or objects in the picture. These feelings are primarily the result of the sparkling highlights and dark shadows produced by bright sunlight.

CINDY ALLEN

To make things worse, the camera has only one eye and consequently cannot perceive depth. If there is a telephone pole 40 feet behind a person when his picture is taken, that pole in the finished photograph will look as though it is growing out of the person's head. The consequence is that an unwanted object steals interest from what the photographer was trying to say in the picture. Almost anything in the background can dominate and confuse a picture if it has no business being there. Distractions can be as common as a light switch on the wall or a "No Parking" sign and still ruin an otherwise good photograph.

Safe backgrounds for most picture situations are a bare wall, clear sky, or open ground. If you use a wall, move your subjects 4 or 5 feet away so they will not cast confusing shadows on the wall. If you decide to use the sky, select a spot where the horizon is relatively free of trees or buildings and take the picture from a low

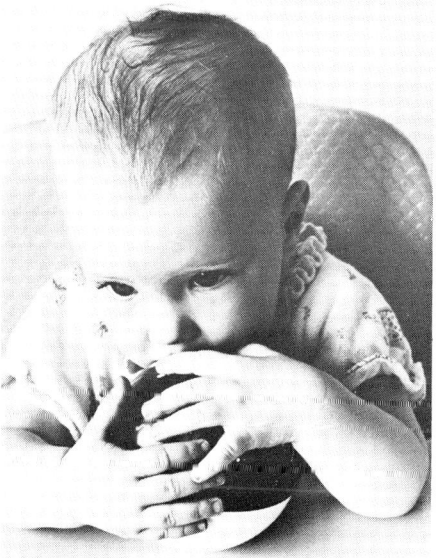

FIG. 7.12. When the contrast between highlight and shadow is reduced the subject takes on a soft, warm, and gentle feeling. Pictures taken on overcast days or in the shade will have such soft lighting and delicate qualities.

DAVID LENDT

viewpoint. If you wish to use the ground, pick up any litter that might be scattered around and take the picture from a high angle.

There often are situations in which the background can help tell the story. To carry out that function, however, the background must be well organized and everything in it must relate to the picture. Avoid any background which seems uniform at first glance but actually is made up of little patches of light and dark. This includes trees, shrubbery, radiators, venetian blinds, figured draperies, and the like. Backgrounds of that sort make pictures seem cluttered.

In general, if you are taking a picture of a dark object, place it in front of a relatively light background. If you tried to photograph a black Angus cow in front of a dark red barn, for instance, you would have trouble in a black and white picture trying to decide where the animal ended and the barn began. The reverse situation is also true. If you arranged to photograph a blonde woman in a white coat against a light background, your picture might turn out to be a face and two hands floating around in space.

FIG. 7.13. It is usually best to have persons face either directly into or directly away from the sunlight. This avoids the harsh shadows that frequently form an unattractive pattern on faces.

PLAN LIGHTING TO FIT SCENE

In addition to keeping your pictures simple and loading them with action, learning as much as you can about lighting and composition and applying that knowledge will do much to make your pictures more meaningful and psychologically interesting to those who see them.

As you consider the lighting question, you must decide what mood you want the picture to portray. Do you want the subject matter to have a strong and forceful appearance, or would it be more appropriate to convey the impression of softness and gentleness? If you decide upon the former, set up the picture in bright sunlight or light the subjects with

FIG. 7.14. With inanimate objects, on the other hand, it is usually better to have the light skim across the surface. This will result in patterns of highlight and shadow, creating the illusion of three dimensions in a two-dimensional photograph. Such lighting also brings out the surface texture of the subject.

PHOTOS AND ART

PHIL WHEATLEY

FIG. 7.15. A single camera cannot perceive or record depth in a picture. When images of objects touch or coincide with each other, the illusion of depth is often lost. Even though there may be great distances between objects in a scene, they may seem to merge in a photograph. This phenomenon creates the illusion that a person has a tree or a lamp post growing from his or her head. Depth and distance can be suggested in a two-dimensional picture by carefully arranging foreground articles and objects so as to enhance scale and perspective.

incandescent light bulbs. In both situations, the light will be intense and direct, resulting in bright highlights and strong shadows. This is a type of lighting that is appropriate for machines, buildings, men at work, and the like. It would not be the lighting to use for a picture of a young girl or a child with a new puppy where you wanted to create the effect of gentleness and affection. To do that, select a spot in the shade, take the picture on an overcast day, or use fluorescent lighting. All of these lighting conditions produce relatively less contrast between highlights and shadows.

Another aspect of lighting that may be subject to control is the angle at which the rays strike the subject.

If there are persons in the picture, have them face either directly toward or directly away from the light source. Either way, you will avoid harsh and ugly shadows and lines on their faces. If, on the other hand, you are photographing an object such as a cake, a building, or a machine, the picture will be more interesting if the light strikes that object from a side angle. This creates the highlights and shadows which will separate the various planes of the object in space, giving it volume and providing the illusion of depth in the picture. This type of lighting also brings out surface texture, illustrating for the viewer whether the subject being photographed is rough, smooth, shiny, or dull.

PLAN COMPOSITION FOR MOOD, STORY

Although composition is a term about which volumes have been written, we will use it here to mean **the arrangement of images within the picture**. As you compose a photograph, you should be less interested in the arrangement as seen without the camera than you are in the arrangement as seen through the viewfinder. When you are doing the camera work yourself, study the scene carefully through the camera's viewing system. As you do so, move the subjects to be photographed, the camera, the lighting, or all three until you are satisfied with the arrangement. If someone else is taking the picture for you, cut a small rectangular hole in a cardboard sheet, close one eye, and study the arrangement this way from the camera position. Again, shift things around until you like what you see.

One quality that people like to see in pictures is repetition of lines, shapes, or objects, so long as there is some variation in the pattern. If, for example, you were

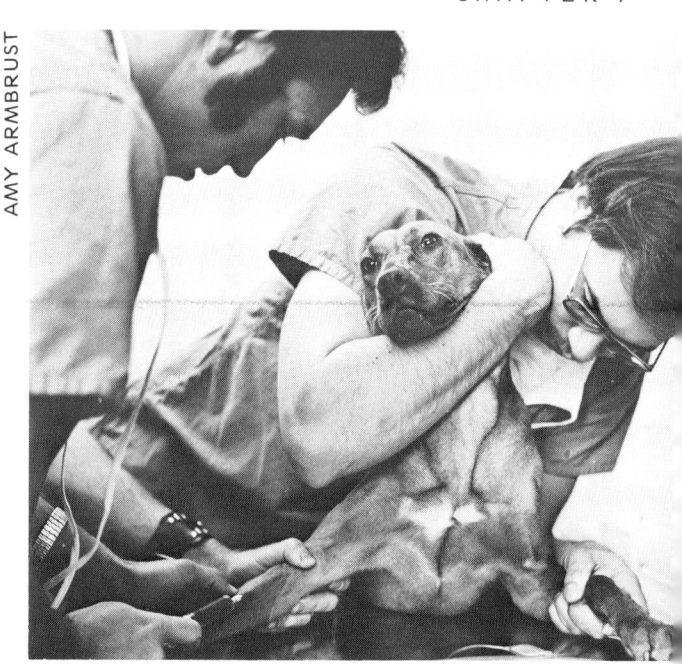

FIG. 7.16. Human interest is difficult to define but its presence in a picture is very nearly guaranteed by an expressive animal. The human interest photo calls up human emotions—empathy, sympathy, anger, outrage, pity—with its remarkable two-dimensional power. The most forceful and memorable photographs generally possess strong elements of human interest.

taking a picture of the winner of the county fair pie baking contest, you might show her in the foreground holding the prize pie while in the background would be a table holding all the other pies in the contest. You could tell the story by photographing just the woman and her pie, of course, but the picture would have greater appeal with the pie repetition feature added.

Another way to make your publicity pictures more attractive to editors and viewers is to arrange the subjects in a spot where there will be a natural framing situation. The simplest example would be to pose a person in a doorway and use the door jamb as your framing device. The framing idea you decide upon does not need to be as obvious as a doorway, and it is not always necessary to have the subject matter completely framed on all sides. Sometimes, just the corner of a building at the edge of the picture is sufficient. A common framing device used by photographers is a tree. Usually,

the trunk is located at the edge of the picture on one side and the lower limbs and leaves complete the frame at the top.

You might find some other aspects of composition useful in setting up a picture. One of these is the shape of the picture itself. In general, the picture's shape ought to fit the subject. That is, if you are picturing a tall object, such as a silo or grain elevator, the photograph probably will be more effective if it is taller than it is wide. Similarly, if you are photographing a horizontal scene such as a bean field or an arrangement of food on a dinner table, a horizontal picture will best fit the subject matter. It is also widely believed that a rectangular picture, either horizontal or vertical, is more interesting to the viewer than a perfectly square picture.

Where you are free to arrange your subject matter, a horizontal grouping in a horizontal format will convey a restful or quiet mood. A vertical arrangement in a vertical picture, on the other hand, is

75

FIG. 7.17. A picture with a vertical orientation of objects or with strong vertical lines conveys a feeling of dignity and a sense of respect.

thought to convey an impression of dignity or strength. A diagonal arrangement through either a horizontal or vertical picture will suggest action to the viewer. For example, if you wanted a picture of a conveyor loading corn into a crib, the picture would suggest more action if it were based on a diagonal line. You could position the camera so that the wagon and the bottom of the conveyor were in the lower left corner with the conveying device running diagonally to the upper right corner where the corn was falling into the crib.

FIG. 7.18. Pictures composed with horizontal lines or with a horizontal arrangement of images will tend to produce a quiet or restful feeling.

DEB SCHULTZ

CANDICE CAVANAUGH

FIG. 7.19. Diagonal lines or a diagonal arrangement of objects will enhance the feeling of action and movement in a picture.

SUMMARY

You are responsible for the pictures you want to place for publicity purposes whether you actually operate the camera or not. Keep them as simple as possible and load them with plausible action so they will seem real to both editors and viewers. Where possible, use lighting, repetition, and natural frames to emphasize subject matter.

FIG. 7.20. Providing a picture with some sort of natural frame is another way of getting reader or viewer interest. A tree, a doorway, or nearly any object can serve as a frame.

SUGGESTED READING

Bethers, Ray. **Photo-Vision.** New York: St. Martins, n.d.
Eastman Kodak Co. **Enlarging in Black and White and Color.** Kodak Publication No. 6-16, Rochester, N.Y.
Eastman Kodak Co. **Flash Pictures.** Kodak Publication No. C-2, Rochester, N.Y.
Fox, Rodney, and Kerns, Robert. **Creative News Photography.** Ames: Iowa State Univ. Press, 1961.
Rhode, Robert B., and McCall, Floyd H. **Introduction to Photography.** (2nd ed.) New York: Macmillan, 1971.
Sidey, Hugh, and Fox, Rodney, **1,000 Ideas for Better News Pictures.** Ames: Iowa State Univ. Press, 1956.
Swedlund, Charles. **Photography: A Handbook of History, Materials, and Processes.** New York: Holt, Rinehart & Winston, 1974.
Time-Life Library of Photography. New York: Time-Life Books, 1972.

You also are encouraged to read carefully the instruction booklet accompanying your camera and the instruction sheet accompanying the film you buy. Both provide reliable information which can be combined with the picture-making guides discussed in this chapter to improve both the technical quality and the content of your photographs.

ARTWORK

JOHN C. HUSEBY

Although the photograph is today's most widely used method of illustration, the drawing or painting still has its place. In some cases, it is an indispensable adjunct to a printed text, whether an advertisement, an editorial, or a straight news account. The choice of illustration depends, of course, on the function it is expected to perform.

The most obvious use for illustration is to provide visual information about things, people, or places. Photographs are used widely for this purpose, but in many instances drawings are more practical (as in a machinery parts catalog), or must be used where photos are not available (as for many historical events). Technical illustration of all kinds also fits in this category. We call such work "descriptive illustration."

Some illustrations, however, have a function beyond that of literal representation; they express a character or establish a mood appropriate to the text they accompany. The skillful artist has numerous devices available to help create such qualities. For example, the artist can select the most appropriate details and eliminate less significant ones; or the artist can employ various kinds of exaggeration, whether of form or action or lighting effect; or resort to symbolism to establish a nonvisual idea. Such illustration could be called "expressive."

A third function for illustration is the

JOHN HUSEBY is Senior Artist in Iowa State University's Publications Office.

"Along the way,
we've solved some pretty
interesting puzzles."

RYUN, GIVENS and COMPANY
Certified Public Accountants

CHAPTER 7

purely ornamental one. The small spot drawings in such magazines as **The New Yorker,** unrelated to the surrounding text, are examples of this function. Such artwork, inserted for the sole purpose of breaking up the monotony of otherwise solid type, is called "decorative illustration."

Here, then, are three different, although seldom clear-cut, functions for the illustrator—description, expression, and decoration. Many illustrations combine all three functions, and most combine two. For example, a high-quality descriptive illustration will probably exhibit some expressiveness also; and any well-trained illustrator should be skilled enough at pictorial composition that the finished work will decorate the page whether that is the artwork's major function or not. In most cases, however, one of the three functions is dominant.

Most professional illustrators are specialists. Those who are on the staffs of agencies or institutions need to be somewhat versatile, but those who work on a free-lance basis establish their reputations for particular types of work.

FIG. 7.21. A simple pen and ink drawing, executed in a free style with a minimum of detail. The effectively contrasting dark areas are drawn and filled in with the same pen in such a way as to provide an interesting and "softening" texture. (Courtesy Wesley Day and Co., Inc.)

FIG. 7.22. This illustration, drawn with a brush rather than a pen, utilizes a greater variety of line than is possible with a pen. (Courtesy **Des Moines Register** and **Tribune.**)

PHOTOS AND ART

The Graphic Artists Guild, a national organization of illustrators, classifies its members into five different groups: general (those doing advertising, editorial, or institutional work); technical; medical; fashion; and book. These are only general groupings, and individual artists are apt to be much more specialized. For instance, one illustrator might do nothing but nature and wildlife subjects, while another concentrates on illustrating children's books, and yet another specializes in science fiction.

STYLE

Within these specializations is another important consideration—the element of style. Each successful artist must develop this quality and, once developed, it is the artist's most valuable asset. It is the one element that makes artwork unique, the one thing that can

FIG. 7.23. An example of the scratchboard technique. A special cardboard, with a smooth surface of fine-grained white clay, is used. The drawing area is covered with black ink and details and textures are produced by scraping the ink away with a special tool. An especially effective technique for depicting various textures, it requires a practiced and disciplined hand. (Courtesy Iowa State University Press.)

FIG. 7.24. A drawing in the "dry brush" technique. The solid black areas are drawn with a wet brush, but the gray tones are produced by dragging a nearly dry brush over the paper. This is a good way to get the effect of gradations of tone without using a halftone screen. Understandably, some of the drawing's more delicate tones might be lost in reproduction. (Courtesy **Des Moines Register** and **Tribune**.)

FIG. 7.25. A composite illustration intended to represent a wide range of professions. Such an illustration is more symbolic than factual, and its irregular dimensions give it a strongly decorative character. It is executed in partly opaque and partly transparent washes, and it is printed as a highlight halftone, requiring a double printing process. The process is thus more expensive than a plain halftone printing job. (Courtesy Iowa State University Publications Art Office.)

place one artist's services in greater demand than another's.

For the art buyer, too, this is an important consideration. Does the particular artist's style suit the buyer's situation? Is it in character with the buyer's product? Will it be attractive to the buyer's audience? Norman Rockwell is not used to advertise rock concert, nor is Peter Max used to sell mutual funds.

Some persons are afraid to use art that is "far out" or extreme in style on the ground that it is faddish and will soon go out of style. In most cases this is a foolish fear. The overwhelming majority of publicity pieces rarely reach beyond the audience of the moment, and a contemporary, up-to-date appearance is nearly always an advantage.

Interest in nostalgia may seem to contradict this rule of thumb. The interest in styles of the past has led progressively from a revival of "Art Nouveau" of the 1890s, to a rage for the "Art Deco" of the 1920s and early 1930s, and even to the styles of the 1940s and 1950s. When such styles are borrowed, however, it is usually in such a special context that it

PHOTOS AND ART

becomes another form of bringing artwork up-to-date.

TECHNIQUE

Closely related to the element of style is the artist's technique. Famous artists whose work appears in full color in

For the best coverage of the Boys State Basketball Tournament turn to your Des Moines Register and Tribune Sports sections!

FIG. 7.26. Exaggeration is not only a device for expressing character, but is also a prime tool for achieving humor. (Courtesy **Des Moines Register** and **Tribune**.)

FIG. 7.27. Though this brush drawing is based on a photograph, it is simplified nearly to the point of abstraction. Little remains but a striking pattern of lines; yet, its subject is immediately recognizable. (Courtesy **Des Moines Register** and **Tribune**.)

New Year's Day Bowl Games

New Year's Day is Football Day, with the country's top college teams battling for bowl game honors. You'll see all the big gridiron action on television, but don't settle for a partial picture of the games. Because it's what goes on behind the scenes — off the field — that explains much of the action you see on TV.

You won't want to miss the sidelights and interviews with players and coaches in the Big Peach Sports Section the morning after the game.

THE ROSE BOWL

CHAPTER 7

national magazines work in paint such as oil color, tempera, acrylic, or watercolor. Such illustrations are expensive to reproduce in print. They are found primarily in national publications or in high-budget advertising or public relations campaigns. On a more modest scale, most illustration is done in black and white. If one or two additional colors can be used, they are added as overlays, but the basic work is conceived and rendered in black and white.

The variety of media available for work in black and white range from simple pen and ink to watercolor wash, pencil, charcoal, felt-tip pen, dry brush, and scratch board, each having its own special effect. In Figures 7.26 through 7.33 are examples of some of these techniques, along with some comments on their uses and some of their limitations.

SUMMARY

A photograph or a piece of artwork can enhance the communication process if illustrations are selected with care and if they are of high quality.

From the publicist's standpoint, it is important to recognize that effective illustration requires photographic and artistic expertise. Some projects demand professional assistance and counsel. Illustration generally requires added forethought and planning, also, because of increased processing and production complexities.

In some instances, illustration is not worth the time, trouble, and expense involved; in other cases, illustration is an indispensable part of the message. In nearly every situation, illustration—the addition of graphic representation to the spoken or printed word—enhances listenership and readership.

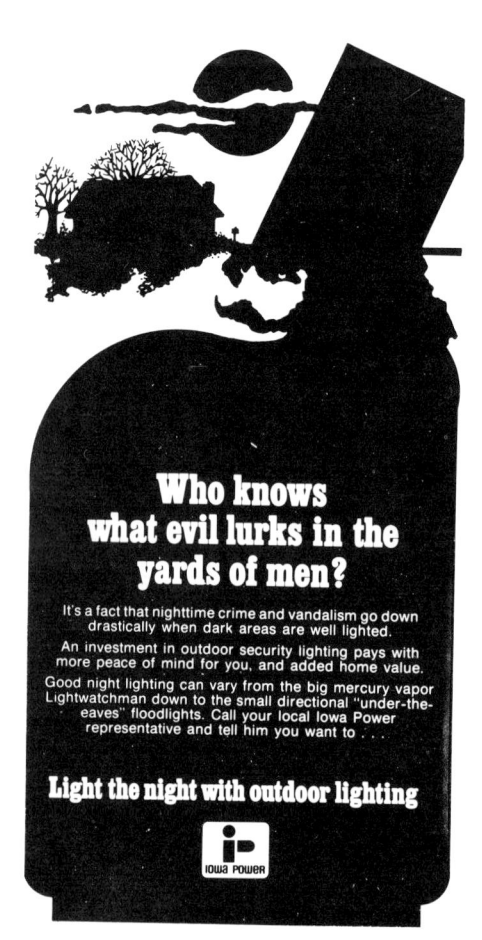

FIG. 7.28. An advertisement that attracts attention by means of the bold black and white pattern of its illustration. (Courtesy The Graphic Corp.)

PHOTOS AND ART

SUGGESTED READING

Mendelowitz, Daniel M. **Drawing**. New York: Holt, Rinehart & Winston, 1967.

Several periodicals may also be of interest:

American Artist (Billboard Publications, New York City)
Communication Arts Magazine (Coyne and Blanchard, Palo Alto, Calif.)
Graphis (Graphis Press, Zurich, Switzerland)
Print (RC Publications, New York City)

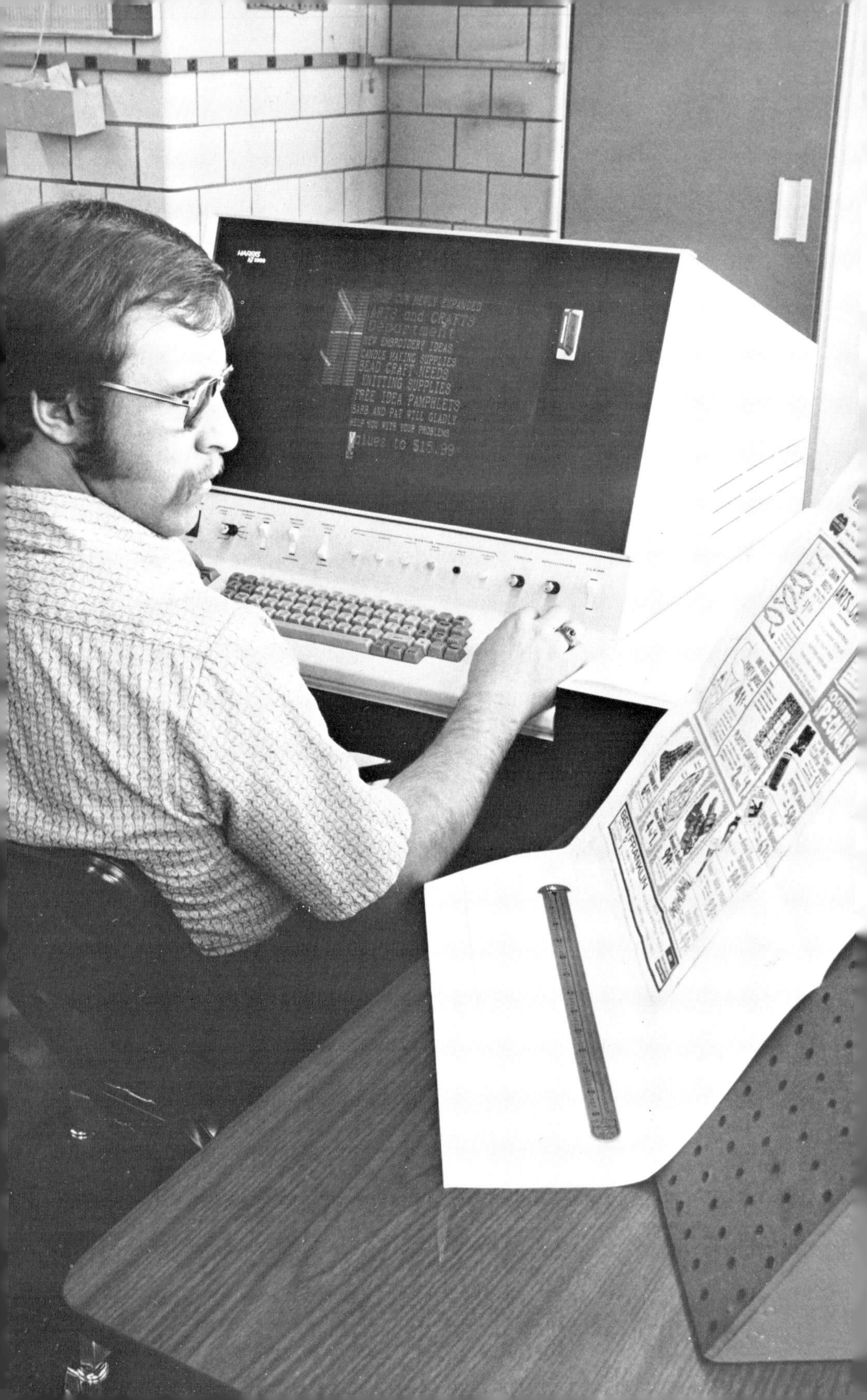
FREE IDEA PAMPHLETS
BEAD CRAFT NEEDS

8

Advertising: publicity you pay for

C. GENE BRATTON

More than $25 billion per year is being spent on advertising in the United States, according to the nation's economy watchers and the advertising industry's trade journals. This amount is expected to rise to at least $30 billion by the turn of the decade, barring unforeseen circumstances.

The money is spent in newspapers, magazines, television, radio, and all the other mass media advertisers use to promote their products, services, or ideas. Advertising expenditures total about 2 percent of the nation's gross national product (GNP) and have for many years.

The total amount spent on a yearly basis may seem fantastic to the uninitiated, but the annual budgets of some of the nation's large corporations are equally impressive.

Advertising Age, the leading trade publication in the advertising field, recently listed Procter and Gamble, Sears Roebuck and Company, General Foods Corporation, General Motors Corporation, and Warner-Lambert Pharmaceutical as the five largest advertisers. In one year alone, Procter and Gamble spent $310 million on advertising (6.3 percent of sales), Sears spent $215 million (1.7 percent), General Foods spent $180 million (8.1 percent), General Motors, $158.4 million (0.4 percent), and Warner-Lambert, $141.7 million (14.6 percent). Four other corporations—Ford Motor Company, American Home Products, Bristol-Myers Company, and Colgate-Palmolive Company—were also listed as having spent more than $100 million on their advertising budgets in one year.

ROLE OF ADVERTISING

Why spend all that money for advertising? Simply stated, advertising is one small part of a greater whole—the marketing system upon which the economy of the United States is based. Advertising is essentially the **voice of marketing.**

In such an economy, mass production is essential. Utilization of mass production, however, demands mass sales in far-flung markets. Mass sales can be achieved only if there is some method of informing prospective users of the availability and desirability of the goods being produced. An old advertising maxim claims, "You can't sell 'em if you don't tell 'em."

C. GENE BRATTON is Associate Professor of Journalism and Mass Communication, Iowa State University, a former industrial editor, retail advertising layout specialist, and newspaper advertising designer and representative. He has conducted numerous advertising workshops for business owners and managers.

Advertising performs this mass communication function. A visualization of its place in the marketing process might look like Figure 8.1.

```
         /\
        /  \
       /    \
      /MASS  \
     /PRODUC- \
    /  TION    \
   /            \
  /   MASS       \
 /    SALES       \
/_____\
   MASS COMMUNICATION
       (ADVERTISING)
```

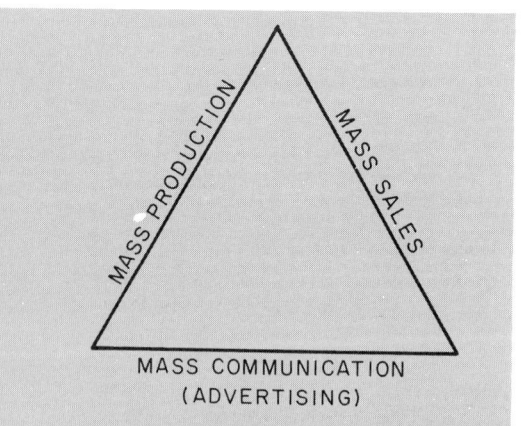

FIG. 8.1. Advertising's role in the marketing process.

The marketing process is generally defined as having two parts: (1) Finding and gathering the raw materials necessary for the production of the finished product; and (2) moving the finished product down the "channel of distribution," through the various middle stages, into the hands of the consumer.

To the publicist, advertising may seem similar to other communication techniques. It contains many of the qualities associated with news, publicity, and propaganda, and it is used widely by public relations specialists. Advertising does have at least three distinguishing characteristics:

1. It is almost always purchased (or provided in return for services of value).
2. The buyer of advertising is assured that the message will be printed or broadcast.
3. Advertising is displayed in such a way that it can be identified as having been paid for.

In some ways, advertising is the most straightforward of all publicity techniques. Whereas the source of the planted news story, the public relations gimmick, or the propaganda device may be hidden, the advertisement is marked as a persuasive message paid for by an individual or organization with a selfish interest. Even in ads with deceptive language, their purpose is seldom mysterious.

FORMS OF ADVERTISING

Over the years, advertising in the United States has developed into many specialized forms, most of which are designed to help move the goods down through the "channel" to the person who finally uses it for his or her own benefit.

Some of these forms the average consumer will never see. **Trade** advertising, for example, is designed to persuade a retailer or wholesaler to stock a certain item for resale to his or her own customers. **Industrial** advertising tries to get a manufacturer to use a specific product in the production of other goods. There are others, but discussion in this chapter will be confined to **consumer** advertising.

Consumer advertising may be generally defined as that form of advertising attempting to get an individual to buy and use a specific product for his or her own benefit, to subscribe to and use a particular service for his or her personal gratification, or to accept and support a specific idea during his or her lifetime. The advertising for Botany suits, for United Airlines, and for the American Cancer Society may be used to illustrate the distinctions.

Consumer advertising may be purchased by a national manufacturer or a local retailer.

It is probably the most carefully prepared form of mass communication today, for two reasons. First, the sponsor behind the advertisement generally has both the time and the money to make certain that the message is prepared for maximum impact and pinpointed toward a precise audience for the greatest possible effect. Second, unlike some other forms of mass communication, there is almost always some quantifiable "feedback" such as profits or losses on the sales ledgers. If the advertisement proves successful, it may be continued and expanded upon. If it fails, it will be dropped and another approach attempted.

The competent advertising man or woman who determines the "copy pitch," or approach that the advertising message should take, is in many ways as much a reporter as the person who prepares an in-depth story for the **Washington Post** or **Time** magazine.

Much information must be gathered, sorted, and digested before the copywriting begins, and the familiar "Five W's and H" of the news story writer (see Chapter 5) are just as important to the advertising copywriter—with some modifications:

Who—Who, precisely, am I trying to sell? Age? Sex? Occupation? Race? Religion?
What—What attitude is this person likely to have? What does he or she already know about the product? What instincts make him or her buy? What will motivate him or her?
When—When is the prospect most apt to need or want the product? Is the year, month, day, or hour important? When should the ad be run for maximum effect?
Where—Where does the prospect live? Where does he or she buy the product? Where will he or she most likely be when watching, reading, or hearing this message?
Why—Why should the person need or desire the product? Why should the product have importance to the prospect? Why should certain instincts, motives, or desires be appealed to or bypassed?
How—How much of the product can be sold at one time? How is the product packaged? How does our competition rate? How will the consumer buy it (will the buyer need credit)? How can we best reach the prospect?

ADVERTISING RESEARCH

Fortunately for the advertising copywriter, five major forms of advertising research have been developed to help get the answers to these and other questions. They are product research, consumer research, market research, motivation research, and media research.

Product research deals basically with the product itself—yours and your competitors'. It is designed to give answers about quality, uses, prices, faults.

Consumer research tries to give an in-depth look at the person who buys and uses the product. Here, the researcher may be interested in marital status, age, sex, religion, or race.

Market research is conducted to help the manufacturer determine the best locations for the sales efforts. Questions about wages, occupations, per-capita income, number of families in the area, and sales of related items, for example, are answered.

Motivation research is the newest of the research forms and is largely psychological. It is based upon the assumption that sometimes the consumer does not really know (or is unwilling to admit) why a purchase was actually made (or not made). This research, usually conducted by a trained psychologist, deals with the subconscious and attempts to find the "real reasons" for some consumers' actions.

Media research is designed to help

the advertiser find the best "carrier" for an advertisement—the medium most likely to reach, and be read, watched, or heard by potential buyers. Most of this research is conducted and paid for by the media themselves. An individual newspaper may survey its "reach" and readership to gain an advantage over other outlets in its trade area. Its competition is then urged to do the same. All such information is then available to potential advertisers to help them select the best media for their messages. The national media—including television, magazines, and newspapers—are continually conducting research of this kind. Age, income, education, sex, religion, lifestyle, depth of interest in the medium, and many other factors are included in the data sought.

Obviously, not all the questions a good copywriter might ask can be answered, but the copywriter will get as many answers as he or she can and will utilize them in preparing advertising copy.

Usually, the person preparing a national advertisement (often an employee of an advertising agency) will have considerable research material nearby while preparing the ad, but the person preparing the local or retail advertisement is ordinarily the employee of a retail establishment or local medium and will have to depend upon personal knowledge of the local business situation, the local media, and potential consumers.

Advertisers at both levels will depend to a great extent upon personal insight. Formal research is an important tool for the writer to use, if possible, but often the ability to look within one's self for motives, desires, and feelings is even more important. It might seem that this approach depends upon nothing more than hunches, but it is based upon awareness of the world as it is—events that are happening, ideas being proposed and accepted or rejected, and the trends of events that are evident. These factors are affecting the copywriter's life and the lives of others. The observant copywriter can better understand others, and, therefore, better communicate with them about the product, service, or idea to be advertised. Many successful advertisements and advertising campaigns have been built upon personal insight, informal research, or a "gut feel" approach in the past.

SELLING "SIZZLE"

Personal insight can also underscore one of the most important elements to be remembered about advertising. Someone expressed it long ago as follows: "In advertising, we sell the 'sizzle' and not the steak." The expression serves as a valid reminder to the advertising writer that a product is bought because of what it will do, or can do, for the buyer, not because of what it is.

A car, for example, is simply a box sitting upon four wheels that can be rotated by an internal combustion engine. It would be difficult to sell the car.

But selling what the car will do for the buyer is a different matter. The advertising copywriter might speak of personal comfort, prestige in the eyes of a peer group, economy, safety for the family, freedom from fear of mechanical failure, a feeling of power at the wheel, or any of a multitude of other attributes. Of course, tangible factors are often put into the advertisement—the warranty, rate of acceleration, high trade-in value—but these are sometimes included only to help the buyer justify and rationalize the buying decision.

What is the *real reason* a woman buys a dress or a man a suit? Why is that insurance *actually* purchased? Does one *really* buy the steak or the sizzle?

AD WRITING

Whether an advertisement is prepared by an agency, a small businessman, or a volunteer publicity chairman, the same general approach should be followed. The writing of the copy should be the culmination of a well-planned, thorough investigation of all pertinent factors—the product, the specific prospect, the "sizzle" or appeal, and the market. In addition, the advertiser must have a clearly defined objective in mind. Is the objective to sell a product, to sell an idea, to improve the image of a company or other organization? After the approach has been determined, the advertiser is faced with the demanding task of phrasing the advertising message.

The importance of the advertising message has been pointed up in countless instances in which advertisers have experimented with different messages in the same media and have realized startlingly different results. For example, one advertiser ran two different ads of the same size offering the same product at the same price in the same issue of a newspaper. One ad resulted in the sale of 1,000 units, while the other sold only 70. In other instances, for example, an ad costing $40 sold three units and an ad costing twice as much sold nearly 70 times as much. A change in the headline on one ad boosted sales by more than 12 times.

Professionals often classify advertising copy into categories: news, reason why, humorous, testimonial, dialogue, narrative, descriptive, and others. The distinctions, some of them subtle, are beyond the scope of this text, although most are recognizable.

More important than this classification is the selection of the words, phrases, and sentences that make up the advertising message. An effective ad demands the same skills as a good lead on a news story. The sentences are usually short, the verbs are active, and the words are few and carefully selected.

An ad might begin with a short, interesting statement of the appeal (or "sizzle") in the headline. This might be followed by an amplification of the appeal and a logical progression of believable information, in simple words, through the end of the copy, where a course of action is suggested.

In advertising, some latitude is possible in the use of partial sentences or unusual capitalization to stress a sales point, but in general the copy should follow the basic rules of good grammar. Unusual usage tends to draw attention to itself and interrupt the copy flow that has been so carefully formulated. Short words, familiar to the reader, are usually best. The copy should be written on a one-to-one (personal) basis, without seeming contrived. While a million persons might be exposed to the message, each individual receives it alone. Write to sell the one and many of the others will buy.

Eight Guidelines

Morton Levinstein, in a trade magazine article several years ago, cited eight guidelines to effective retail advertising. Although his remarks were directed toward merchants, they are helpful to anyone engaged in creating an advertisement.

1. The purpose of advertising is to sell—not to satisfy the personal ambitions of the advertising man, the artistic aspirations of the artist, or the vanity of the firm.... Advertising should try to sell and not call unnecessary attention to itself, its cleverness, or its flamboyant originality.
2. Every advertising man should assume that the customers do not want to read his advertisement. Therefore, he should make reading it as easy as possible.... If we write our ads with no illustrations beforehand, and make up our minds that people are not eagerly looking forward to our ads, the burden is on us to do a better selling job.
3. Think of the customer as essentially egotistic and self-centered. He is in-

terested primarily in himself. Therefore, show what you can do for him.
4. Make ads simple and easy to read. What you don't say is often as important as what you do say. Unless a thing is really important, leave it out. It is better to have three important statements in an ad than six important ones mixed with fifteen that are not.
5. Ideas are important in advertising. Give your ads plenty of thought. Have definite reasons for doing what you do. Space is expensive. If you cannot give a good reason for running an ad, don't run it. When you have something worth saying, that is the time to advertise.
6. Be yourself. Give your ads a personality. Let them express the individuality of your store, so that the people who read your ads will feel that your store is composed of human beings and not bricks, showcases and store fixtures.
7. Don't be dogmatic. All rules can be broken, including these. The only hard and fast rule in advertising is that there is no hard and fast rule. Be flexible in your thinking. Don't be afraid to be different.
8. Don't use advertising to cover up your past mistakes. Good advertising will not help move bad merchandise. Such advertising is expensive because it will not produce results, and it also gives people the wrong impression of your store. Sell the merchandise the people want to buy, at the time they want to buy it, and at the prices they want to pay for it.

AD LAYOUT

The task of laying out an ad bewilders the nonprofessional unnecessarily. It need not, if the neophyte keeps in mind the major function of the layout—to make the ad as easy to read as possible. Accomplishing this calls for an emphasis on simplicity. Leaf through any newspaper or national magazine and you will find that the layout of most ads is quite standard. They contain one main headline, a dominant illustration, a copy block, and a trademark or business signature. Such sameness in layout does not mean that the professionals lack talent or imagination. It means, instead, they usually conclude that the most effective layout is the simplest.

To prepare an ad for the print media (see Figs. 8.2 and 8.3), follow this procedure:

1. Use a layout sheet large enough to accommodate the ad and still leave room for printer's instructions in the margins.
2. Include name of advertiser, medium, date of insertion, and size of ad in the upper right-hand corner. (For newspapers, ad size should be listed in columns wide and inches deep—2 cols. x 5 inches. For magazines, ad size should be listed in fractional page units—¼ page, ½ page.) Circle instructions to the printer.
3. Rule in borders to exact size of ad.
4. Paste proofs of illustrations in exact location desired in final ad. If proofs are not available indicate position and size of illustration with blocked-out area.
5. Letter headlines and other larger type in approximately the same size as desired in final ad.
6. Indicate body copy with horizontal, parallel lines. Key copy blocks with circled letters corresponding to actual copy on copy sheet (see 8, below).
7. Indicate position of trademark, product name, or company name.
8. On an 8½ x 11-inch copy sheet, type the copy desired and key it to correspond with location on layout sheet. Do not try to type the copy line for line. The printer will handle this for you.
9. Indicate information included in 2 in upper right corner of each copy sheet.

TYPE SELECTION

At some stage in the preparation of an ad layout, one has to give thought to type faces and type sizes. According to the professionals, certain type faces are more suitable for women's items, others are masculine, some can help promote a feeling of prestige or the urgency of a sale, and still others can help build a mood or setting for the product or service being advertised. The subject is too complex to cover in this chapter, but the nonprofessional can get assistance from the printer, who should also be consulted on matters such as the use of color and white space.

Type sizes, on the other hand, are relatively easy to understand and should concern anyone who wishes to communicate with a printer. Because of the many small sizes he works with, the printer's measurement is the point, of which there are 72 per inch. The printer's 72-point type is 1 inch high, 36-point type is ½ inch, and 5½-point type is about 1/14 inch high. Typically, the body type (the "straight matter") in a newspaper's news section is 8-, 9-, or 10-point, and many headlines in both ads and news are 14-, 18-, 24-, 36-, or 48-point sizes. Column and picture widths and depths are also measured in points, although the printer will usually express them in picas. A pica is equal to 12 points, or 1/6 inch.

ADS IN OTHER MEDIA

No attempt will be made to deal comprehensively with the physical presentation of radio, television, direct mail, or outdoor advertising in this chapter, although the principles of good advertising hold true in all these media.

With both radio and television advertising, the assistance of a professional may be required. Because the broadcast message is presented in a more intimate manner than the print message, a more personal tone is incorporated whenever feasible. And, because the message is short and fleeting, even more stress is given to simplicity. A typical commercial would contain just one strong, simple benefit repeated with variation.

Radio and television offer the advertiser several exclusive tools and techniques, such as various forms of animation, singing commercials, echo chambers, and other sound effects that reinforce the selling message. Some can be used without inflating production costs, but others may be prohibitively expensive under normal conditions.

Direct mail has so many forms and design factors to be considered that unless a person is dealing with a simple postcard or personal letter, even a professional may hesitate to attempt its design without the aid of the postmaster, an artist, and a good printer. Purpose, format, paper, color, fold, enclosure, and mailing list are all of great importance. Potentially the most effective, direct mail advertising is also the most expensive of the mass selling media and should be approached with care.

Outdoor advertising, with a desired limit of 8 to 10 words (including sponsor's name), is considered by some to be among the most difficult of all ad forms to effectively design. Colors, locations, messages, traffic flow, speed of traffic, lighting, and illustrations are among the factors to be considered.

CHOOSING A MEDIUM

At some time during the process of forming the advertisement, it is necessary for the advertiser to decide upon the proper medium to carry it to prospective customers. The decision is a major one, because unless the proper audience is reached, most of the expended creative effort—and money—will be wasted. The selection process is not necessarily easy.

A national advertiser has available some 1,800 daily newspapers, 9,300 weekly newspapers, 9,750 magazines, 6,950 radio

Copy A

9 Helvetica
10 Condensed
/13

Pancake Days is a joint venture of all Boy Scout troops in Lyon County. All proceeds will be used for next summer's activities. Tickets are available from the scout who will visit your home this week or at the auditorium's south entrance during Pancake Days.

*Illustration
Metro Mat Service
4144 Sept. 72 M.M.S.*

36 Helv. Bold Cond. —

12 Helv. Bold —

10 Helv. Cond. —

18 Helv. Bold —

10 Helv. Cond.

18 Helv. —

FIG. 8.2. The copy sheet and the layout sheet have been prepared according to the standards discussed in the text. The layout is the same size as the completed ad will be. Type faces, type sizes, and line length have been indicated to assist the printer in building your ad the way you want it to appear. Make sure the printer has the type faces and sizes you specify. If you do not wish to mark up the type, the printer will do it for you and will be glad to discuss makeup problems with you. Note that complete information has been given concerning source of illustrations. The completed ad resulting from this layout is shown on the succeeding page.

2 col. x 7 inches
Affiliated Men's Club
Register Tuesday, April 2

18 Helvetica Bold

3rd Annual Boy Scout

PANCAKE DAYS

Three Consecutive Saturdays
April 6, 13 and 20

PANCAKES
and
SAUSAGES

(All You Can Eat)

$1.50

Open 6 a.m. to 10:30 a.m.
Civic Auditorium Basement

Ⓐ

36 Helvetica Reg (Cond.)

AFFILIATED MEN'S CLUBS

3rd Annual Boy Scout

PANCAKE DAYS

Three Consecutive Saturdays
April 6, 13 and 20

PANCAKES and SAUSAGE

All You Can Eat!

$1.50

Open 6 a.m. to 10:30 a.m.
Civic Auditorium Basement

Pancake Days is a joint venture of all Boy Scout troops in Lyon County. All proceeds will be used for next summer's activities. Tickets are available from the scout who will visit your home this week or at the auditorium's south entrance during Pancake Days.

AFFILIATED MEN'S CLUBS

stations, more than 600 television stations, and 320,000 outdoor advertising signs. There are also the cards in buses and subway trains, motion picture advertising, calendars, novelties, and direct mail, to name only the major media. A large American business firm may use several or nearly all these outlets. How the selection is made is a highly sophisticated process and we will not deal with it in depth in this text, but the relative advantages and disadvantages of the media should be noted.

Newspapers

The newspaper industry is the largest of the communications media in the United States. The approximately 1,800 daily newspapers have a total circulation of more than 62 million, and the 9,300 weeklies have a combined circulation of approximately 25 million. The industry has survived the emergence of magazines, radio, and television and remains the leader in total advertising revenue, attracting about 30 percent of the advertising dollar.

Not utilized by national advertisers to a great extent today, newspapers remain the primary promotional vehicles for retail advertisers. It is estimated that 70 to 80 percent of all department store advertising is in newspapers, along with virtually all grocery store advertising.

Newspaper advertising has these major advantages:

1. Penetrability—Typically, the newspaper that has no newspaper competition reaches 75 to 90 percent of the homes in the area where it is published.
2. Flexibility—Newspapers may be selected in any or all of the specific areas where a national advertiser has distribution.
3. Breadth of audience—Virtually everyone, regardless of income or occupation, reads a hometown or area newspaper.
4. Timeliness—The advertiser can inject immediacy into advertising through up-to-date newspaper ads.
5. Adaptability—Because the message can be reread, it can be of virtually any length or contain any amount of detail.

Newspaper advertising also has disadvantages:

1. Short life—Today's newspaper is dead when the next one appears.
2. Inferior reproduction—Although vastly improved in recent years, newspaper reproduction (printing quality) is not as good as that in magazines because of the lower quality of paper and the high-speed presses used.
3. Expense for national advertiser—To achieve national coverage through newspapers, an advertiser must deal with many papers. Even the largest papers are essentially community papers serving at most a major metropolitan area, a state, or a region.

Television

Television is the newest and most flamboyant of the advertising media and is considered the most effective by many advertisers. The more than 600 commercial television stations beam programs into approximately 96 percent of American homes, and the typical family will have its set turned on about 7 hours each day.

Of the more than $4 billion spent annually on television (nearly 20 percent of the total spent for all advertising), about 85 percent is contributed by national or regional advertisers and 15 percent by local advertisers. Television time is classed as network, spot, and local. **Network** refers to full, alternate, or multisponsorship of network-originated programs. **Spot** is the purchase of programs or announcements on several stations without regard to network affiliation. **Local** is the purchase of programs or announcements on one or more stations in a single market by businesses in that market.

The advantages of television are:

1. Audience size—Prime time network television offers the advertiser the largest audiences of any medium.
2. Exclusive features—Television is unique among media in that it combines sight, sound, and motion.
3. Personalization—Personal selling is considered more effective than any other type.
4. Breadth of audience—Television provides an audience similar to that of newspapers. It reaches more young persons than newspapers, but there is evidence that it remains less popular among the highly educated.
5. Market penetration—Television probably penetrates more homes in each market than do newspapers, but its exposure is considerably different. The reader can digest all the content of all the newspapers available in a market. He can view the offerings of only one television station at a time and thereby is denied exposure to whatever is being aired by other stations.
6. Audience selectivity—Although television probably reaches as broad a segment of the population as any of the mass media, it can offer selective audiences. By tailoring content and by carefully selecting time periods, the television advertiser can reach predominantly male, female, or young audiences, for example.
7. Integration of advertising with nonadvertising—The advertiser can relate the content of the program to his or her product, and popular entertainers can be used as commercial presenters. Their involvement usually heightens interest in the commercial.
8. Exclusive appeal to small children—Television is the only medium of mass communication that communicates with children before they themselves can verbalize. (For a philosophical discussion of this fact, see Chapter 16.)

Some of the disadvantages of television are:

1. Initial cost—Although there is evidence that television is an economical medium on the basis of cost per viewer reached, the initial cost is high. It is beyond the budget of most advertisers, both local and national.
2. Short life of advertising message—The broadcast advertisement lives only 10 seconds, 30 seconds, or 1 minute, in most situations.
3. Inability to deliver complex messages—The brevity of broadcast ads makes it difficult for the advertiser to present detailed product information.
4. Difficulty of measuring audience—Rating services and other types of surveys are used to measure broadcast audiences. These rely on sampling methods which provide only estimates of audience size, whereas the exact circulations of print media can be verified.
5. Clutter—The tendency to jam three or four commercials, a station-break announcement, a public service announcement, and other material into just one program break is annoying and confusing to many viewers. The product misidentification rate is high and the number of commercials offered seems to be constantly increasing.

Magazines

Of the approximately 9,750 magazines in this country, only a small percentage are a major factor in advertising. They include some 300 so-called consumer and farm magazines such as **Time, Woman's Day, Reader's Digest, Farm Journal,** and **Successful Farming** plus about 2,500 business and trade publications. Business publications are written for highly selective audiences and may be classified as either horizontal or vertical. The horizontal publications are aimed at individuals, such as engineers or personnel officers, doing the same kinds of work in various industries. Vertical publications are aimed at all individuals employed in the same business, such as everyone in the petroleum industry, whether a vice-president or an apprentice.

One-issue circulation of the approximately 300 consumer and farm publications totals more than 200 million. The 2,500 business publications have about 45 million subscribers. About 8 percent of all advertising is done in magazines and most of this is purchased by national advertisers. More than 5.5 billion copies of magazines are published each year in the United States. When television attracted many of the blue chip national advertisers, the magazine industry looked to some of the smaller firms, including companies with regional, rather than national, distribution. To attract these advertisers, many magazines now offer zoned or regional editions. **Reader's Digest** has 10 regional editions; **Farm Journal** offers more than 40 regional or demographic editions.

In recent years, several controlled or free-circulation magazines have been successful. These are distributed free to audiences tailored to satisfy certain classes of advertisers. Most of these magazines are business or farm publications. Also in recent years, small circulation magazines of all stripes have found the going tough and some have succumbed to higher paper and postage costs.

The advantages of magazines include:

1. Audience—An above average audience in terms of income, education, social position, and buying power.
2. Longevity—A longer life than newspapers.
3. Quality—A much better quality of ad reproduction than newspapers.
4. Audience selectivity—Through selecting the right magazine, an advertising message can be aimed at men, women, professional people, certain income groups, or any other audience.

The disadvantages of magazines include:

1. Limited market penetration—Magazines deliver national and regional audiences, but they do not offer extensive penetration of any one territory.
2. Lack of timeliness—Since advertisers must plan anywhere from two weeks to as much as several months in advance, magazine advertising is generally not immediate.
3. Lost circulation—There is some waste circulation since only those advertisers whose products are available in all markets realize maximum efficiency from magazine advertising.
4. Cost—Large amounts of money are involved. Despite the fact that the per-reader cost of a magazine might be quite small, the dollar outlay often reaches into the tens of thousands and can prove a hindrance to a smaller company.

Radio

Radio, counted out by many observers when television began to flex its muscles in the 1950s, not only has survived but has grown. Today about 7,600 AM and FM stations are broadcasting in the United States and nearly 370 million sets are in operation, including more than 93 million in automobiles. Yearly, radio receives about 6 percent of the total advertising dollars with nearly two-thirds coming from local advertisers.

As an advertising medium, radio can best be compared with television, sharing several advantages and disadvantages. The advantages include personalization of approach, use of program talent to deliver advertising messages, and selectivity of audience. The disadvantages include the short life of the message, an inability to present complex information, and difficulty in determining size of audience.

The radio commercial, however, usually carries less impact than its television counterpart because it cannot offer sight and motion. And, although many radio stations reach farther than competing television stations, their audiences are generally smaller.

Radio does have some advantages over television. The initial cost of radio advertising is low (most local advertisers can afford it) and radio reaches more out-of-the-home consumers than any medium except outdoor advertising. Listenership is especially high among commuters on their way to and from work and persons at work or play outdoors during warm weather. In addition, more than any other medium, radio can achieve impact without receiving the full attention of the consumer. A homemaker, for example, can be sold by radio while ironing or doing dishes; a lathe operator can receive advertising messages while machining a part.

Outdoor Messages

Outdoor advertising is the only major medium in which expenditures have remained relatively static in the past few years. This is at least partly due to a widespread movement to restrict the placement of billboards on American highways. The federal government now offers bonus highway funds to states that regulate outdoor advertising on the interstate highway system.

About 700 outdoor advertising companies or plants are responsible for about 320,000 signs located in approximately 15,000 cities. They base the cost of an outdoor location on the number of potential viewers who pass the location daily. Plant owners offer the advertiser package deals of several signs which assure exposure to a specific percentage of the population in a local market. A Number 100 showing supposedly exposes a population the size of the entire market to the advertiser's signs in a 30-day period.

Although outdoor advertising expenditures represent less than 1 percent of the total advertising outlay, some types of businesses and noncommercial organizations make heavy use of some form of outdoor advertising. At the local level, banks, hotels, motels, and restaurants find it a valuable medium. Nationally, gasoline and oil companies and soft drink companies use it extensively.

Only about 5 percent of all outdoor signs that one sees are controlled by the organized outdoor advertising industry. The others, including signs above shops, motels, and eating places, are controlled by individual firms and are not included in industry statistics.

Outdoor advertising's advantages include geographical flexibility, wide audience, repetition, and relatively low cost per impression. Among the disadvantages are the speed with which the sign is passed and the inability to express any but the shortest message.

Direct Mail

About 15 percent of the advertising dollar is spent annually on direct mail. More than one-quarter million businesses use this form of advertising, and it is an important medium for noncommercial agencies such as churches and political parties. Some firms spend more money on it than on any other medium. Book publishers generally spend nearly half their advertising budgets on direct mail. Other heavy users include automotive dealers, drug companies, clothing stores, and investment brokers. Another mass communication medium,

ADVERTISING: PUBLICITY YOU PAY FOR

the magazine industry, also is a heavy user of direct mail.

Direct mail offers several advantages: The advertiser can select the audience carefully, can personalize the message to an unusual degree, can use a wide variety of formats, and can measure the response with considerable effectiveness.

The disadvantages of direct mail include its cost (in part, due to postage rates), the problem of securing and maintaining mailing lists, and the attitude of the public toward direct mail.

ADVERTISING COSTS

How much does advertising cost? As with most other items offered for sale, the price depends upon the kind and quantity purchased. But there is another factor, too—the size of audience reached. Before examining some typical charges for the various media and the methods by which advertising is sold, let us quickly review this subject from the standpoint of the individual businessperson or merchant. What does advertising cost in relation to other business costs?

As pointed out earlier, the total amount spent on advertising in the United States equals about 2 percent of the gross national product. This figure—2 percent of gross sales—is a rule-of-thumb figure frequently used by business personnel in establishing an advertising budget. There are wide variations, of course. Some business firms will spend a tiny fraction of 1 percent of gross sales; others may spend 6 or even 8 percent. But many fall in the bracket between 1 and 4 percent of gross sales.

Some businesses will spend more than others. Entertainment and luxury items will be on the high side of any comparison. Food, despite its large ads, will be on the low side, percentagewise. Persons who maintain that the average businessperson spends 15 or 20 percent of gross sales to buy customers through advertising are "grossly" misinformed. Certainly, at times one merchant will spend more than at others—in getting a store established or in introducing a new line of merchandise. Typically, though, advertising expenditures will be fairly stable in relation to gross business. The merchant will use advertising to help level out business cycles. If an advertising program is well planned a businessperson will tend to overadvertise in periods when business is normally slow and underadvertise in times of ready sales.

The merchant must decide where to spend the advertising dollar and quite naturally wants to know where it will do the most good. Each situation is different, depending upon media available, costs, the advertiser's particular needs, and many other factors. Below are some of the cost yardsticks an advertiser will use in making advertising decisions.

Newspapers

Local newspaper advertising is usually sold at the column-inch rate. A column-inch is an area 1 column wide and 1 inch deep. A paper 8 columns wide with 20-inch-long columns will, therefore, offer for sale 160 column-inches of advertising in a full-page ad. On small community newspapers, this may cost less than $1 a column-inch and the page might cost less than $100. On a metropolitan newspaper, this same page would cost several thousand dollars. This reflects the differing circulation. (National advertising appearing in newspapers is billed by the agate line. There are 14 agate lines per column-inch; but this is jargon of importance only to those who deal in the business.)

The yardstick used to measure comparative costs of newspaper advertising—larger circulation papers versus smaller ones, taking into account their varying advertising rates—is known as the milline rate. This is the cost of sending one agate line to one million readers. It can be figured by multiplying the agate line rate by one million and dividing by the circulation. Smaller newspapers customarily have higher milline rates than do metropolitan newspapers, but publishers of smaller newspapers maintain that their products are more thoroughly read.

Magazines

Almost all magazine advertising is billed at the page rate or fraction thereof. A full-page black and white ad in a general consumer-type magazine with a circulation of 7 million may run in excess of $50,000. Color will cost more. But a page in a business magazine with 25,000 circulation may cost less than $1,000. Again, it is a matter of circulation and the cost per thousand is the standard measure used to compare costs of magazines. This is calculated by multiplying the full page cost by 1,000 and dividing this figure by the magazine's circulation. The cost per thousand for some of the major consumer magazines may range from $2 to $5. In more selective magazines of smaller circulation, the costs may go as high as $25 to $50, but the advertiser interested in that market may find the higher cost quite the best deal.

Radio and TV

The advertising rate structure of the broadcast media is far more complex than that of the print media. Rates are based on potential audience and on units of time and time of day. Broadcast audiences fluctuate greatly throughout the day, and the fluctuation is more pronounced among television viewers than among radio listeners. Television is primarily a nighttime medium; radio a daytime medium. Network and station rates are scaled to take into account the general patterns of listenership—the greater the number of listeners, the higher the rate. The most expensive time, the so-called prime time, on television comes from 7 to 10 P.M. Peak listenership on radio, on the other hand, comes between 6 and 10 A.M. The advertiser decides on the kind and number of listeners or viewers to be reached and the relative costs of reaching them. As we mentioned, television tends to be a tool for national advertising, whereas radio is more generally used for local advertising.

The cost of commercial time on a radio station located in a town of 7,500 may be as low as $3 to $5 per minute. In a city of 250,000, the cost may range from $50 to $70 per minute, depending upon the time of day. At the other extreme, the cost of a half-hour show (including time, talent, and production) on one of the national television networks may run $150,000 or much higher. During this time, the sponsor may have no more than three one-minute commercials which, under these circumstances, makes the actual commercial announcements cost at the rate of $50,000 or more per minute.

Cost per thousand is the measure used to determine the relative expense of television and radio advertising. This informs the advertiser of the cost of reaching a thousand homes with one commercial minute and is calculated the same as cost per thousand for magazines, except that any talent expenses are added to television time costs.

SUMMARY

This chapter has attempted to provide a general picture of the advertising industry and to present information that may be of help if you are ever called upon to produce an advertisement. If you do find yourself in this situation, be sure to take advantage of the expert services that are available, usually at no cost to you. (The advertising agency usually receives its pay, in the form of a 15 percent commission, from the media that run the agency ads.) The advertising departments of the various media are staffed by well-trained, experienced professionals whose main job is to assist advertisers. Take your problems to these experts. Be frank with them. Supply them with accurate, complete information and ask their advice. Usually, it will be extremely valuable. In many cases, these persons will undertake the entire chore of preparing an advertisement or a campaign. It is still important that you understand the principles of effective advertising, however, so that you can evaluate their work, either as a publicist or as a consumer. (Also, see Chapter 15.)

SUGGESTED READING

Bedell, Clyde. **Your Advertising.** Park Ridge, Ill.: Clyde Bedell, 1953.

Dunn, S. Watson. **Advertising: Its Role in Modern Marketing,** 2nd ed. New York: Holt, Rinehart & Winston, 1969.

Kirkpatrick, C. A. **Advertising: Mass Communication in Marketing.** Boston: Houghton Mifflin, 1959.

Klepner, Otto. **Advertising Procedure,** 6th ed. Englewood Cliffs, N.J.: Prentice-Hall, 1973.

Levinstein, Morton. "Eight Ways to Strengthen Your Advertising." **Automotive Retailer,** June, 1946.

"The New World of Advertising." **Advertising Age,** Nov. 21, 1973.

Sandage, Charles H., and Fryburger, Vernon. **Advertising: Theory and Practice.** Homewood, Ill.: Irwin, 1967.

Sizing up

2

the mass media

It is important for both the publicist and the consumer to understand how the media operate, their strengths and their limitations, their capabilities and their handicaps. Such knowledge is necessary to enlightened criticism and effective publicity alike.

THE WALL STREET JOURNAL

"All the News That's Fit to Print"

The New York T

What's News—

CHRISTIAN SCIEN

The Washington Post

, Congress work on

WEDNESDAY, JANUARY 8, 1975

Los Angeles Times

dnap Victim's Party ins W. Berlin Vote

es Moines Register

ur Anarchists Are Freed in Effort Save Leader of Christian Democrats

DELAYS OIL TARIFF

THE MILWAUKE

Tuesday, March 4, 197

y Reports Hospital

THE NATIONAL OBSERVER

(DELETED)

Bubbles at TV, Dogs...

The Detroit News

AMERICA'S LARGEST EVENING CIRCULATION

e Cedar Rapids Gaz

Chicag

DELAYS $2 OF OIL

THE MINNEAPOLIS STAR

ROL

THE ELECTR MUSE

brings depression warning

9

Newspapers: the heavy local coverage medium

WILLIAM F. KUNERTH

Newspapers are the backbone of most publicity campaigns. They maintain their position in the face of media research studies that show the American public:

1. Spends more time attending to the electronic media—especially television—than to newspapers.
2. Gets most of its news from television.
3. Places greater credibility in news offered by the broadcast media than that read in newspapers.[1]

Many newspaper partisans will argue with the accuracy of these findings, particularly points 2 and 3. Even if they are accurate, today's publicist still considers newspapers the basic vehicle for the transmission of messages.

There are several reasons for this, probably the most important of which are access, content and capacity, and coverage.

ACCESS

The 1,800 daily newspapers in the United States have a combined circulation of nearly 63 million. The more than 9,000 weekly, semiweekly, and triweekly newspapers have about 30 million circulation. These are the general circulation publications. In addition, several hundred specialized newspapers are aimed at ethnic, religious, political, and other target audiences. In numbers and geographic spread, newspapers are the most accessible of the media.

CONTENT AND CAPACITY

The newspaper is a favorite of publicists because it is the basic information medium and because it has a huge appetite for news. The bulk of the material publicists feed into the information channels is in the form of news. Much of it carries the tag, "News Release." Newspapers concentrate more on informing and less on entertaining than any of the other mass media. And,

WILLIAM KUNERTH is Professor of Journalism and Mass Communication, Iowa State University, former news editor, reporter, and advertising manager for several community newspapers in Wyoming and South Dakota, former general manager of the Students Publishing Company at Northwestern University, and former editorial faculty adviser to the **Iowa State Daily**.

1. The Roper Organization, Inc., **What People Think of Television and Other Mass Media, 1959-1972** (8th in a series of studies conducted in conjunction with the Television Information Office), 1973, pp. 2-3.

they can accommodate much more such material in their pages than can the competing media. As a result, newspapers—even the metropolitans—can usually find room for a story or a calendar item on the upcoming meeting of the camera club or the women's garden club. An event need not be exceptionally newsworthy to merit publication in a newspaper.

COVERAGE

In general, newspapers are unequalled in their ability to cover specific markets. The typical daily newspaper is delivered into about 80 percent of the homes in the city it serves. It is read daily by about 75 percent of the adults in the community. This appears to be the case regardless of the editorial quality of the publication. It is a long-established habit for most families to subscribe to the local paper. Even its sharpest critic is likely to consider it an essential ingredient in his or her life.

Although newspaper penetration varies from city to city, the medium does offer the highest degree of individual market saturation of any of the mass media. In competitive, metropolitan areas, city coverage may be as low as 30 percent of the households. In communities with monopoly newspapers, it will generally range from 75 to more than 100 percent. For example, the **New York Daily News** circulation within the city totals 41.3 percent of the households; the **Des Moines** (Iowa) **Tribune**, 72.7 percent; and the **Rapid City** (S.D.) **Journal**, 100.2 percent.[2]

Although 96 percent of American homes are equipped with television and radio receivers, broadcast stations cannot claim the same kind of coverage of a local community that its newspaper can because of the competitive situation. The broadcast audience is highly fragmented in almost every market. Such is not the case with newspapers. Of the more than 1,500 daily-newspaper cities, just 182 are served by more than one daily and in fewer than 50 of those cities are the additional papers published by totally separate and competitive firms.

Most communities are served by one newspaper publishing company whose output may be a weekly, a single-edition (morning or evening) daily or, in many metropolitan markets, a morning-evening-Sunday combination.

Although proponents of widespread free expression have reason to be concerned about the monopolistic aspects of the newspaper industry, the situation does allow for efficient, near-saturation coverage of most communities and their environs.

OTHER ADVANTAGES

Other advantages of the newspaper as a publicity medium are:

1. The broad socioeconomic audience it serves. Newspaper readership cuts across most occupation and income groups although it falls off sharply among those persons of very low economic status.

2. The variety of material covered in its columns. In addition to straight "nuts-and-bolts" news, the newspaper contains a smorgasbord of information covering the business world, agriculture, sports, and social activities. No matter what area of activity a publicist in engaged in, newspapers probably cover it.

---

2. From **The Annual Geographic Penetration Analysis of Major Print Media, 1974-75.** American Newspapers Markets, Inc., Thomas A. Sinding, Founder, Northfield, Ill., pp. 326, 528, 654.

3. These and other results of a Newspaper Advertising Bureau, Inc., study were reported in **U.S. News and World Report,** Apr. 29, 1974.

NEWSPAPERS: HEAVY LOCAL COVERAGE

3. Its ability to handle complex, lengthy material. Statistical reports, financial statements, and the intricacies of complicated narratives can be presented more effectively by newspapers than by the broadcast media.
4. Its permanence. As with other print media, messages in newspapers can be saved and referred to repeatedly, if necessary.

DISADVANTAGES

The major disadvantage of newspapers in the eyes of the publicist is probably the lack of large-circulation, nationally distributed publications.

Although newspapers tend to saturate their own markets, not one offers an impressive national circulation package. There are no strong national newspapers in the United States as there are in many countries, especially the densely populated European nations.

Only a handful of general circulation newspapers have coast-to-coast distribution in the United States—the **National Observer** (weekly), the **Wall Street Journal**, the **Christian Science Monitor**, and the **New York Times**. Their circulations, ranging from 185,000 to approximately 1.4 million, are spread thinly across the country when compared with competitive national media such as magazines and network television.

Unless the publicist is dealing with an event or issue of interest to the domestic news services, such as the Associated Press or United Press International, he or she has to work with a large number of units if the message is to be spread nationally through newspapers. (For a more detailed treatment of the news services, see Chapter 12.)

Other Disadvantages

Other disadvantages are:

1. Hasty and selective readership. Although a newspaper may guarantee delivery of its product into 80 percent or more of the homes in a community, the readership of that product is far from thorough by most of its subscribers. Average readership of daily newspapers is 30 to 45 minutes. The typical pattern of many readers includes a quick scan of front-page news, a thorough look at the sports or society section, and a rundown of favorite comics.
2. Mediocre reproduction. For economic reasons, newspapers are printed on low quality paper and on high-speed presses which use fast-drying inks. Naturally, the quality of reproduction suffers, especially when compared with that of magazines. The problem is most acute in reproducing full color photographs.
3. Lack of appeal to the youth market. Although they offer a varied fare, newspapers do not attract a large readership among youth. The very young tend to become addicted to television while most teenagers appear to favor radio.

DEALING WITH NEWSPAPER EDITORS

In dealing with newspapers, the publicist may find that he or she is supplying material to newspapers of different sizes, from the **Ree Heights** (South Dakota) **Review** (circulation 250) to the **New York Daily News** (weekday circulation, 2.1 million).

The news operation of many of the "Ma and Pa" weeklies is often taken care of by one person—the editor. This party probably also carries the title of publisher. And, he or she may be advertising salesperson, printer, circulation manager, bookkeeper, and janitor. The publicist may be sure that a release will reach the proper person on a small weekly (2,000 or fewer circulation) if it is mailed to the editor.

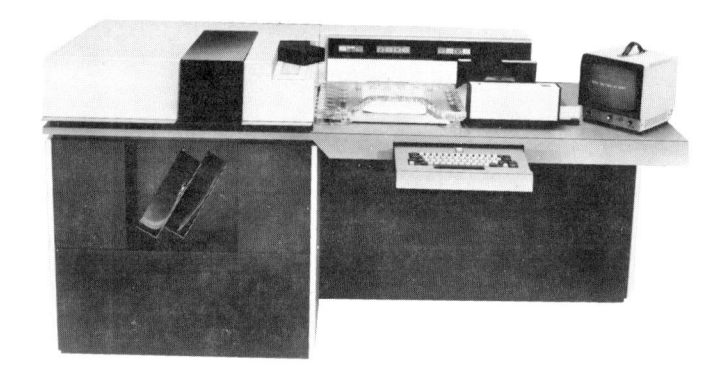

On large weeklies and semiweeklies (3,000 to 5,000) and on small dailies (5,000 to 20,000), the person in charge of the news operation may be called the editor, managing editor, or news editor. The best bet is to send releases to the managing editor. Often, the editor is the person in charge of the editorial page and the news editor may handle national news only.

On medium and large circulation dailies (25,000 and up), there is usually a raft of specialized or departmental editors in addition to the sports and society editors often found on even the smallest papers.

Before submitting specialized material to the larger papers, the publicist should check the staff listings of these papers to determine whether there is a particular editor who might be interested in the story.

The usual list of special-interest editors includes such areas as amusements, books, business-financial, education, farm, fashion, feature, food, garden, home furnishings, music, radio-TV, religion, society, sports, Sunday, travel, and women's, in addition to city and state and wire editors.

The titles and specialties change with the times. In recent years, former women's editors have become home and family editors and many newspapers have added environmental and consumer affairs editors to their staffs.

The dailies generally process straight news on a geographical basis. Subeditors may include city, suburban, state (or regional), and wire or telegraph (national and international) news. The managing editor in an operation of this size usually coordinates the entire newsgathering and processing effort. Straight news releases sent to the managing editor will be relayed to the proper subeditor. The release may move into print faster, however, if sent directly to the appropriate editor. (See the discussion of gatekeeping in the newsroom in Chapter 3.)

FIG. 9.1. The CompuScan Optical Character Reader (OCR) is one example of technological innovation in the printing industry. The machine can "look at" typewritten pages and "tell" a typesetting computer what size type to set on what length of line and with what spacing between lines. It is a timesaving device because it can eliminate the need to manually "reset" a reporter's copy into type. Instead, the reporter's copy can be run through the OCR and into the typesetting computer.

CIRCULATION NOT THE ONLY CRITERION

One might assume that publicists are interested only in reaching the largest possible number of persons with their messages. With that thought in mind, consider the newspaper statistics in Table 9.1.

If the publicist is intent on numbers only, it is unlikely he or she will bother with weekly newspapers. One must deal with more than 9,000 publications to realize a circulation of 30 million. With one-fifth as many papers (1,778 dailies) the publicist can reach twice the audience (62 million). Even better, 605 Sunday papers deliver a circulation of 50 million.

FIG. 9.2. Datatype Corporation's desk top OCR scans typewritten copy at a rate of approximately 110 characters per second and converts the information into computer language. A Character Reading Terminal (CRT), with a televisionlike display tube and an operator keyboard, can be used in conjunction with the OCR to make corrections and other editorial changes in the copy.

The fact is, publicists do "bother with" weekly newspapers even though they do not offer as many readers as the dailies. Numbers are not the only criterion of the farsighted publicist. He or she may submit material to weeklies for any or all of the following reasons:

TABLE 9.1. Newspaper Numbers and Circulations

	Number	Total Circulation
Morning Dailies	337	26.0 million
Evening Dailies	1,441	36.4 million
Sunday Editions	605	50.0 million
Nondailies (weeklies, semi-weeklies, triweeklies)	9,000(+)	30.0 million

Source: Editor and Publisher Yearbook, 1973.

1. The likelihood that they will use the material. Many weeklies are understaffed and often have trouble filling the "news hole" each issue, whereas most daily editors are faced with selecting about one-fourth or one-half the editorial material available to fill each day's issue.
2. The likelihood that the release may be read if it is used. Readership of weekly newspapers is intensive. The 8- to 20-page edition of the typical weekly will be checked from cover to cover by a large share of its readers as compared with the average half-hour readership given to the 60- to 100-page metropolitan daily.
3. Audience composition may be important. Weekly newspapers deliver a large segment of the rural and small town population. On certain occasions, publicists may consider this a vital target audience. They might be working for a politician who is promoting a piece of farm legislation or a company selling equipment to care for large lawns and gardens.

So, the publicist is interested in audience composition as well as audience size. In selecting media, he or she will probably also be interested in the chances that the material will be used and read and in the nature of the audience it will reach.

SPECIALIZED NEWSPAPERS

Publicists generally use newspapers to reach broad segments of the socioeconomic spectrum, but there are specialized publications that go to highly tailored audiences. These include more than 200 black newspapers (with an estimated 4.1 million circulation), 250 in foreign languages, and 275 American Indian newspapers. In addition, there are religious, political, labor, trade or occupational, and other newspapers aimed at fairly homogeneous groups. These publications may have local, state, regional, or national coverage.

So, the publicist can use newspapers to reach special audiences—the black community in New York City or Baltimore, members of the Lutheran Church across the United States, Republicans in the Midwest, or labor union members in Illinois.

Also deserving of mention are the misnamed "underground" newspapers, most of which have been established since the mid-1960s. The original underground newspapers were organs of political commentary published anonymously during the pre-Revolutionary War period. Today's underground press continues to stress political issues; but its writers, publishers, and editors are identified in their publications, which are published out of well-known locations. They certainly cannot be considered underground. Many, such as **Rolling Stone**, with a circulation exceeding 250,000, are financially well supported and have established credibility among their readers.

If a publicist were interested in reaching a young, politically and socially liberal audience, the undergrounds would be logical vehicles.

DEFINING AND IDENTIFYING NEWSPAPERS

Newspapers tend to be defined or identified on several bases: content, format and paper stock, audience, and coverage pattern. The typical newspaper is envisioned as containing objective reports of current happenings supplemented by interpretive stories, editorial commentary, and a small package of entertainment materials.

Most newspapers are full sheet (6 to 8 columns wide and about 20 inches deep) or tabloid (4 or 5 columns wide by about 15 inches deep) and printed on wood-pulp-based newsprint.

The conventional newspaper is aimed at all literate residents of a community—small town to metropolis—and its surrounding area. In general, the circulation pattern of a newspaper coincides with its trade area. Persons who shop in a community are the most likely subscribers to its newspaper.

Now that all the general attributes of a newspaper have been outlined, it must be pointed out that many publications identified as newspapers fall outside these limits. These publications may be partisan and biased, rather than striving for objectivity in their news columns. They may be packaged in a non-newspaper format on slick paper, rather than newsprint. Their audiences may be homogeneous, rather than mixed; and they may be scattered across the country, rather than located in a limited area.

It is probably helpful to place newspapers in two classifications—general interest (or general circulation) and special interest (all others generally identified as newspapers).

Newspapers are, of course, also classified on the basis of their publication frequency, whether daily (at least five times each week), Sunday, or nondaily (weekly, triweekly, semiweekly).

By locale, newspapers are identified as metropolitan, urban, suburban, and community. The greatest growth in recent years has been among the suburban newspapers. While the circulations of most metropolitan dailies have fallen off, many former country weeklies have become healthy, large-circulation suburbans. The trend among metropolitan papers has been closedowns and mergers. In the suburban and medium-sized daily fields, chain ownership and consolidation of printing facilities have grown. Improvements in electronic printing technology—computerized typesetting and page makeup and large capacity, high-speed offset presses—may have paved the way for a more active, prosperous community press. These advancements have made it possible to establish newspapers without the major capital investments necessary in the past. Today, a small newspaper needs only the equipment necessary to transmit copy to a central printing plant.

OTHER OPPORTUNITIES

Although most of the publicist's efforts will probably be aimed at placing news releases in newspapers, the medium does offer other opportunities for expression.

In addition to supplying newspaper editors with completely written stories, the publicist may offer story ideas—especially to the editor of the local newspaper. The bulk of such ideas would naturally relate to the publicist's area of interest. However, if he or she develops a professional attitude about news (and that should certainly be the case), a publicist may in fact be supplying an editor with story suggestions outside the publicist's own bailiwick.

The same applies to editorial ideas, although this is a more sensitive area than news. Publicists should not pester editors with suggestions that they write editorials supportive of this organization or that project. But if a significant issue arises which the publicist believes is deserving of editorial comment, he or she could relay the idea to the editor. Editors are individuals. Some are receptive to suggestions; others are not. The publicist has to play the individual situation by ear.

One of the functions of the press is to serve as a sounding board for the average citizen. The letters-to-the-editor section provides that forum. On occasion, a publicist may find it helpful to write a letter to the editor or encourage someone else to do so. Certainly, this outlet should not be overused, but it should be considered when one feels it is important to impart a point of view that probably would not be expressed in the news columns. The most effective letters to the editor are restrained, factual, and brief. Long, emotional diatribes seldom have any influence.

Local columns, regardless of their quality, tend to receive high readership and provide an easy climate for the discussion of sensitive issues. The publicist should be alert to situations in which a column item might be helpful. The publicist, obviously, should not harass or pressure the columnist to run self-serving items but should restrict such suggestions or requests to significant issues of general concern.

Most newspapers run calendars of events. The publicist may use these instead of, or in addition to, news coverage of an event.

In addition to their news sections and their specialized departments, many newspapers carry regular and seasonal supplements. Most large dailies offer a Sunday or weekend feature magazine and a television or entertainment supplement. Seasonal editions often include fashion, real estate, business, education, sports, garden, and home furnishings.

SUMMARY

Newspapers, for so many reasons, including their access, their content and capacity, and their coverage, remain the backbone of most publicity campaigns and a staff of life to publicists, professional and amateur alike. Although there is no one "national newspaper" to compete with other national media, the newspaper is truly the best medium for concentrated local print coverage.

SUGGESTED READING

Charnley, Mitchell V. **Reporting,** 3rd ed. New York: Holt, Rinehart & Winston, 1975.
Crump, Spencer. **Fundamentals of Journalism.** New York: McGraw-Hill, 1974.
Raskin, Jonah. "The Underground Press." **Change,** Mar., 1974.
Schoenfeld, Clarence A. **Publicity Media and Methods: Their Role in Modern Public Relations.** New York: Macmillan, 1964.
Tebbel, John W. **The Compact History of the American Newspaper.** New York: Hawthorn, 1963.

10

Magazines: something for everyone

RICHARD L. DISNEY

The magazine is one of the most useful of the media for many purposes and one that is too often overlooked by nonprofessional publicists.

You will find the magazine's special virtues—its versatility, intensity of readership, ability to pinpoint special audiences—mentioned in some detail in Chapter 8. It is sufficient here to suggest that, whatever your interest, there is a magazine to match it, with a ready-made audience waiting to hear what you have to say, if you say it well enough.

Since 1741, when the first magazines

RICHARD DISNEY is Associate Professor of Journalism and Mass Communication, Iowa State University, a Phi Beta Kappa graduate of the University of Oklahoma, and former faculty member at Montana State University and the University of Wisconsin.

in the United States came into being, their numbers have grown until in the mid-1970s we have a total of approximately 10,000, as well as another huge group of "house" publications issued by corporations and other institutions. There may be as many as 17,000 of these.

The first things about the magazine field that are likely to strike an acute observer are the volume, the range of content, and the utter lack of uniformity among American magazines. **Reader's Digest** boasts a United States circulation of more than 17 million and another 11 million abroad; and there are publications that print fewer than 1,000 copies per issue. Some are color-splashed; some are drab. Some are works of art; some are shabby. There are magazines for bakers and for scuba divers, for astrophysicists and for bibliophiles, for lonely hearts and for probation officers.

We cannot, however, get an adequate concept of the impact of magazines on their readers and on society merely by counting.

In 1974, it would have cost you nearly $53,000 to buy a page of advertising in **Reader's Digest**, which counts out to less than $3 per 1,000 issues. At the same time, it would have cost you $10 per 1,000 copies to reach the readers of **The Atlantic** with a page of advertising. The major buyers of advertising, obviously, believe there are real differences between the kinds of persons on the subscription lists of the two magazines. (For a variation on this discussion, see Chapter 8.)

One way we might measure a magazine's influence would be to determine how "influential" its readers are. Most authorities agree that among the "influentials" are the country's editorial writers. A study was made some years ago of the reading habits of editorial writers and it disclosed that they did read intensely in the large-circulation news magazines. But high on their reading lists also were **Harper's** and **The Atlantic**. Neither has a circulation that comes close to 500,000. Moreover, a significant number of these editorial writers read **Commonweal**, whose circulation is less than 30,000. Opinion leaders have written for, and have read, such magazines since magazines began. Today, as always, we can trace the development of many important public discussions from ideas that appeared first in relatively small journals of opinion or "quality" magazines, then filtered into the more popular magazines and into newspapers.

THE MAGAZINE OFFICE

The editorial offices of the very largest magazines are impressive. Those of most publications, however, will surprise the average visitor—especially one who makes the mistake of trying to compare them with newspaper offices. A magazine's printing plant may be spectacular (if it does not contract to have its printing done elsewhere), but its editorial offices may house but a handful of editors and a few secretaries. Many of the small magazines are edited from offices that include one editor and, perhaps, one secretary.

One of the important reasons for this relatively small size of magazine editing and writing staffs is the fact that "outsiders" provide so much of the content of many magazines. The publications use materials they get from corporation officers, governmental officials, economists, social and political experts, scientific and technological specialists, professional free-lance writers, publicity agents, public relations personnel, information specialists for various groups, and others.

One survey of editors of magazines listed in **The Writer's Market** indicated that more than half used free-lance materials. Some magazines fill only 10 or 15 percent of their space with such materials; others take nearly 100 percent from outsiders.

This means many editors are willing—and eager—to use fact packed news items and feature articles from professional and amateur publicists. Moreover, even if you know from study of **The Writer's Market** or other references that a magazine seldom uses anything other than staff produced material, you may be sure that editors are happy to receive (and may even be willing to pay for) ideas for stories that their own editors will write.

Careful analysis of the magazines that cover the topics you are publicizing will show you whether you will be wisest to submit articles and items of your own, or whether you should offer only ideas. Similar analysis also will tell you whether the articles you submit should, or must, be accompanied by photographs or other illustrations. Some magazines refuse to use anything in certain departments or sections unless they also can use pictures.

WRITING RULES

One of the cardinal rules for the writer who wants to be published is this: **Study your market.** The dictum applies with particular emphasis to one who wishes to be published in a magazine. Our earlier emphasis on the range and variety of magazines will already have suggested this. Those readers who have paid their money for **Popular Mechanics** differ in many ways from the self-selected readers of **Saturday Review** or **Successful Farming.** If you hope to please the readers of a particular magazine, you must know what the special interests of those readers are. Professional writers expend much time and energy trying to discover just who it is they are writing for.

As a writer or a publicist, you can do several things that will help to simplify this task. You can learn whatever you can about an editor and his or her interests. You can study one or several of the references and directories that describe magazines and their needs. You can study issues of a magazine itself.

Personal contact with an editor may be the quickest and surest way of coming to understand what that editor will buy. But it is not crucial; most would-be authors overrate the importance of such a personal relationship. Many writers never see the editors who accept their material.

Several compilations are designed specifically to help the person who works with magazines in various ways. Some of these works are directed specifically toward the writer. Others are not but hold valuable information for the inquiring writer.

Two books addressed specifically to the writer and to helping the writer explore markets are:

The Writer's Market—Published each year in Cincinnati by Writer's Digest, Inc.

The Writer's Handbook—Edited by A. S. Burack and published in Boston by The Writer, Inc.

Two magazines of importance to the writer are **The Writer** and **Writer's Digest.** They offer articles designed to instruct or inspire would-be authors. Each month they carry news of changes in the magazine field, changes in personnel, office addresses, and changes in what editors are seeking.

One reference has been designed specifically for the publicist interested in getting materials into the periodicals published by business corporations for their employees, clients, and others. Among other things, it describes specific topics that particular publications are looking for. The reference work is **Gebbie House Magazine Directory,** published in Burlington, Iowa, by the National Research Bureau, Inc.

Another group of references, designed for advertisers but holding significant clues for writers, includes **Ayer Directory of Publications, Business Publication Rates and Data,** and **Consumer Magazine and Farm Publication Rates and Data,** all of which are described in further detail in the Appendix.

Useful as these references may be, however, they are not enough. The ultimate clue to what a magazine wants—lacking an editor to tell us—is the magazine itself. No intelligent writer, unless working under very strange circumstances, will attempt to write for a magazine without first reading it carefully. If, among the many frustrations that give an editor ulcers, one can be said to lead the rest, it is probably receiving a well-researched, handsomely written story that might fit another magazine but is patently unsuitable for the editor's.

Professional writers do not read stories merely to enjoy them, or articles (except when gathering data for their own stories) solely to obtain information. They read to see how the other writer worked. They analyze techniques.

Nor do they read only the articles or stories. They read everything. They read magazines' departments to see who the editors are writing to. They read advertisements and attempt to visualize the age, sex, income, church affiliation, and other characteristics of an ad writer's target audience. They look at the letters to the editor to discover who cares enough about what the magazine is doing to comment on it.

The publicist who has completed a thorough study of a magazine has a firm grasp of something called "slant." Some persons feel that a slanted story is one that warps or distorts the information it presents, and that to say a magazine is slanted is to say that it it untruthful or biased. However, when we talk of slant we mean something quite different—the special interest a magazine and its readers share in a subject or in several subjects. We are talking about the special approach to that subject that readers have come to expect.

A reader buys **Better Homes and Gardens,** for example, because he or she expects to find within its covers articles that deal with home, garden, and family. If the reader chooses **Good Housekeeping,** he or she anticipates that some of the content will be similar, some quite different. A reader is not distressed to find the approach to the topics covered is not the same. Once could say that every good magazine has a theme song and that the writer who wants to be published in that magazine will write a tune that harmonizes with the theme song.

WRITERS AND EDITORS

Because writers and editors may never see each other, communication between them becomes especially important. Certain amenities, if observed, make the communication quicker and easier. These amenities regulate the pattern of communication between writer and editor and the form of the manuscript that an author submits.

Basically, the only thing an editor cares about is what the author produces. If it is good and suits the magazine's needs and the editor recognizes this, it is purchased. Otherwise, it is rejected. This means that letters telling an editor why an author wrote a piece, or explaining parts of the piece, are not only superfluous but self-defeating. An editor does not care why an author wrote a story. The central concern is what the readers will make of it. It is possible that rare circumstances may call for an explanation by the author of something that would not interest readers. A cover letter may then be desirable. Otherwise, the manuscript and its package will explain themselves if they follow accepted procedure.

The package that an editor receives should, in general, contain the following items:

1. Cover sheet (Fig. 10.1)—This, in effect, is a sales device. It offers a hint of the author's competence and of the story's content.
2. Manuscript. (See examples in Fig. 10.2.)
3. Self-addressed, return envelope.
4. Adequate return postage, clipped to return envelope.
5. Pictures or other illustrations, if appropriate, fully explained and adequately protected. No amateur snapshots, please.

The entire packet goes into a manila envelope. If the manuscript is slender enough, it may be folded once. Usually,

MAGAZINES: SOMETHING FOR EVERYONE

```
              To be paid for at
              your usual rates or
              returned to:


          Diane Dior
          2118 Sunset
          Ames, Iowa



          She's Not Getting Any Older

          by Diane Dior

                          Note:

              This article is about an Iowa woman who has a unique way of staying young --
          she makes bridal dresses. The article contains approximately 500 words.


              Georgia Mullex, Ames, has more than just a grandmotherly hobby. She's been
          making dresses for 20 years and through that activity stays vital and "alive."


              The article should appeal to adults concerned with their elderly parents'
          welfare and to the elderly themselves-- Georgia is one of them.


              The following pictures are inclosed:
                 1. Fitting time.
                 2. Delicate handwork is part of the process.
```

FIG. 10.1. The cover sheet.

however, the envelope should be 9 x 12 inches—large enough to hold the unfolded manuscript flat. Finally, the package should be weighed to verify the postage required. Editors do not appreciate having to pay "postage due" on unsolicited manuscripts.

QUERIES

When you have a story that you think the editors of a certain magazine will like, should you write them about it? The answer to the question varies. If the editors don't know you, they can't know until they see your work whether they can trust you as a reporter and writer. If, however, you have a clear picture of what you have to offer, a well-written query can save you time. It may even elicit helpful suggestions from editors and make the finished product better serve their purposes. A good query letter will indicate an article's theme, demonstrate the slant and tone of the story, and show off the writer's ability as a reporter and wordsmith. A poorly written query is the sure road to refusal.

Diane Dior
2118 Sunset
Ames, Iowa

500 words

SHE'S NOT GETTING ANY OLDER

By Diane Dior

She's 70 going on 20.

Georgia Mullex, an Ames, Iowa, senior citizen, has a unique way of staying young. She doesn't golf; she isn't chairman of the woman's group.

She designs and creates bridal dresses...for young brides.

"Each time I hear the romantic wedding details I get excited all over again," says Georgia, a woman so tiny that she has to stand on tiptoe to "fit" some of the brides. And she's outfitted about five bridal parties a year for 20 years -- more than 100 in all. It's no wonder Georgia still enjoys life so.

"I enjoy the girls and I stay useful," says this woman with snow-white hair and snapping eyes.

(more)

FIG. 10.2. Page 1 of a manuscript.

A WARNING

One magazine practice that puzzles nonjournalists is the refusal to accept multiple submissions. If you have a story that is perishable, why not offer it to several magazines at the same time and accept the offer of the first, or highest, bidder?

Very nearly without exception, it is not done. Editors, under such circumstances, run the risk of competing for the same story or, worse, accepting the same story for publication at approximately the same time, but in different magazines. Through the years, the rules of the game have developed to this point, and if you intend to write for the magazines, you will be obliged to play by the rules of the game or be barred from the field.

SUMMARY

With their numbers and their range, their diversity and their ability to speak directly to audiences with narrowly and sharply defined interests, magazines offer a magnificent challenge and an opportunity to the publicist and seemingly endless opportunities to the alert consumer of the mass media. The publicist who learns how to use them will significantly expand his or her ability to communicate information and ideas. The consumer who becomes familiar with their diversity and breadth will be better informed through his or her access to a variety of points of view.

SUGGESTED READING

Ford, James L. C. Magazines for the Millions. Carbondale: Southern Illinois Univ. Press, 1969.

Peterson, Theodore. Magazines in the Twentieth Century, 2nd ed. Urbana: Univ. of Illinois Press, 1964.

Wolseley, Roland E. The Changing Magazine: Trends in Readership and Management. New York: Hastings House, 1973.

―――. Understanding Magazines. Ames: Iowa State Univ. Press, 1966.

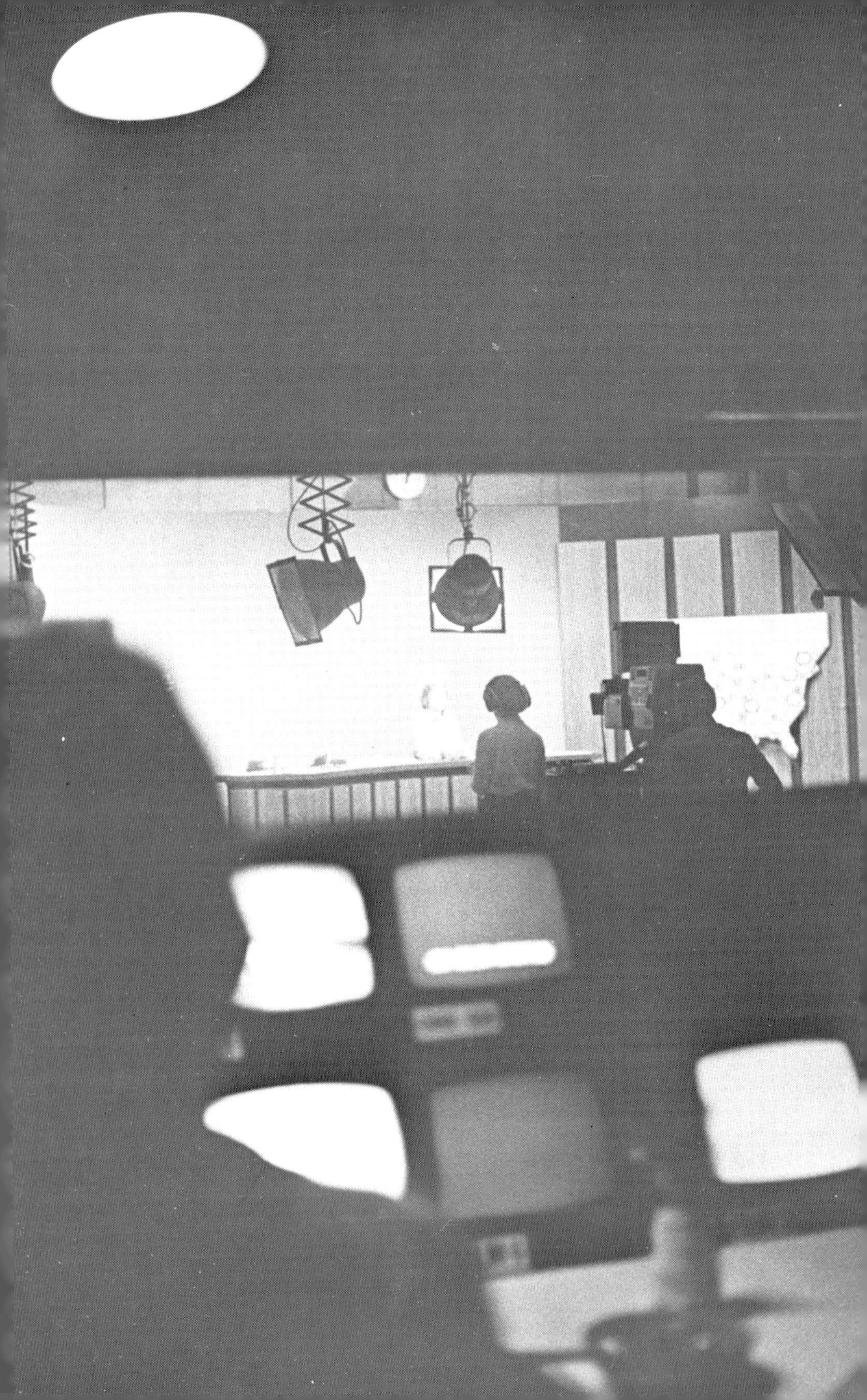

11

Radio and television: the pervasive media

JACK D. SHELLEY

He struggles out of bed at 4:45 A.M. "Those first 10 minutes are tough, but once I get going it's okay," he says. "After 20 years, you get used to it."

By 5:30 A.M. Bud Chaldy, news director of KASI Radio, Ames, Iowa, is at the municipal building chatting with police, firefighters, and highway patrol personnel about what's happened overnight. At 6 A.M., he's reached the station and has begun a frenzy of activity: Clearing a nightlong accumulation of copy from the United Press International (UPI) teletype machine; recording national and international news feeds from UPI's audio wire service; and taping offerings from the Iowa Radio Network (IRN) audio news exchange, while feeding down the line the statewide stories he's picked up and exchanging information with other news directors about what's likely to happen today.

Between feeds, he's typing up news gathered at the municipal building, selecting copy from the teletype, putting in order the tape cassettes he'll use from UPI and IRN. And, at 6:25 A.M., the whirlwind pauses for five minutes while he sits down at a microphone and airs the first of eight newscasts he delivers daily. He does all his own news writing and reporting, prepares special broadcast reports on city council meetings, and does a weekly local public affairs program.

In early afternoon, he takes a nap and comes back to the station for later newscasts. During football and basketball seasons, he doubles as a "color" man for broadcasts of the local high school games. Chaldy describes his administrative responsibilities as "practically nil. We have what I'd call a one-and-a-half-man news staff," he explains. "One announcer works about half-time on news." There are no labor unions at the station, and Chaldy describes his working relationship with owner-manager Dale Cowle as "ideal."

Ed Planer reaches his office in the

JACK SHELLEY is Professor of Journalism and Mass Communication, Iowa State University, former news manager of station WHO and WHO-TV in Des Moines, former president of the International Radio-Television News Directors, and former president of the Associated Press Radio and Television Association. A war correspondent with extensive service in World War II, Shelley headed the WHO radio news bureau, which twice was honored as the best in the nation by the Radio-Television News Directors Association. He is a recipient of the "Honor Medal" of the School of Journalism of the University of Missouri and of the Mitchell Charnley Award of the Northwest Broadcast News Association (University of Minnesota) for "distinguished service to broadcast journalism."

huge Merchandise Mart in Chicago at about 9 A.M. and plunges immediately into details of a job that is "almost entirely administrative, plus general oversight of major editorial decisions." He does no in-person or telephone news reporting, no writing of news copy ("I'm not allowed to under our union contracts") and airs no newscasts.

Planer is news director for WMAQ-TV, owned and operated by the National Broadcasting Company (NBC) in the nation's third largest television market. Local newsgathering is carried out by a task force of some 32 writers, reporters, and desk personnel. To meet WMAQ-TV's local newscast needs and to service NBC with midwestern coverage for its national network, nine camera crews of three persons each (cinematographer, sound specialist, and light specialist) are on the go, each accompanied by a reporter. Four full-time specialists operate equipment developing hundreds of thousands of feet of color newsfilm monthly. Before the film is aired, it passes through the hands of 7 film editors and 13 assistants.

In all, Planer rides herd on a television news staff of close to 120, not counting a few more persons who work exclusively in news for WMAQ Radio. A large portion of his day may be spent dealing with seven locals of four labor unions. Whatever the staff member's role, a labor union has jurisdiction, and dealing with careful delineation of job responsibilities is so much a fact of life that NBC keeps a fulltime labor negotiation specialist on the scene to help Planer and other station executives.

The contrast between Bud Chaldy's and Ed Planer's working days illuminates the spectrum in American broadcast news operations today. Indeed, Chaldy's one-and-a-half-man staff is larger than many; a 1973 survey by Vernon Stone and James Hoyt of the University of Wisconsin-Madison concluded: "The typical small-market radio station has no one working full-time in news." Yet the three national radio-television networks (ABC, CBS, NBC) spent a reported $159,264,000 on news in 1972, most of it payroll for more than 3,000 workers. Another $275 million was reported spent by individual radio and television stations for local news coverage.

SOME SIMILARITIES

With such a range in manpower and expenditures, describing a "typical" broadcast station news operation is an exercise in futility, but there are some commonalities. Let's look at several job categories.

The most widely used title for the individual who heads the news staff of a radio and/or television station is **news director**. He (there are few women news directors, although the number is growing) is the opposite number of a newspaper's managing editor.

Most news directors report directly to the station **general manager,** whose role in broadcasting is similar to that of a newspaper publisher. News directors hire and fire members of the news staff, fix salaries, and allocate pay raises on the basis of a budget approved by the general manager. News directors plan work schedules, oversee purchase of newsroom equipment, and set general news coverage policies and priorities.

Depending on size of staff, news directors may play an active role in the reporting and writing of news, shooting and editing of television newsfilm, and they may even be the principal newscasters for their stations. In larger cities (such as Planer's) they may be almost entirely administrators.

Television news, with its vastly greater requirements for manpower and equipment, has developed some recognizable job titles seldom found in radio.

An **assignment editor** schedules

reporters and motion picture camera operators to cover news stories in the television station's service area. As the assignment editor balances available personnel against estimated news values, his or her decisions have a critical effect on the accumulation of picture and word information from which the final newscast is fashioned. Typically an assignment editor spends the working day with telephones and radio microphones used to dispatch camera crews around the city and environs, making minute-by-minute decisions as information from many sources makes new story material available.

Conferring repeatedly with the assignment editor, the television **news producer** takes the finished product from writers, reporters, film and videotape editors, and literally puts a newscast together. The producer amy have much influence on the assignment editor's decisions, but typically the producer's key role lies in making final editorial judgments as to what does or does not go into the newscast from the available copy and visuals. He or she also "orchestrates" the material, so that when the newscast goes on the air it has balance, continuity, unity, and sustained interest for the viewer.

Across the industry, the **anchorman** or **anchorwoman** is the highest paid person in broadcast news—and also the least secure, because anchorpersons "live" or "die" by the audience ratings. They read the newscast on camera and lead into film and other segments voiced by other personnel. Increasingly, two anchorpersons may share this role on a single newscast.

The smaller the news staff, the less precision about job titles and work descriptions, particularly if no labor unions are involved. Likewise, staff members of a "small" news operation are expected to perform a wider variety of tasks. Many television news reporters for medium- and small-sized stations operate silent and sound motion picture cameras, edit film, write stories, and deliver news on the air as well. At all but the largest radio news operations, it is commonplace for everyone on the staff to do in-person and telephone reporting, use battery operated tape recorders for interview and actuality coverage, edit the tapes, write and assemble copy and tape materials, and then deliver a regular schedule of newscasts.

BROADCAST NEWS SOURCES

Virtually every radio and television newsroom is equipped with one or more wires of Associated Press (AP) and United Press International (UPI). Stations without network affiliations rely on the wire services for nearly all information about what is going on outside their local coverage areas. Both AP and UPI offer 24-hour-a-day "broadcast wires," written for easy oral delivery and organized into convenient, 5-, 10-, or 15-minute newscast formats. The "rip-and-read" stations, with little or no professional news staff, air wire service copy with only the addition of such local news as they have been able to come by. (The wire services are discussed in more detail in Chapter 12.)

Professional news staffs, even if small, usually organize available news sources in the community into "beats" which they cover either in person or by telephone. Many will have "stringers"—correspondents who report news and perhaps shoot film—in communities outside the station's home city

Affiliated stations carry not only the national newscasts offered by their radio and television networks, but they also can arrange to tape record news reports fed down the line specifically for use in local programs. Both AP and UPI offer "audio services" complete with network-style radio newscasts or individual news reports which the station may use locally; both also provide picture wires and color slides (sent by mail) for use as backdrops for the on-camera anchorperson.

By mail, telephone, and in person, hundreds of prepackaged news items or suggestions for stories cascade into even the smallest of broadcast newsrooms each day, in addition to those from sources already mentioned. They come from public relations firms, government agencies, special interest groups, political figures, aspiring entertainers, and little old ladies who are unhappy with the neighbors' kids. The contest for a share of precious newscast time never ends.

SOME DIFFERENCES

Among the more than 7,600 radio stations operating in the United States, differences in staff size and audiences are approximately as great as those between such newspapers as the **New York Daily News** (daily circulation 2.1 million) and the weekly **Ute** (Iowa) **Independent** (circulation 517).

AM (for Amplitude Modulation) radio stations, for example, range in assigned power from 100 watts all the way to a declining number of 50,000-watt "clear channel" giants. The 100- and 250-watters at the bottom of the power scale often don't expect to be heard outside their local communities. Even if their signals pushed farther, they would run into a buzzing swarm of interfering transmissions from other stations, licensed to use the same spot on the AM band of roughly 540 to 1600 kiloHertz. Strong and weak, there are some 4,400 AM radio stations in America.

"Clear channel" 50,000-watters operate on frequencies that have been set aside for interference-free reception. When the friendly protection of nighttime darkness allows their signals full range, they can be heard for thousands of miles.

So you may be twiddling the dial some bitter winter evening in Minnesota and hear booming over the airwaves, loud and clear, the voice of an announcer at WSB, Atlanta, telling you it's a pleasant 70 degrees there. But the approximately 3,200 FM (for Frequency Modulation) stations are more alike in coverage patterns than their AM counterparts. Operating on a band of 88 to 108 megaHertz, FM transmissions are primarily limited in reception by the line of sight from the antenna atop the station's transmitter tower. While this tends to limit the coverage area of most FM stations, there are compensations: FM is not subject to interference with other stations and is, in most respects, static-free as well. Tune the AM band during a thunderstorm and you may not be able to find a usable signal because of crashes of lightning-caused static; switch to the FM band and hear the difference. (The sound on your television set also tends to be static-free because television's audio signal is an FM transmission.)

Despite certain technical superiorities, FM radio was much slower to develop in the United States than was AM. The story of American radio until well after the end of World War II was almost exclusively concerned with AM, but a boom in the late 1960s and early 1970s altered a longtime trend for FM to be considered merely a secondary, auxiliary service. For the first time in American radio history, some FM stations now figure prominently in audience ratings in their markets.

There is somewhat less diversity among the nation's more than 600 television stations than among radio operations. However, it is a long way from KYUS-TV, Miles City, Montana, whose published commercial rate for a one-time, one-minute commercial is $30 for prime time, to WCBS-TV, in New York City, where the comparable rate is $16,000.

RADIO AND TELEVISION: PERVASIVE MEDIA

The biggest difference is not so much how far KYUS-TV's transmissions reach compared to WCBS-TV's. Actually, television signals generally cover roughly the same distance from the transmitter (given equal tower heights) because of the way the Federal Communications Commission (FCC) has allocated channels and power and because television, like FM radio, is line-of-sight transmission. The difference lies in the number of available viewers crowded under the invisible tent of WCBS-TV's radiated waves—a market of more than 6 million television households, compared with about 7,000 households for KYUS-TV.

It is the function of market size, translated into available viewers who may be "sold" to a potential advertiser for so much cost per thousand, that produces the contrast between the staff of a TV station in the wide-open spaces and that of another station in the megalopolis. There is not a great difference in the number of square miles they reach, but prairie dogs don't buy the products television commercials advertise.

Even so, no television station is as small in staff size as the smallest radio station. Despite increased automation, television still requires lavish use of personnel compared to radio. Virtually nowhere is there anything in the news and information services of television quite comparable to the one-man news staff often found in grassroots radio.

Another characteristic of most television stations is important to any individual or organization trying to get a story told on the tube: The overwhelming majority of U.S. television stations are jointly owned and operated with radio stations, and share the same staffs. Hundreds of broadcast ownerships grew up in the same way: First an AM radio station; later an FM station; finally a television license. There may be separate program directors and sales managers for the three licensed broadcast operations, but all typically operate in the same building and most of the staff work in all three media. There are exceptions, but not many.

So, if you want to get your newsworthy item or viewpoint used on the kind of broadcast outlet we have just described, it helps to know that the executive who heads the television station's news staff is usually also news boss for the associated FM and AM radio stations as well. And most of the news personnel who work with him are contributing to the reporting, writing, and presenting of news for all three stations, too.

It is also useful to remember, when dealing with radio-only broadcast outlets, that because of some of the differences we have mentioned, radio tends to multiply its diversity. Stations in the same city may seek to reach widely different parts of the total available audience. If you are pushing a message intended for senior citizens, for example, don't make much effort to get it on a station noted for rock music, aimed at teenagers.

PUBLICITY CHECKLIST

Whenever you take a message or a news item to a station in the hope it will be broadcast, here's a handy checklist:

1. **Know your station.** Make a list of all broadcast stations in the area you are trying to reach. Such standard reference works as **Broadcasting Yearbook** and the radio and television editions of **Standard Rate and Data** are available from many libraries or you can probably borrow one for a short time from a nearby broadcasting outlet. (These guides are described in the Appendix.) Familiarize yourself with each station's coverage area, operating hours, size and nature of its staff, and schedule of news and public affairs broadcasts.

2. **Know the adudience.** Learn what kinds of audiences area stations are trying to reach. You may notice some make almost no effort to attract the kind of person whose attention you are seeking. While some stations may have the transmitter power to reach farther, they may seek to appeal to certain residents of only one city; others may try to serve a large and heterogeneous audience.

3. **Know your contact.** Even when a station has a large staff, there will usually be just a few persons you can effectively approach. A fairly typical organizational chart indicates a great many staff members are not directly concerned with information content. (See Figure 11.1.)

As we have seen, all but the smallest stations do have news directors; if one does not, simply ask for the person who has most to do with information for the station's newscasts. Any item you seek to have used on the station's regularly scheduled newscasts or any suggestion for an editorial or a public affairs program should be presented to the news director. If he is not the person directly involved with the broadcast you have in mind, he can quickly direct you to that individual.

If you are seeking a free public service announcement, ask to see the program director or a member of his or her staff. As a general rule, the two persons most likely to be the decision makers when you are trying to get a noncommercial informational message on the air are the news director and the program director. Unless the station's staff is extremely small, or unless you know the individual personally, do not bother the general manager.

4. **Make your contact personal.** Being normal human beings, broadcast executives are more likely to pay attention to a request made in person. So, if the number of outlets you are trying to reach makes it feasible, make direct, personal contacts with the news directors and program directors. Set this up by phoning in advance for an appointment; midmorning and midaf-

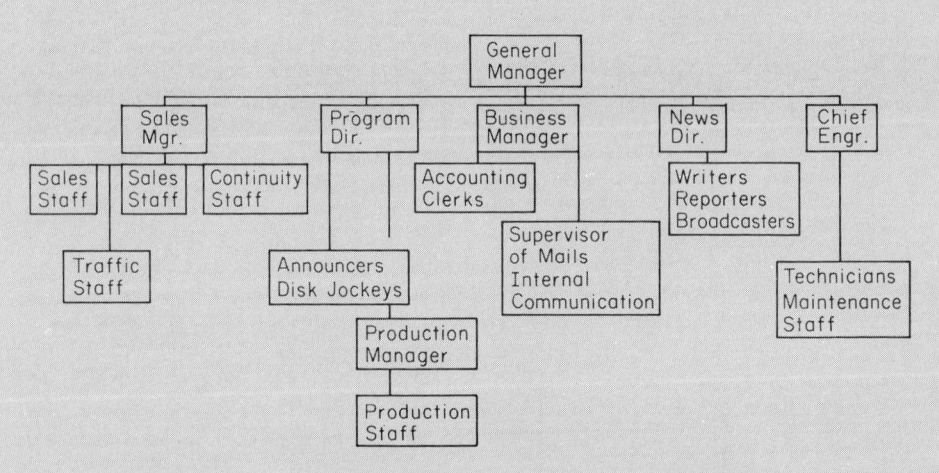

FIG. 11.1. A typical organizational scheme for a local broadcasting operation. The job titles and lines of authority vary sharply from small, radio-only, to combined AM-FM-TV complexes. In the latter case, separate sales managers and program directors are often assigned for differing media.

ternoon tend to be the least hectic times of day for them. And if you are able to meet personally, keep the conference brief because these are busy people. Bring with you a concise written statement of the information you seek to have aired, and leave it with the station executive as a record for his files, keeping a copy for yourself.

Sometimes an item you hope to have broadcast may be considered usable both on a regularly scheduled newscast, and also as what broadcasters sometimes call a "plug." That is a free announcement, carried somewhere in the station's regular program schedule (often in a spot where they have not sold a commercial message) and read on the air by a station announcer or disc jockey. If you hope for both kinds of usage, see that copies of your material go to both the news director and program director.

In that case, prepare a news-style, moderately detailed report for the news director and a separate, shorter "plug" for the program director. Stick to the most important essentials in this "plug"; read it aloud after you have written it to make sure it will not take more than 30 seconds. (Occasionally, a spot announcement of this kind might be allowed to run 60 seconds, but don't count on it.)

5. **Don't overlook opportunities.** Today's broadcast schedules, especially in radio, frequently include time set aside for public service announcements. Many stations have "datebook" or "calendar" periods scattered through the day, and they will carry almost any legitimate advance announcement about events of public interest at these times. Open-line telephone shows are heard on hundreds of radio stations; they may offer you a chance to call in with a helpful word about the activity or event you wish to promote. Man-on-the-street interview shows may serve the same purpose.

However, audience surveys show that an item carried in a regularly scheduled newscast is heard by far more persons than the kind of "plug" discussed here. So, if you have a choice, make newscast use your first priority. And if the news director doesn't think your item is of sufficiently widespread interest to make the news, ask if the station has some other scheduled program it might fit. Sportscasts, homemakers' news, health and medical programs, and club calendars are examples.

6. **Remember your competition.** There are many chances for an energetic person to get his or her message on radio or television today. But you are unrealistic if you do not keep in mind that your precious message is in rugged competition with literally thousands of others also trying to get just a little of that air time.

No broadcaster has yet squeezed more than 60 seconds out of a minute or expanded an hour beyond 60 minutes. Time is the only thing he has either to sell or give away. A news director can air only a handful of the literally thousands of items available for use and must make decisions on the basis of his or her experienced news judgment. Program directors spend hours dealing with appeals for worthy causes seeking air time. It may be hard to believe, but many of those other causes seem to them to deserve exposure just as much as yours. So, after considering the competition. . . .

7. **Don't complain.** If your item doesn't get on the air, don't waste the broadcaster's time with loud complaints. Pressures of news and other commitments often upset even the most carefully laid programming plans. Try again.

And don't be offended if the station staff has rewritten the material you submitted. This often is necessary to fit requirements of time, style, or format applying to the program in which it is used.

But, if the item has been used, show your appreciation. Write or telephone a brief thank-you message to the station executive responsible. You may also want to send a copy of your letter to the station manager for his files.

8. **Remember broadcasting is a business.** Every American commercial broadcaster is in business to make a profit; if a profit is not realized, nobody on the staff get paid. So don't request free publicity for an item involving a commercial activity that ought to be the subject of a paid advertisement. One almost guaranteed way to lose the goodwill of a broadcaster is to hit him up for a free "plug" and then buy a paid advertisement for the same cause in the local newspaper.

9. **Remember mechanics.** Learn how to submit your story to broadcast media in a form meeting minimum professional standards. Two of the best concise, inexpensive manuals on radio and television newswriting methods are broadcast news stylebooks published by the Associated Press and United Press International. They are available from many college book stores or from: United Press International, 220 East 42nd Street, New York, N.Y. 10017; or The Associated Press, 50 Rockefeller Plaza, New York, N.Y. 10020.

PREPARING COPY

Here are some generalized tips on preparing information for broadcasting stations:

1. **Make your copy clean.** Type your release. A hand-written item is almost certain to hit the wastebasket. Write on one side only of 8½ x 11 typing paper; double or triple space; put only one informational item on a single page; and make sure every station gets a clear, legible copy.

2. **Make it short.** Broadcast news items rarely run more than 60 seconds; 30 seconds is more usual. Set your typewriter margins for a 65-space line. Sixteen typed lines of this length will require 60 seconds to deliver at a moderate pace.

3. **Use modified conversational style.** Broadcast information is delivered orally, so make it easy for the announcer or newscaster to read your copy aloud. Use short, simple sentences, with subject and verb in clear, direct relationship. Try to average no more than about 20 words per sentence. Avoid long, complex structures with clauses that require a listener to sort things out in his or her head. Remember, the listener cannot see your copy.

4. **Talk it out.** Read your copy aloud in a strong, "broadcaster-type" delivery after you have written it. Notice difficult combinations of vowels and consonants or the breath control problems you may have handed the person who has to deliver such material on the air. Correct these shortcomings before submitting your material to a station. Reading your copy aloud will tell you more about its broadcast quality than almost anything else you can do.

FAIRNESS, EQUAL TIME

There is a significant difference between broadcasting and printed publications in the United States in terms of what is often called "access"—the opportunity to get your point of view across through the media. The United States Supreme Court, in June, 1974, unanimously upheld the right of a newspaper to refuse a political candidate's demand that his reply to a critical editorial be printed in the same paper that attacked him.

Yet five years earlier the Supreme Court unanimously upheld the Federal Communication Commission's "Fairness Doctrine." It requires radio and television stations to offer reply opportunities to persons whose honesty, integrity, or character have been attacked in connection with discussion of a controversial topic on the air. Indeed, the FCC's "personal attack" provision requires broadcasters to notify the subject of such an attack of the date and time the attack was broadcast, and to send the person or persons involved a tape, script, or summary of the attack within seven days. Then the broadcaster is expected to afford the subject a reasonable opportunity to reply—on the same station that carried the critical comment.

When it comes to political candidates, the regulatory power of the federal government over electronic media has required, almost from the beginning of broadcasting, an even-handed opportunity of access. Section 315 of the Communications Act of 1934, the basic statute under which American broadcasters operate, sets forth clearly that whenever radio and television stations make time available to a political candidate, they must offer time **on an equal basis** to all other legally qualified candidates for the same office. Again, there is nothing comparable to this requirement for newspapers, magazines, and other print media. (See also Chapter 15.)

If broadcasting is part of the "free press" in America, as we often are told, why is it so much less free to refuse airtime to points of view with which owners of radio and television stations may not agree? The rationale has emerged from several situations and philosophies dating back to the early twentieth century.

As radio developed, governments around the world recognized the need for some kind of international agreement, allowing electronic signals (that blithely ignore national boundaries) to be allocated in orderly fashion. To play its role under an international radio treaty, a nation had to have some means of control over broadcast frequencies within its own borders. It was logical, therefore, that the United States Congress, in the Radio Act of 1912, made it illegal for anyone to operate a radio station without a license from the Secretary of Commerce.

But Secretary of Commerce Herbert Hoover found his hands legally tied when he attempted to exert licensing control in the mid-1920s. The resulting electronic interference, as hundreds of stations broadcast whenever and wherever on the dial they wished, supported a further point: The government must be able to allocate frequencies. It was contended that the broadcast spectrum was so limited that only a certain number of stations could ever operate effectively, whereas (in theory, at least) anyone could start a newspaper.

Further, from both a national security and a philosophical base, it was strongly felt that control of the air waves over which these far-ranging signals travelled must be in the hands of the people of the United States, through their government. Hence the language of the Communications Act of 1934, to "provide for the use of (radio transmission) channels, but not the ownership thereof, by persons for limited periods of time, under licenses granted by federal authority...."

A seven-member Federal Communications Commission was established by the act, its members appointed by the President for seven-year terms with Senate approval. Today, the FCC licenses broadcast operations in the United States, allocates frequencies, and has regulatory authority over cable television in addition to many other nonbroadcast responsibilities. The 1934 act directs the FCC to issue licenses on the basis of the "public convenience, interest, or necessity."

The act also states that the commission does not have "the power of censorship" and shall not "interfere with the right of free speech by means of radio communication." But in the 1940s and

1950s, the FCC steadily increased emphasis on requirements that broadcasters allow a wide variety of points of view to be expressed on their stations (whether they agreed with them or not) and the courts upheld such regulatory actions, climaxing with the "Red Lion" decision of June, 1969.

Writing the U.S. Supreme Court's opinion upholding the "Fairness Doctrine" in that case, Associate Justice Byron White declared, "Although broadcasting is clearly a medium affected by a First Amendment interest . . . differences in the characteristics of new media justify differences in the First Amendment standards applied to them. . . . Where there are substantially more individuals who want to broadcast than there are frequencies to allocate, it is idle to posit an unabridgeable First Amendment right to broadcast comparable to the right of every individual to speak, write or publish."

The "Fairness Doctrine" has evolved over decades of FCC rulings on specific questions dealing with broadcasters' performance. It is broadly based on the FCC's contention that a licensee has an obligation to allow presentation of contrasting viewpoints, dealing with a wide variety of controversial issues of public interest. In 1974, the commission completed a three-year review of the doctrine, which many broadcasters had opposed as both an infringement on First Amendment rights and a reflection on their integrity as responsible media operators. But when the review was concluded, the FCC made it clear the doctrine was to be retained, for the time being at least, but without being expanded.

Perhaps the most widely debated application of the "Fairness Doctrine" occurred in the late 1960s when a young attorney named John Banzhaf III persuaded the FCC to issue a ruling that broadcasting cigarette commercials amounted to trying to persuade the public on an issue of a controversial nature. The commission agreed, to the dismay of the advertising industry, and for some years required that stations carrying cigarette commercials also broadcast a number of antismoking messages free of charge. The requirement finally ended when Congress passed a law banning all cigarette advertisements from the airways. In the report summarizing its "Fairness" review in 1974, the FCC said that in the future it would apply the doctrine to commercials only if they explicitly raised issues of controversial importance.

Beyond its debatable influence in pressuring broadcasters to allow a variety of viewpoints to be aired over their stations, what does the "Fairness Doctrine" mean to you, if you have a cause to promote? To the advocate of a controversial issue, the doctrine can be a two-edged sword. Let's say you are chairman of the committee backing passage of an impending school bond issue, and you persuade the manager of the local radio station to carry an editorial urging a "yes" vote next Tuesday. That's a fine accomplishment, but not altogether in your favor. For under provisions of the "Fairness Doctrine," the group trying to get out a "no" vote can go to the manager and demand a chance to have its negative view also aired on the same station. And, if the manager has good reason to believe airing your viewpoint will subject him or her to a whole series of demands from various groups, he or she may decide the whole thing is too much of a headache and not carry any editorial expressions of opinion at all on the matter. The manager can still report public statements and developments regarding the bond issue in the station's newscasts, relying on professional staff judgments about news values, and still avoid "Fairness Doctrine" complications.

ABOUT CABLE TELEVISION

As through-the-air television spread rapidly across the United States in the 1940s and 1950s, viewers who lived near mountain ranges or in sparsely settled rural areas were frustrated in their efforts to pick up the electronic pictures so many of their fellow Americans were enjoying. Palm Springs, California, for example, was cut off from television signals out of nearby Los Angeles by the mountains rising between them.

An enterprising businessman thereupon erected a large receiving antenna atop a nearby peak and offered to connect any television set in Palm Springs to his antenna for a modest monthly charge. Business boomed, and his customers happily watched clear pictures from 10 Los Angeles stations.

That is how what was first known as Community Antenna Television (CATV), later more often called Cable Television, got its start. From a single small system in 1948, cable grew by 1974 to approximately 3,000 operating systems serving more than 5,400 communities, with applications pending or approved to build some 3,400 more systems. Those in operation were reaching more than 22 million persons—more than 10 percent of the television homes in the nation.

California is the state with the largest number of cable subscribers—more than 1.1 million homes and business places. The largest single system in 1974 was San Diego's, with about 74,000 subscribers in and near the city.

After much backing and filling, the FCC issued rules in early 1972, asserting clearly its regulatory authority (although leaving the power to issue cable franchises in the hands of local governments) and saying the commission wanted "to get cable moving." Many of its rules, however, protected the interests of conventional broadcasters, limiting the number of distant signals a cable operator may import into a community. The FCC also prohibited cable operators from importing programs that would duplicate what a local television station was offering.

By the 1970s, many local cable systems (450 in 1974) originated their own local live programming, averaging about two hours a day. Typical offerings included local sports events, public affairs shows, and coverage of city council and school board meetings. But since most cable operators avoided trying to compete head on with the local broadcast station, cable news operations were comparatively few and modest. The FCC ruled that cable systems with more than 3,500 subscribers must originate local programs, but a court action delayed enforcement.

Optimistic predictions that cable television and other technological developments will make America a "wired nation"—and that every household would be served by perhaps hundreds of channels offering news, entertainment, and services—have been heard during the 1960s and 1970s. The FCC requires that all new systems in the 100 largest television markets have at least a 20-channel capacity and three free channels. The latter would include one channel each for educational and municipal government use, plus one for "public access." These "access channels" have generated excitement among some who see them as open forums, available at last to anyone who wants to speak his or her mind. But others have responded with the put-down: "With all those other channels, who'll pay any attention?"

So, if you want to sound off on the cable, it seems safe to say that:

1. Wherever there are newer systems with local, live program originations and access channels, you or your group can probably get on the wired tube.

2. Cable television presentation techniques are substantially the same as those for conventional broadcasting.
3. Until cable commands a much larger audience than it did in the mid-1970s, you had better recall and heed a time-honored rule for the broadcast publicist: Remember your competition!

SUMMARY

Even before the age of the transistor, radio and television were pervasive media. With the advent of solid-state devices and the rugged dependability and miniaturization they make possible, radio and television are virtually everywhere. Farmers listen to FM music in the comfort of their enclosed tractor cabins, youngsters are accompanied by radio receivers built into headsets or mounted on bicycles, AM and FM stereo receivers in a wide price range have become commonplace in the American home, and tiny television receivers can rest atop protuberant stomachs while others are plugged into automobile cigarette lighter outlets.

Since the first national study of television habits was conducted in 1959 by The Roper Organization, Incorporated, there has been a steady and uninterrupted increase in the "American public's regard for television and approval of its performance."

Among the college-educated, newspapers have maintained a lead over television as the major source of news, but the gap has been narrowing. And, since 1961, television has consistently been judged by survey respondents as the "most believable news medium."

The publicist or consumer who fails to appreciate the diversity of the broadcast media is likely neither a well-informed agent of change nor a constructive mass media critic.

SUGGESTED READING

Adler, Richard, and Baer, Walter S., eds. **The Electronic Box Office: Humanities and the Arts on the Cable.** New York: Praeger, 1974.

Bliss, Edward, Jr., and Patterson, John M. **Writing News for Broadcast.** New York: Columbia Univ. Press, 1971.

Chester, Giraud; Garrison, Garnet R.; and Willis, Edgar E. **Television and Radio,** 4th ed. New York: Appleton-Century-Crofts, 1971.

Dary, David. **Radio News Handbook,** 2nd ed. Blue Ridge Summit, Pa.: Tab Books, 1970.

———. **TV News Handbook.** Blue Ridge Summit, Pa.: Tab Books, 1971.

Fang, Irving E. **Television News,** rev. ed. New York: Hastings House, 1972.

"In Cable Franchising, the Cards Are Being Played Closer to the Vest." **Broadcasting,** 86, No. 5 (Feb. 4, 1974), 48.

Kahn, Frank J., ed. **Documents of American Broadcasting,** 2nd ed. New York: Appleton-Century-Crofts, 1973.

Mitchell, Curtiss. **Cavalcade of Broadcasting.** Chicago: Follett Publishing Co., 1970.

Pember, Don R. **Mass Media in America.** Chicago: Science Research Associates, 1974.

Sloan Commission on Cable Communications. **On the Cable: The Television of Abundance.** New York: McGraw-Hill, 1971.

12

The wire services and syndicates

LORRAINE WECHSLER

A look at the by-lines and credits in a newspaper shows that much, perhaps most, of the material in the news columns comes from outside the newspaper office. Stories are attributed to an assortment of news services. Regular features like political columns, comic strips, astrology charts, and medical advice come from syndicates. Even editorials, which presumably reflect the opinions of the editor, are sometimes purchased from a service or have come in the mail from a pressure group. Publicists and news consumers need to know something about these many sellers of information competing for space in newspapers and time on the air.

NEWS SERVICES

Only a small percentage of newspapers and broadcast news departments can afford to have reporters in the can afford to have reporters in the

LORRAINE WECHSLER is Assistant Professor of Journalism and Mass Communication, Iowa State University, a former writer for **Current Biography,** a former staff reporter for a foundation-financed education project, and a reporter for **The Oak Ridger,** Oak Ridge, Tennessee. She is also a former journalism instructor and Assistant Director of Public Relations for Hunter College.

nations' capital or overseas. Only a few more even assign reporters to the state capitals to cover state governments. For regional, national, and international news nearly all rely on the two major American news services, the Associated Press (AP) and United Press International (UPI). For broadcast media, the other major sources of news are the news staffs of the three national commercial networks.

Large newspapers (more than 100,000 circulation) often also buy as many as six or seven supplemental news services. Some of these are the wire services of metropolitan papers. The 1960s saw the rapid growth of these supplemental wire services when hundreds of newspapers began to receive by teletype the news gathered by the staffs of large newspapers such as the **Los Angeles Times,** the **Washington Post,** the **Chicago Daily News,** and the **New York Times.** These major newspapers, in competition with AP and UPI, maintain bureaus of their own in Washington, D.C., and send reporters to cover news throughout the world.

This competition has resulted in more access to news from more sources. For example, while AP and UPI failed to dig out the story for the more than 1,700 newspapers that used one or both of their services, 200 newspapers across the country that subscribed to the **Los**

133

Angeles Times-Washington Post news service had access to the stories of the two Post reporters who uncovered the Watergate scandals in 1972 and 1973. The Post won a Pulitzer Prize for that investigation.

Thirty-four news services are listed in Editor and Publisher International Yearbook for 1974 as being used by daily newspapers in the United States. Some are foreign wire services, such as the British-owned Reuters and the French Agence France-Presse, or foreign newspaper services, such as that of The Times of London. Others offer specialties such as financial news or home and family news. Some are the services of groups of newspapers under a single ownership that maintain news bureaus in major cities. Examples include the Knight News Service and the Scripps-Howard Newspaper Alliance. Familiar credit lines over news features in many papers are the North American Newspaper Alliance (NANA) and the Newspaper Enterprise Association (NEA), which, like UPI and the Scripps-Howard Newspaper Alliance, is owned and independently operated by the E. W. Scripps Company.

Even small papers can afford to carry this additional coverage of world and national affairs because they pay for the services according to circulation (as they do for AP and UPI). A small paper can get the daily mail service of the New York Times or the Christian Science Monitor for approximately $100 a month, while a large paper taking the daily wire service of the New York Times pays several thousands of dollars a month.

Mail service is for background, analysis, or feature material of longer-term interest. Some mail service stories are a week or more old before they are published by a client newspaper.

Many newspapers and broadcast newsrooms have rows of AP, UPI, and other news service teleprinters (or teletypes) printing words on continuous rolls of paper. The news arrives at a speed of about 66 words a minute by way of leased telephone wires, ocean cable, radio, and communication satellite. Some teletype machines also deliver punched tape for typesetters that automatically set the stories in columns of type. Other wires deliver pictures to those who buy the AP or UPI wirephoto services. Larger papers may subscribe for additional wires from AP and UPI, such as stock market tables that come by high speed transmission on typesetting tape, a full sports wire, or a business news wire.

Recently improved wire service receivers are smaller, faster, and quieter than the noisy teletypes. Some are designed to feed electronic signals directly into a typesetting computer where an article can be stored until it is "called up" on a Video Display Terminal (VDT) for editing refinements. The new technology eliminates the bulk and the clatter of the teletypes as well as the jobs of some printers.

Both major wire services transmit broadcast wires especially written for reading on the air and including frequent short news summaries. Those small stations whose announcers "rip and read" the broadcast wire news summaries rarely credit the wire services.

The AP and UPI news pouring into newsrooms comes from a network of wire service bureaus and clients. These range from a declining number of one-person offices in small cities, where the wire service representatives get most of the news by phone and from local papers, to the well-staffed, computerized New York, Los Angeles, and Chicago offices where news from around the world is selected, edited, and transmitted to the media 24 hours a day. Stories of state or regional interest are shared on regional wires without going through New York. If a local story has wider interest, the state bureau offers it to New York or a regional office for national or even worldwide use.

Once written or phoned into the office,

WIRE SERVICES AND SYNDICATES

stories are edited and transmitted in minutes. The wire services now use computers to store, sort, and send out stories. A reporter types a story into a video display terminal (UPI) or a cathode ray tube (AP). A small television screen above a keyboard displays the copy, and the reporter makes changes, erasures, and additions electronically by using the keyboard. A press of a button stores the report or sends it thousands of miles on the wires. Editors in other bureaus can call the story up on other screens for editing and further transmission. New equipment moves the stories at speeds of more than 1,000 words a minute compared with the teletype speed of about 66 words a minute.

AP and UPI are also using such technological innovations in picture transmission as laser beams and electrostatic recording processes.

History

News by wire service goes back to 1848 when AP, the oldest and largest wire service, began as a cooperative newsgathering association of six New York publishers. It remains a membership organization, with the board of directors elected from among the members and member newspapers expected to contribute locally written stories when they are of wider interest.

The UP was founded in 1907 to sell news to competitors of AP-member papers. A third competitor, International News Service, founded by William Randolph Hearst in 1909, was absorbed by United Press in 1958. The resulting UPI depends on its own staff correspondents, but also gets help and news tips from reporters on the staffs of subscribing newspapers.

The two services vie for the business of the nearly 1,800 daily newspapers and the more than 8,200 radio and television stations in the United States as well as for clients overseas. At the end of 1973, AP was ahead in number of newspaper clients, claiming 1,265 to UPI's 1,140, and UPI was ahead in broadcast subscribers, with 3,627 to AP's 3,402. Worldwide, AP says it has more than 8,500 subscribers and UPI says it has 6,622. Well over a third of United States dailies take some of the services of both AP and UPI.

The two largest of the metropolitan newspaper wire services are the **Los Angeles Times-Washington Post** and the **New York Times** service. Each claims more than 200 subscribers in the United States and more than 350 including overseas customers. The **Chicago Daily News,** with more than 100 subscribers, offers the oldest of these services, begun in 1896. One of the newest was formed in 1973 to offer news by wire from the combined staffs and bureaus of the Knight newspapers, the **Chicago Tribune** and the **New York News,** as well as news features from the weekly **National Observer.** The news services that send news features by mail have many hundreds of subscribers.

How They Compete

Unlike the supplemental news services, AP and UPI operate with a deadline every minute. Reporters try to beat the rival service with the latest in breaking news. And since AP and UPI sell to newspapers with a variety of political and social editorial positions, they emphasize objectivity as well as speed.

If an editor takes both services, he or she will use the latest story available on an important event. If two stories are at hand, the editor will probably run the one that is more interesting or more nearly complete. Often the editor combines two or more accounts.

The need for speed combined with the policy of objectivity makes it more difficult to add the interpretation and background often necessary to give meaning to events. For this reason, the wire services also send out authoritative news analyses and background stories. Both wire services transmit thoughtful, well-researched stories on complex issues as well as breaking news. They recognize that newspapers cannot compete with the broadcast media in getting the news out fast, in covering a space flight as it occurs, or reporting the unfolding elements of a disaster. Newspapers, however, have the advantage of more time and space to explore the significance of news.

Regional News

Most papers in small cities and towns, however, make little space available for anything but local news. For them, the AP and UPI provide a state wire that carries state and regional news and a digest of a national and world news. On the state wire, a story of the war in the Middle East may be reduced to a few paragraphs of late developments, while heavy rains that damage crops in a farm state will get extensive coverage in that state. Even when they get the shortened news wire, most editors print only a small part of what is sent.

In a critique of the Dubuque (Iowa) Telegraph-Herald, as an example of a middle-sized daily newspaper (circulation 41,000), Ben H. Bagdikian called the paper's use of the regional abbreviated service "the most significant and obvious weakness in the paper." He argued that most newspaper readers want "more analytical and interpretive articles" on the main events they have already heard about on radio or television newscasts.

To meet the need for analysis, most editors believe it is their responsibility to print syndicated columns representing a range of political positions. They buy a "conservative" political column to balance a "liberal" column.

SYNDICATES

Editors choose columns from syndicates. The syndicates are businesses—many of them offshoots of large newspapers and newspaper groups—that package and sell newspaper features and supplemental material. In its "Feature News and Picture Syndicate Directory," **Editor and Publisher International Yearbook** for 1974 lists 358. They range in size from one-man offices offering single features to giants like the Hearst Corporation's King Features Syndicate, which sells 166 features in 38 languages to 3,330 newspapers in 109 countries. Among other large syndicates are United Features, owned by Scripps-Howard Newspapers, and Publishers Hall, with ties to the **Chicago Daily News** and **Sun-Times.**

Boyd Lewis, the retired former president of the Newspaper Enterprise Association, one of the largest syndicates, has described syndication as the golden idea of Samuel Sydney McClure in 1884. "Noting that the large newspapers were buying and serializing fiction from their writers for $100 to $150, McClure reasoned that if he could induce 100 editors to pay $5 for each story, he could earn more for the writer and pocket a neat profit." McClure's idea worked and later he added recipes, comics, humor, puzzles, columns, and other features.

By the turn of the century, because of the "economic magic" of syndication, newspapers could afford to print more than "the mere brute facts" from the press association wires. Competitors appeared and syndication grew, as did the range of offerings. Newspapers now buy the famous names and best talents for a fraction of the earnings of the writers and artists. They offer comic strips and cartoon panels and columns on just about everything—food, science, religion, antiques, bridge, golf, love, health, ecology, consumerism, foreign affairs, politics, and more. They buy photographs and illustrations and editorial cartoons. Large papers generally have their own editorial cartoonists, but smaller papers will choose syndicated editorial cartoonists whose views are similar to the papers' editors.

The best read syndicated features in most newspapers are the comic strips, and all the syndicates combined offer some 275 strips and another 200 or more cartoons and comic panels. Comic strips began as "funnies," but by the 1930s most strips were not humorous. Adventure and violence took over. After World War II, some strips began to burlesque or satirize politics and society. Al Capp's "Lil Abner" and the late Walt Kelly's "Pogo" were among these. More recently, humor and fun have returned to the strips, notably in Charles M. Schulz's "Peanuts," which some consider philosophical as well as funny.

WHERE TO SEND NEWS

The syndicate office is not the place for the publicist to deliver his news. Frank Clark, business manager of the Register and Tribune Syndicate, says, "Millions of dollars in public relations money is wasted by sending press releases to syndicates. We throw away bushel baskets of press releases every week." Clark advises publicists to send their material to the authors of the syndicated features—food news to the cooking columnist, garden news to the garden columnist, financial news to the money management writer. If an item is sent in care of the local newspaper that carries the author's material, the item will be forwarded to the author.

The local offices of the AP and UPI, however, are good places to send news releases and invitations to newsworthy events. The publicist may also want to send news to other local services, such as city news wire associations, minority press cooperative bureaus, or such state news cooperatives as the Iowa Daily Press Association.

SUMMARY

The wire services and syndicates are often not recognized as mass communications media. Because they are so pervasive and because they are used by so many mass media outlets, wires and syndicates provide much of the national and international information received by a significant portion of the American public. They provide many of the entertainment, self-improvement, and indepth features devoured by the public every day.

For many, the wire services and syndicates represent a mysterious aggregation of electronic gear and highrise offices. They are, however, essential elements in the flow of information; they are not impossible to penetrate or to understand; and their functions are important to the publicist and the information consumer.

SUGGESTED READING

Editor's Note: Surprisingly little has been written concerning the wire services or the syndicates and press associations in recent years. Lorraine Wechsler's chapter is the most up-to-date treatment available.

Bagdikian, Ben H. "The Little Old Lady of Dubuque." **New York Times Magazine,** February 3, 1974, p. 14.
Lewis, Boyd. "The Syndicates and How They Grew." **Saturday Review,** December 11, 1971, p. 67.
MacDougall, A. Kent. "Wire Services: AP and UPI." **The Press.** Princeton: Dow-Jones Books, 1972.

The consumer

3

and the press

A free society cannot endure without a free press, and the freedom of the press ultimately rests on public understanding of . . . its work.
—**A Free and Responsive Press: The Twentieth Century Fund Task Force Report for a National News Council,** 1972.

Congress shall make no law respecting an establishment of religion, or prohibiting the free exercise thereof; or abridging the freedom of speech, or of the press; or the right of the people peaceably to assemble, and to petition the Government for a redress of grievances.—**First Amendment to The Constitution of the United States, ratified December 15, 1791.**

Horace Greeley

...O Rare Don Marquis · Edward Anthony

The Muckrakers 1902-1912

McCORMICK OF CHICAGO

BENJAMIN FRANKLIN · CARL VAN DOREN

HORACE GREELEY
Nineteenth-Century Crusader by GLYNDON

CITIZEN HEARST

13

Journalism's revolutionary past, present, and future

RODNEY T. FOX

The press in the United States is a very human institution reflecting vividly the history, tradition, and culture of America. Consequently, it ranges in quality and performance from the superb to the—well, the entire press is not always at its best.

In its finest aspects, the press protects the nation from threats of dictatorship and tyranny, it supplies citizens with facts and opinions they must have if they are to govern themselves wisely, it fights for justice and for wise international policies, and it educates and enlightens.

How the press evolved into the vital institution it is in American life, and how it achieved its peculiar colors and flavors can be explained historically. And it is a vigorous, bumptious, sometimes shocking history out of which has emerged a vital

ROD FOX, Professor of Journalism and Mass Communication, has been a member of the Iowa State University faculty since 1936. A former community newspaper editor and daily newspaper reporter, he is the author of **Agricultural and Technical Journalism,** coauthor, with Hugh Sidey, of **1,000 Ideas for Better News Pictures,** and coauthor, with Robert Kerns, of **Creative News Photography.**

and central current in the mainstream of American life.

The American free press was born in the seething crucible of the revolutionary eighteenth century. That was a period in Europe and America during which men were setting their minds free from ideas that had held them in bondage for centuries. Great philosophers rebelled against the notions of absolutism in government and in the chruch. They argued that man is free and that although he had set up government to better his lot, he retained final authority. And they argued that to exercise wisely his sovereign authority man needed access to all facts and ideas in a great common marketplace of ideas. And the philosophers believed that man is rational and thus able to select the good and the true rather than the false and the bad in such a free marketplace.

The American Revolution was a great flowering fertilized by such philosophies. One of the products of the Revolution was a press free from government control and designed to serve as a common marketplace of facts and ideas. To make sure that the press was free to criticize government itself—to serve as a watchdog of government—the founders recognized that the press could not be a part of government or supported financially by it. Such ideas about freedom of the press eventually were embodied in the First Amemdment to the Constitution.

But we are getting ahead of our story. Long before the First Amendment was written, long before the Declaration of Independence, some Colonial journalists were struggling toward a free press in spite of rigid laws. For instance, in the first real attempt to publish a newspaper in what is now the United States, Benjamin Harris, in 1690, brought out an issue of **Publick Occurrences** without bothering to obtain a license as required by law. Four days after it appeared it was suppressed by the governor and his council because it contained "reflections of a very high nature." The authorities did not consider it proper for the people to know about public affairs. It was 14 years before another attempt was made to publish a newspaper.

By 1721 James Franklin, elder brother of Benjamin, dared publish the **New-England Courant**. Eventually James was thrown in jail, but his attempt marked new daring. It also gave young Benjamin his journalistic training. His later exploits as a journalist are well known.

By 1734 John Peter Zenger, publisher of the **New York Weekly Journal**, had the courage to criticize bitterly the tyrannical Governor William Cosby. Zenger spent nine months in jail awaiting trial on a charge of libel, which then meant any criticism of authority. Zenger's case before a jury was won when the renowned lawyer Andrew Hamilton argued for the admission of truth as a defense. That was a long step forward from the traditional British idea that "the greater the truth, the greater the libel."

As revolutionary fervor intensified in the colonies, a segment of the press stimulated the patriot cause, and the patriot press became of paramount importance to the movement. Samuel Adams and Thomas Paine used the press widely for their incendiary exhortations. The **Boston Gazette** did much to prepare the minds of the people for independence. Isaiah Thomas is supposed to have hung the lantern in the tower of the Old North Church and then returned to editing his flaming **Massachusetts Spy**. But the press of that period was not free. While public sentiment protected the patriot press from government action, that same public sentiment, coupled sometimes with mob action, silenced papers whose editors remained loyal to their king. Tory editors shut up or fled to Canada or England.

Without the press it is doubtful whether the Revolution would have occurred and been brought to a successful conclusion. At the end of the war, the press—free from government restriction—exploded with vitality. The number of papers increased rapidly and the press became an increasingly important factor. It played a leading part in determining the direction the infant republic took.

PARTY PAPERS

The first great task undertaken by the press concerned two rival philosophies struggling to determine national direction. The two factions quickly developed into political parties and each encouraged newspapers to promote its cause. Both parties subsidized their favorite publications, and sometimes the party in power found ways to provide government aid to some helpful paper.

The first spectacular journalistic clash was between John Fenno, favored editor of the conservative Federalist party, and Philip Freneau, spokesman for the liberal Anti-Federalist party. Fenno spoke for George Washington and Alexander Hamilton. Freneau, America's first lyric poet, was appointed by Thomas Jefferson. Other colorful editors of the period included such characters as

Benjamin Franklin Bache, called "Lightning Rod Junior" in honor of his famous grandfather; Peter Porcupine (his real name was William Cobbett), who later dug up and stole Thomas Paine's bones; and Noah Webster, of dictionary fame. The journalism of the period, led by these and other vigorous editors, was marked by violent partisanship, shameful name calling, unprincipled and often false charges, and frequent physical combat between rival editors.

Disturbed by the violence of the attack by the liberal newspapers against the Federalist administration and by a war scare, Congress passed the Alien and Sedition Acts during the John Adams administration. The acts, intended to silence criticism of the Federalist administration and its officials, was quite contrary to the notion that the press should serve as a watchdog of government. The acts constituted the first great testing of the free press idea. Fortunately, violent public reaction against the acts was a factor in electing liberal Thomas Jefferson. He did not enforce the acts and eventually they lapsed.

In spite of the reprehensible quality of much of the journalism of the period, newspapers succeeded in spreading before the people the basic ideas of both major factions and, in spite of the briefly enforced Alien and Sedition Acts, served well as watchdogs of government.

PENNY PAPERS

The birth of the modern American press in the early 1830s resulted from vital changes in the American nation. The kind of newspaper that emerged was popularly appealing in content, in contrast to the rather stuffy and politically obsessed papers preceding them. In the new kind of papers, crime and scandal stories, interestingly written, made people want to read (and Americans were rapidly becoming literate). The papers sold for one penny, much cheaper than traditional prices. As a result, the penny papers attracted big circulations, advertisers became aware of the value of buying space to reach the large audiences, and the press discovered it had a new financial resource in paid advertising. No longer did papers need to be subservient to political parties for financial support.

The first three great penny newspapers—Benjamin Day's Sun, James Gordon Bennett's Herald, and Horace Greeley's Tribune—were leaders in journalism for many years. They were in commanding positions as the events that led to the Civil War developed, and they along with the rest of the press were important during the war.

An interesting aspect of the pre-Civil War period was the emergence of a protest press favoring abolition of slavery. Elijah P. Lovejoy, an antislavery editor in Alton, Illinois, stubbornly insisted on his right to publish what he considered to be the truth. For his insistence on exercising freedom of the press, he saw four of his presses thrown into the Mississippi River and eventually he was murdered. William Lloyd Garrison, with his Liberator, was a powerful voice. He once was mobbed as were several other abolitionist editors.

In the North, some Copperhead newspapers, those with pro-Confederate or antiadministration views, suffered from official action, and many were closed by mobs. In the South, the press suffered much during the war and the years following Northern victory.

The years following the Civil War came to be known as the Golden Age of newspapers. It was a period in which railroad building was at the heart of explosive western expansion. It was a period marked by exploitation of natural and human resources, by the acquisition of vast fortunes, by financial booms and busts, and by much suffering. But it also was a time of great material achievement, and newspapers participated in the exciting action. Many of them became very rich and powerful. Perhaps more than typical was the paper of James Gordon Bennett, Jr. He spend much of his life on his palatial yacht from which he successfully directed the New York Herald he inherited from his father. Young Bennett is memorable because he indulged such personal pasttimes as stripping naked and driving powerful horses at breakneck speeds. But other highly successful editor-publishers of the period included such great and dignified figures as Charles A. Dana of the New York Sun and Whitelaw Reid of the New York Tribune.

YELLOW JOURNALISM

Perhaps the most flamboyant period of journalism history involved the brief but dramatic rivalry between Joseph Pulitzer and William Randolph Hearst. Because both publishers used yellow ink on a popular comic feature, their style of reportage became known as Yellow Journalism. With his New York World, Pulitzer developed what then was known as a "new journalism" marked by extra good news reporting, magnificent editorials, shrewd promotion, and shocking sensationalism. Hearst, supported by ample money derived from his father's vast fortune, and his New York Journal challenged Pulitzer's growing New York supremacy. The resulting contest flared in lurid coverage of Cuban affairs that eventually resulted in the Spanish-American War. Very probably that war never would have occurred had it not been for the extreme sensationalism of Hearst and Pulitzer and their imitators. Just as sensationalism had built success for the early penny papers, it built success for the giants of Yellow Journalism.

MUCKRAKING

The excesses of Yellow Journalism were among several factors that spurred a counterreaction in the press. Some magazines and newspapers turned to reform crusades in a movement that became known as muckraking. Such writers as Lincoln Steffens and Ida M. Tarbell attacked public corruption and the evils of monopoly. Upton Sinclair in his book, The Jungle, shocked the nation with his descriptions of filth in Chicago meat packing plants. That book, along with other exposés, helped initiate responsible controls over newspaper advertising which, for a century, had been characterized by appeals from quack doctors and patent medicine manufacturers. In 1912, a law was passed that required that paid items resembling editorial matter must be labeled "advertisement."

MAGAZINES

The fact that the great thrust of the muckrakers was carried in such magazines as McClure's, Cosmopolitan, and Colliers calls attention to the development of a powerful new factor in journalism. Although magazines had existed from Benjamin Franklin's time, they did not become large and powerful until about the 1890s. Then the great mass circulation magazines evolved in response to a demand for national, or at least regional, advertising media in contrast to the merely local coverage provided by newspapers. That surging new trend arose because mass production had developed a demand for widespread dissemination of advertising to sell products nationally; and it came at a time when railroads made rapid distribution of goods possible. Favorable postal rates had also been established and new printing techniques had made production of vast circulation magazines feasible.

After more than a half century marked by the success of huge circulation magazines, the scene has changed. Several of the big circulation magazines, such as Life, Look, and the old Saturday Evening Post, have ceased publication, victims of higher postal rates, the desires of advertisers for more specialized publications, and for other causes. Several huge circulation magazines with special appeal continue to be successful, but the magazine field seems dominated by increasing numbers of specialized publications.

Wars and other periods of great national tension especially threaten the unbridled exercise of freedom of the press. So it was that World War I saw passage of laws resembling the Alien and Sedition Acts. At the close of the war the most repressive features of those laws were repealed, but a "red scare" and superpatriotism engendered by the war remained to hamper full expression of freedom of the press.

JAZZ JOURNALISM

Somewhat in reaction to the excitement of World War I and the sense of frustration and boredom that followed it, a supersensational period of journalism developed. This new "jazz journalism" was introduced to the United States by Joseph Medill Patterson and his New York Daily News. The News' tabloid format was copied by many other papers whose products were devoted largely to sex, sin, and sensation expressed in lurid headlines and photographs which were occasionally fakes. The coming of the Great Depression, followed by World War II, called for calmer and more sedate newspapers, and the character of the American press again changed in response to the times.

During the 1920s, radio broadcasting got under way and developed into a powerful medium for dissemination of news. By the time the nation established something resembling equilibrium after World War II, television had arrived. Today television and radio bear a large portion of the responsibility for news dissemination. The "electronic press" also competes for a substantial share of the advertising dollars the free press in America must obtain in order to function, or even to exist.

Because the number of channels on which the electronic media can operate are limited, it has been necessary for government to establish a system of licensing stations to provide for orderly use of the airwaves. (See Chapter 11 for a more detailed treatment of station licensing.) While this system is based on the physical aspects of broadcasting, and any control of program content by means of license restrictions is prohibited, some uneasiness has been felt at times because the licensing system constitutes a potential vehicle for government influence over radio and television programming.

FREEDOM AND TENSIONS

Freedom of the press survived the high tensions, the largely military censorship, and general difficulties of World War II only to emerge into a long and confused Cold War period. Threats to freedom arose because the nation was almost continually at war and because of recurring periods of hysteria such as that memorialized by the antics of Senator Joseph McCarthy. The end of the American involvement in the war in Viet Nam was followed by increased tension resulting from the Watergate upheaval.

In general, the press seems to have developed a deep sense of responsibility, although there is considerable disagreement about the nature of newspaper responsibility. Great publications like the **New York Times**, the **Washington Post**, and other newspapers; magazines; and electronic media have shown initiative, intellect, and courage in digging out and reporting government scandals and malfeasance.

When the history of the American press for the remainder of the twentieth century is written, what will it say? Already the idea of a free press has been rejected in most of the world: in Russia, China, much of Latin America and Africa, in Spain, in Greece, and in other places. Will it survive in the United States?

Knowing something about the problems, criticisms, and dilemmas of today's press should help to understand its behavior as well as to predict its future. Such problems are far too many to list here, and they are too complex to discuss in depth in this chapter, but mentioning some of the more provocative ones may be valuable.

TODAY'S PROBLEMS

Monopoly is a problem with the press because it is financially not feasible for more than one newspaper to be published in most cities, just as it is not economically desirable to have more than one telephone company or more than one waterworks in a city. In almost all cities and towns there is one newspaper; sometimes it owns the leading television station. The number of major cooperative news-gathering agencies in the United States has been reduced to two (see Chapter 12). Many chains own large strings of newspapers and/or stations. With the limited number of sources from which to readily obtain news, does the average citizen obtain as wide a range of information and opinion as when news gathering was as competitive as in the days of Fenno and Freneau, of Greeley and Bennett, of Pulitzer and Hearst? Is it now easier for an individual or a group or a government to control such a limited number of information channels? Or do news gatherers, unharried by intense competition, have a better chance of doing a complete and fair job?

With the number of easily available news sources reduced until, in effect, most persons use only one major source of news, a strong case has been made that the news content of a paper or station should be as objectively presented as is humanly possible and that comment and opinion should be plainly labeled as such. "Give the citizens the raw materials and let them make up their minds without influence from those who control the press," it is argued.

Critics point out that it is impossible to be "absolutely" objective. And some, like the "new journalists" of the 1960s, argue that the presentation of the reaction of the reporter is an essential ingredient of a news story. The new journalists attempted to demonstrate that the devices of fiction writing as applied to news enhances its readability. While the new journalism of such writers as Tom Wolfe and Norman Mailer may have been a phenomenon of the 1960s, its impact still seems to have some influence on some news presentations.

A person who owns a printing press or broadcasting station has vast power advantages over those who do not. Are those powers being fairly and justly used? Should individuals and groups with something to say be able to force owners to provide access to the press? How can the press be free of government control if officials have the power to force control of access and to supervise their versions of fairness?

If the press is to be free to serve as a watchdog of government, it must not be a part of that government or financed by that government. So the founding fathers left the press to be operated by private enterprise motivated by a desire for profit. But sometimes there is conflict between the role of the press as a profit-seeking business and its role as an institution of the democratic process. Does that conflict sometimes result in biased news in favor of advertisers and business versus the general welfare and interest of the public?

The right of the press to fully cover crimes so that the people may be informed of how their police and courts are functioning has been confronted by the rights of the accused to a fair trial with jury members unprejudiced by extensive pretrial publicity. That question is very complex.

The credibility of the press often is questioned. In the scurry to cover vast quantities of news rapidly, some factual errors are inevitable. Critics charge that the press slants the news deliberately and the press denies such charges; but not everyone accepts the denials.

Because of its role as the bearer of bad tidings, the press is constantly criticized. When the press publishes reports about American massacres of civilians in an already unpopular war, or about extreme malfeasance in the White House, or about unpleasant racial situations, there is a tendency for some readers to blame the press rather than those reported about. Yet if the press is to do its total job of informing citizens it must report bad news as well as good. Can the press, if it is to tell the whole truth, permit itself to be too much swayed by public opinion? To what extent can the press run counter to widespread public opinion and stay alive and well?

SUMMARY

To question the validity of the eighteenth-century philosophies from which American ideas of a free press and other institutions were forged would be to question the very foundations of the Amercian government, society, and way of life. It is not within the scope of this chapter to do that.

But profound questions may be asked about the press today as to whether it is fulfilling the functions assigned to it by the founding fathers. Through two centuries the American press, in spite of its faults, has done its job well enough that the American system of government has somehow survived. Is the press functioning well enough today so that the political, social, and economic systems of the United States will continue to survive and to seek justice and fairness and decency for all Americans and for a better world order? Does the press fully furnish the common marketplace of ideas with all significant facts and opinions? Does it adequately watch government? These questions demand thoughtful and continuing appraisals by professional and lay persons alike.

SUGGESTED READING

Emery, Edwin. **The Press and America**. Englewood Cliffs, N.J.: Prentice-Hall, 1962.
Hohenberg, John. **Free Press, Free People: The Best Cause**. New York: Free Press, 1973.
Mott, Frank Luther. **American Journalism: A History, 1690-1960**, 3rd ed. New York: Macmillan, 1962.
Rutland, Robert A. **The Newsmongers: Journalism in the Life of the Nation, 1690-1972**. New York: Dial Press, 1973.

The Newspaper Iowa Depends Upon

Des Moines, Iowa, Friday Morning, August 9, 1974—Two Sections   Price 15 Cents

NIXON RESIGNS

'Bitterness'

Gerald Ford Taking Oath At 11 Today

By James Risser and George Anthan
Of The Register's Washington Bureau

WASHINGTON, D.C. — Richard ...ous Nixon, thirty-seventh President ...he United States, resigned from office ...ursday night.

Vice-President Gerald R. Ford, 61-...ar-old former Michigan congressman, ...ll be sworn in as President at 11 a.m. ...time) today in the Oval Office of ...ite House.

...ixon, his presidency irretrievably scarred ...and with impeachment and conviction in ...ss all but certain, thus became the first ...tive to resign in the republic's 198-year...

...15-minute television speech to the nation, ...his face drawn and expression sombre, ...longer had "a strong enough political base ...gress" to warrant continuing his fight ...peachment.

'No Bitterness'

...essed gratitude to those who had stood ...ring his long ordeal and added, "I leave ...terness toward those who have opposed

...xon said he was leaving the presidency ...dness" but with satisfaction that with ...the new president "leadership in Amer-...good hands."

...ident said he had "never been a quitter" ...igning was "abhorrent to every instinct of ...

...have continued the fight, he said, would ...y absorbed" his time during the months ...the nation would need "a full-time presi-...

...did not acknowledge any guilt in the ...-over-up, a principal charge against him in ...ent proceedings, but admitted he had ...stakes in the handling of the Watergate ...

Faint Smile

...an American flag pin in his lapel as he ...the 61-year-old President read slowly and ...rom his prepared speech, occasionally ...th a faint smile as he spoke of his hopes ...n would unite behind Mr. Ford and con-...for the goals of peace and international ...fostered by the Nixon administration.

...that his family — a dejected group ...decision hard and remained secluded — ...ly opposed his resignation. But he said ...best interests of the nation demanded ...

...of his accomplishments in ending Amer-...nt in the Vietnam war and in helping ...ast War, he said he was confident that ...make the world a safer place to live, ...that he would continue working for ...of his life.

"God's Grace"

...ed his last message as President to ...ople with a prayer:

..."s grace be with you in all the days...

...who had repeatedly vowed not to ...proliferating scandals that engulfed ...dministration, plans to fly to San ...today after he formally submits his ...Secretary of State Henry Kissinger ...rd takes the oath of office.

...elected by Mr. Nixon to be the new ...President after Spiro T. Ag-...contest to an income tax evas-...d on Oct. 10, 1973.

...becomes the first person ever ...sident without having been elect-...either the presidency or vice-pre-...

...d's choice for vice-president is ex-...top officials for the first time...

Please turn to Page Ele...

14

The press and society

EDMUND G. BLINN

Spiro T. Agnew's most often quoted speech was his Des Moines attack on the television networks, a speech followed a week later by another attacking liberal newspapers.

The gist of Mr. Agnew's comments was that the networks and the liberal newspapers were biased against the Nixon administration and that their handling of the news was solid evidence of that prejudice. He called for the American people to "let the networks know that they want their news straight and objective." Citizens, he said, would never trust government to have the same power over public opinion as did a handful of television news producers and commentators whom he described as "a tiny, enclosed fraternity of priviledged men elected by no one.... It's time," said Agnew, "we questioned [such power] in the hands of a small and unelected elite."

In Montgomery, the then Vice-President attacked the New York Times and the Washington Post as newspapers enjoying virtual monopolies as opinion disseminators in their respective cities.

EDMUND BLINN is Professor of Journalism and Mass Communication, Iowa State University, a former reporter and editor for newspapers in Massachusetts, Connecticut, South Dakota, and Iowa, and former production editor for the Iowa State University Press.

The result of media monopoly, said Agnew, was that some of those who enjoyed it "have—let's face it—grown fat and irresponsible."

The Vice-President was not alone in his anger nor in his charges. Every day some persons are wounded directly or indirectly as a consequence of stories in newspapers and magazines or on radio and television, and every day wounded persons react in anger to such stories.

It is easy to sympathize with many of them and to understand why they respond as they do. But to accept such charges as valid without examination is to seriously undermine the public information role performed by the nation's press. Critics, and especially wounded critics, need a clear understanding of the press and its interrelationship with society—with us.

As the late U.S. Supreme Court Justice Felix Frankfurter wrote:

A free press is indispensable to the workings of our democratic society. The business of the press ... is the promotion of truth regarding public matters by furnishing the basis for an understanding of them. Truth and understanding are not wares like peanuts or potatoes.... I find myself entirely in agreement with Judge Learned Hand that neither exclusively, nor even primarily, are the interests of the newspaper industry conclusive; for the industry serves one of the most vital of all general interests: The dissemination of news from as many different sources, and with as many different facets and colors as possible. That interest is closely akin to, if indeed not the same as, the interest protected by the First Amendment; it presupposes that right conclusions are more likely to be gathered, out of a multitude of tongues, than through any kind of authoritative selection. To many this is, and always will be, folly; but we have staked upon it our all.

We tend to regard the press as we might a parent; as merely being present. Yet both are indispensable. Like our parents, the press is part of each of us. We turn to it for the information we need in order to perform the tasks of our lives and of the society in which we exist. And those persons who operate the press try to give us what we must have and what we desire in the way of information.

In this vital relationship, the consumer's role as reader, listener, or viewer is as important as the part played by the journalist. If the consumer demands only entertainment, the press, in the long run, may offer less enlightenment. Only a demanding, aggressive, interested society can create and sustain an intelligent, responsible, and worthwhile press.

The building of a constantly improving mass society and its press requires that press and society criticize each other. The press carries out its duties daily in this regard through editorial pages, critical columns, interpretive articles, and special radio and television programs. The public performs its critical function through individual howls of rage, complaining letters to editors, cancelled subscriptions, threatening telephone calls, and through the words of self-appointed critics of the press in the government, institutions of higher education, politics, and neighborhood pubs. Such criticism may be formal or informal but, so long as it is knowledgeable and constructive, it is important and necessary.[1]

In August, 1973, another response to mounting criticism of and frustration concerning press performance began operations as the National Press Council. The council is a private and independent institution financed by the Twentieth Century Fund and designed to hear and investigate complaints concerning news reporting in the press and to report its findings. It is the first national press council in the United States; Minnesota has a state council and a handful of communities have local councils. The 15 national council members are laypersons and professional journalists, although the chairperson must always be a lay member.[2]

The press is a reflection of society. It is efficient or inefficient, venal or honorable, stagnant or growing, sensitive or indifferent, liberal or conservative, contemptible or praiseworthy, depending upon the person sitting in judgment and the portion of the press being examined. Yet, it is possible to formulate a list of its presumed responsibilities as well as a list of the major criticisms commonly hurled at it.

As is true of most persons and institutions, the press accepts criticism reluctantly. In 1946, the Commission on Freedom of the Press, funded by

---

1. In response to an increased swell of criticism in the late 1960s and early 1970s, many newspapers established an office of ombudsman. Newspaper ombudsmen investigate and make judgments on complaints against the represented publication by members of the public. Generally, the ombudsman reports his or her findings in a signed column.

2. See **A Free and Responsive Press: The Twentieth Century Fund Task Force Report for a National News Council** (New York: Twentieth Century Fund, 1972).

publisher Henry R. Luce and Encyclopaedia Britannica to inquire into and report on the "present state and future prospects of the press," issued its largely critical findings. The report became the subject of immediate debate, with much of the press opposing its conclusions. Over the years, however, there has been little disagreement with the commission's listing of what it regarded as the responsibilities of the press (the commission used the term "requirements"). The commission said society required of the mass media:

1. A truthful, comprehensive, and intelligent account of the day's events in a context which gives them meaning.
2. A forum for the exchange of comment and criticism.
3. The projection of a representative picture of the constituent groups in the society.
4. The presentation and clarification of the goals and values of the society.
5. Full access to the day's intelligence.

Innumerable formal discussions of press responsibility have been held in the interim, but most have turned upon the principles listed in the commission report. Society must have a press that will supply facts (information) as the basis for rational discussion and debate so that society can make intelligent decisions on issues that affect its well-being.

ADVERTISER PRESSURE

Within this context, then, let us identify and evaluate the criticisms most commonly directed at the press. Foremost among them is the charge that, where content is concerned, the press is overly susceptible to audience and advertiser pressure. Critics say this causes the sensationalism of news to attract larger audiences, and hesitation to discuss issues or report information that advertisers want suppressed or ignored.

These criticisms are not new. When it became apparent that men could become wealthy as mass communications entrepreneurs and that advertising was big business, the raw material was there for the critics to examine and denounce.

The rapid changes taking place in twentieth-century society are bringing with them corresponding changes in our press system—changes that make the criticisms less pertinent now than they once were. Two of the most noticeable changes in media operations are the rise of monopoly ownership and revised methods of distribution. These new conditions have substantially reduced (but not altogether eliminated) the practical necessity for sensational treatment of the news by alleviating much of the pressure from audiences and advertisers.

Although there exist some not altogether effective economic and governmental obstacles to monopoly ownership of magazine, radio-television, and book publishing enterprises, monopoly ownership of the newspaper press throughout the nation has become a fact of life. Competing newspapers are to be found in only a few major cities and in even fewer small towns.

Nearly every American reads a newspaper each day. Most Americans read their hometown newspapers, almost all of which operate without direct newspaper competition. A certain amount of rivalry obviously exists among the various media for audience attention and for the advertiser's dollar. It is not necessary, however, for the monopoly publication to bow to pressures on the part of anyone, even the largest of advertising buyers. If newspaper space is important to the seller of goods (and there is abundant evidence that it is), it is sufficiently valuable in the competitive business world to make the seller unwilling to withdraw advertising for nearly any reason.

As our systems of transportation proliferated and our urban society became more concentrated and affluent, newspapers developed home delivery systems for most of their sales. The great majority of readers today purchase newspapers on a weekly, monthly, or even annual basis. The foundation for most newspapers' circulation claims is this virtually guranteed list of subscribers that fluctuates little in response to exclusive or sensationalized stories. Only in the largest of our cities, where competitive situations still exist, do newsstand sales depend, in any substantial way, on exciting front pages.

MONOPOLY OWNERSHIP

Even as improved transportation and increased monopolization were making the press less vulnerable to some criticisms, they were creating situations which many responsible observers now view with growing concern. These critics see the increase in monopoly ownership of the communication media as a threat to what Judge Learned Hand called "right conclusions" which, he said, are "more likely to be gathered from out of a multitude of tongues." This necessary diversity of voices is not encouraged by monopoly, the critics point out. Intensifying the problem, they claim, is the fact that newspaper publishers and the proprietors of radio and television stations, as well as the owners of book and magazine publishing concerns, are largely alike in their social, educational, and economic backgrounds and thus in their interests, values, and beliefs.

The Commission on Freedom of the Press said in its report that "the agencies of mass communication are big business, and their owners are big businessmen." Robert Lasch, a journalist, is more specific:

In real life industrialists and department store managers do not pound on the publisher's desk and demand favorable treatment. They do not have to. An owner who lunches weekly with the president of the local power company will always grasp the sanctity of private ownership in this field more readily than the public-ownership ideas of a few crackpots. With the best of will, he may tell himself that his mind is open. Yet, as a businessman whose concerns are intimately bound up with those of other businessmen, he has a vested interest in maintaining the status quo.

More recently, Dan Lacy of the American Book Publishers Council pointed to what he felt was the same narrowing effect in another area of mass communication, that of the news magazines:

The difficulties of starting and sustaining a magazine in this field have brought it about that there are only three news magazines of large national circulation—**Time, Newsweek,** and **U.S. News and World Report** . . . —that editorialize a great deal. All of these, despite some minor differences among them, reflect substantially a uniform point of view, that of the dominant business community to which their owners and advertisers and no doubt the majority of their subscribers belong.

Nor is the problem limited to the print media. William Rivers and Wilbur Schramm note:

Most radio and television operations are large business units, and their executives are nearly always among the business leaders of their communities. Motion pictures have long been characterized by extraordinarily large incomes for top executives and performers. Thus the possibility of class bias permeates the media, through entertainment as well as information.

The view that limiting the number of voices in communication necessarily narrows one's range of information has not gone unchallenged. It has been argued, for example, that the competing publication is not necessarily the better publication. Carl E. Lindstrom, at one time a managing editor in a competitive newspaper situation, cites two publishing firms operating four newspapers—the **Des Moines Register** and **Tribune** and the **Minneapolis Star** and **Tribune**—in monopoly situations as serving their areas in "distinguished" fashion. He adds: "It is worth noting that where monopoly is associated with enterprise and imagination, as in Des Moines and Minneapolis, there exists also the will and incentive for research and experimentation, both of which are usually the liveliest where there is vigorous competition."

As critics have observed, the problem of monopoly is intensified by the decline in the number of domestic news services and by the growth of newspaper chains. (See Chapter 13.)

MECHANICAL UNIFORMITY

One additional influence that tends to rob the news of individuality is widespread newspaper adoption of the mechanical device known as the Teletypesetter. By automating type composing machines, the Teletypesetter has converted copy editing from an important task to an annoying expense. Wire service copy (from AP and UPI) comes to the automated newspapers on punched tape, ready to be run through the typesetting machines. Any copy changes that would add missing facts, localize the story, or broaden perspective would slow production and add to costs. As a consequence, many publishers of automated newspapers frown on any additional steps other than proofreading for typographical errors. Although the development of computer technology for newsroom use promises to replace the Teletypesetter and restore the editing function to its former high priority, the new hardware is expensive and thus impractical for many smaller newspapers. On many an American newspaper today the copy desk does little but produce headlines, and some newspapers require their reporters to write local stories on typewriters that punch tape for the automated typesetting machine as the story is being written. So, whether you live in Caribou, Maine, or Carlsbad, New Mexico, your national and international news diet is likely to be about the same.

MASS MEDIOCRITY

Still another severe criticism is that mass media are guilty of purveying a calculated and consistent mediocrity that degrades rather than uplifts mass tastes. One of the major premises of the student revolt of the 1960s was that a materialistic society produces cultural blandness, at best, and an ignoble populace, at worst. Student critics tended to blame what they referred to as "the establishment press" for that blandness and that ignobility. At issue is what the social critic of any generation refers to as the tastelessness of what he or she reads in magazines and newspapers and sees and hears on radio and television.

Newton Minow, a former chairman of the Federal Communications Commission, shocked the broadcasting industry by charging that television programming was a "vast wateland." Although Minow's voice was but one of many raised in criticism of mass media performance, such complaints tend to ignore the fact that the question is not one-sided. Two powerful forces are involved:

The social critic's laudable desire for a constantly more enlightened and edified populace; and the economic necessities of the business of mass communication. The quandary is this: Is it possible to raise the level of popular taste without risking economic ruin through loss of the mass audience?

David Manning White, a professor of journalism and expert observer of popular culture, has written:

> As the college enrollments have continued to increase enormously in the past ... we see ... indicators of their impact on the mass media. For example, in 1960, the number of paperback books in print was 6,800, and in 1970 the number had increased **twelve times** to 81,000. Granted that several thousand were kitsch of no conceivable value, still one is skeptical about the old saw that bad art drives out good when we note seventeen different paperback editions of Jane Austen's **Pride and Prejudice**.

In at least one other instance, White saw signs of a higher level of mass culture developing with the assistance of the mass media. In February, 1969, he reported, CBS telecast Shakespeare's **A Midsummer Night's Dream** in competition with ABC's movie of the week (**Spartacus**) and NBC's "Bonanza." Shakespeare reportedly attracted 13.7 percent of the audience, ABC 37 percent, and NBC 40 percent. White noted that the CBS production "was delightfully performed for an audience of 20 million men, women, and children." He added:

> This figure can be interpreted two ways, depending on one's expectations. It can be compared invidiously with the thirty-five million who elected to watch the simplistic homilies of **Bonanza**; but I prefer the observation that more individuals saw this particular Shakespearean comedy than the Globe Theater could seat in 10,000 performances.

ROLE OF CRITICISM

Criticisms of any public or semi-public institution tend to bring about desirable change. Mass media are not unaware of the criticisms leveled at the press, since they are called upon to report those criticisms. And it can be assumed that the media are at least as responsive to criticism as other institutions with public responsibilities and private economic concerns. At this time, however, the press has a long way to go to wipe out its inadequacies. Monopoly remains, as do vestiges of subservience to economic pressures. Certainly, the survival of much that is printed, broadcast, and filmed will not be a credit to our civilization.

By its nature, the press is particularly vulnerable to criticism. It offers itself regularly to intense public scrutiny in a manner unique among the many and diverse units of an industrialized society. The aeronautical engineer, for example, operates in comparative privacy; even some legislators are practically anonymous. By way of contrast, the newspaper reporter, the magazine writer, and the radio and television broadcaster offer their work for daily examination and evaluation by the consuming public. The journalist's work, moreover, must be performed under the pressure of relentless deadlines.

As you are exposed to the output of the mass media, you may find grounds for disagreement—stories that are disturbing, or factually inaccuarate, or obviously prejudicial. The Commission on Freedom of the Press found many such disorders during its inquiry. In finding faults, however, the commission also discovered strengths that are still discernible. Said the commission:

> Private enterprise in the field of communications has achievements to its credit. The American press probably reaches as high a percentage of the population as that of any other country. Its technical equipment is certainly the best in the world. It has taken the lead in the introduction of many new techniques which have enormously increased the speed and variety of communications. Whatever its shortcomings, the American press is less venal and less subservient to political and economic pressure than that of many other countries. The leading organs of the American press have achieved a standard of excellence unsurpassed anywhere in the world. It is necessary to keep these general comments in mind in order to see the criticisms in proper prespective.

It is noteworthy that few, if any, serious critics have suggested, even in their more agonizing moments, that the basic structure of the American press system should be altered. A free press is so much the foundation of our political orientation that, even as critics object to media inadequacies, they cannot bring themselves to suggest the most apparent alternative—government-enforced standards.

PUBLIC MISUNDERSTANDING

Freedom of the press, an almost sacred American principle, receives public support insofar as the public understands its meaning. It is an unfortunate fact—and a cause of constant social tension—that many fail to grasp the concept in its breadth and depth. A CBS poll reported in 1970 showed that 55 percent of a nationwide random sample of adults would deny to mass media the right to report stories "the government feels... harmful to our national interest." And a survey by Newsweek revealed that 47 percent of the Americans queried believed that national security was more important than press freedom.

The results of these studies have been a source of anxiety to those concerned with maintaining basic American freedoms. They claim that democracy has no meaning without freedoms of speech and of the press. The Supreme Court has validated this standard by extending a "preferred position" to First Amendment freedoms when they are competitive with other rights. The late U.S. Supreme Court Justice Benjamin Cardozo wrote of freedom to think and communicate that "it is the matrix, the indispensable condition, of nearly every other form of freedom."

The men who wrote the Constitution and its Bill of Rights believed in the "self-righting" theory of political organization. That is, they believed that if the people are given access to all shadings of opinion they will eventually ascertain truth. The press was conceived to be a "partner in the search for truth."

NEWER PRESS THEORIES

In recent decades, however, a somewhat different theory of the press's role in society has begun to emerge in answer to the problems posed by modern conditions.

Terming this new concept the Social Responsibility Theory, Fred Siebert, Theodore Peterson, and Wilbur Schramm, authors of Four Theories of the Press, say that as a result of monopoly conditions:

> No longer is it easy for the press to be a free marketplace of ideas.... As the Commission on Freedom of the Press said, "protection against

government is not now enough to guarantee that a man who has something to say shall have a chance to say it. The owners and managers of the press determine which persons, which facts, which versions of these facts, shall reach the public." This uneasiness is the basis of the developing Social Responsibility Theory: That the power and near monopoly position of the media impose on them an obligation to be socially responsible to see that all sides are fairly presented and that the public has enough information to decide; and that if the media do not take on themselves such responsibility it may be necessary for some other agency of the public to enforce it.

The question, of course, remains as to how irresponsible mass communicators may be persuaded to accept their responsibilities to the community. The professors who wrote **Four Theories** are not specific on this matter, nor was the Commission on Freedom of the Press. At least two other theorists, however, advance ideas that may be fruitful.

One theorist, Dan Lacy, rejects the notion of direct government control, but advocates expanded federal or foundation support for television, radio, and books, and to a lesser extent for movies and magazines. Of newspapers, however, he says:

> I believe it is the part of wisdom to accept as inevitable the trend toward monopoly of newspaper ownership in all but the largest cities, and to attempt to offset its disadvantages in part by enlarging the distribution of information and views through other media and in part by encouraging in the press a professional sense of serving as a common carrier of news and opinion.

The other theorist, Professor J. Edward Gerald, discusses professionalism in journalism at length. He observes that the practice of journalism is not regarded as a profession. He points out, however, that First Amendment guarantees probably forbid formal professional status for journalists by prohibiting any attempt to restrict entrance to the field. He contends that professional standards could nonetheless be enforced through industry agreement on those standards and through education for the field. It is obvious that, although we insist that freedom of the press continue, we are seriously concerned that press performance improve to meet our growing needs for responsible reportage.

PRESS PROFESSIONALISM

The schools of journalism are important to the continued development of a sense of professionalism, of social responsibility, in our press system. In their more than half a century, the schools have moved from a primary concern for journalistic techniques to a more sophisticated appreciation of communication and governance processes and their relationships. Contemporary graduates are likely to have a firm sense of profession.

The core of the professional sense in the newsperson is his or her news judgment, which is akin to the physician's diagnostic function. In both are centered the true professional's use of knowledge, experience, and moral and ethical standards. While their diagnoses may be, and frequently are, questioned, the odds favor the accuracy of the judgments of the physician and the newsperson in their own fields. As the medical school attempts, in essence, to produce a better medical diagnostician, so the journalism school strives to graduate a better news analyst.

SUMMARY

It could be argued that, although former Vice-President Agnew may have been correct concerning national network and newspaper bias, he was guilty of attempting to subvert the delicate relationship between the communications media and American society. Many journalists believe that Agnew was trying to discredit not only news personnel, but the press system which, despite short-term inadequacies, has in the long haul of 200 years served as the major barrier to governmental tampering with the rights of the citizenry.

Throughout the early 1970s, the press provided testimony to the wisdom of Thomas Jefferson's statement that, should he be forced to the choice, he would prefer a free press without government to government without a free press.

The decisions to be made about the press in a free enterprise system are in the hands of the consumer, whose responsibility is clear. Since an adequate system of mass communication is vital to the welfare of democratic society, public understanding of that system and public judgments concerning its performance are crucial.

SUGGESTED READING

Barron, Jerome A. **Freedom of the Press for Whom?** Bloomington: Indiana Univ. Press, 1973.

Commission on Freedom of the Press. **A Free and Responsible Press: A General Report on Mass Communication: Newspapers, Radio, Motion Pictures, Magazines, and Books.** Chicago: Univ. of Chicago Press, 1947.

Emerson, Thomas I. **The System of Freedom of Expression.** New York: Random House, 1970.

Emery, Michael C., and Smythe, Ted Curtis. **Readings in Mass Communications: Concepts and Issues in the Mass Media,** 2nd ed. Dubuque: Wm. C. Brown Co., 1974.

Gerald, J. Edward. **The Press and the Constitution, 1931-1947.** Minneapolis: Univ. of Minnesota Press, 1948.

———. **The Social Responsibility of the Press.** Minneapolis: Univ. of Minnesota Press, 1963.

Gross, Gerald, ed. **The Responsibility of the Press.** New York: Fleet Publishing Corp., 1966.

Hachten, William A. **The Supreme Court on Freedom of the Press: Decisions and Dissents.** Ames: Iowa State Univ. Press, 1968.

Hohenberg, John. **Free Press, Free People: The Best Cause.** New York: The Free Press, 1973.

Krieghbaum, Hillier. **Pressures on the Press.** New York: Thomas Y. Crowell Co., 1972.

Lacy, Dan. **Freedom and Communication.** Univ. of Illinois Press, 1961.

Lasch, Robert. "For a Free Press." **Atlantic Monthly,** 173 (June, 1944) 6.

Levy, Leonard W. **Legacy of Supression.** Cambridge: Harvard Univ. Press, 1960.

———, ed. **Freedom of the Press from Zenger to Jefferson.** Indianapolis: Bobbs-Merrill Co., 1966.

Lindstrom, Carl E. **The Fading American Newspaper.** Garden City, N.Y.: Doubleday & Co., 1960.

Nelson, Harold L., ed. **Freedom of the Press from Hamilton to the Warren Court.** Indianapolis: Bobbs-Merrill Co., 1967.

Peterson, Theodore; Schramm, Wilbur; and Siebert, Fred S. **Four Theories of the Press.** Urbana: Univ. of Illinois Press, 1956.

Phelan, John, ed. **Communications Control: Readings in the Motives and Structures of Censorship.** New York: Sheed and Ward, 1969.

Rivers, William L., and Schramm, Wilbur. **Responsibility in Mass Communication,** rev. ed. New York: Harper & Row, 1969.

Rosenberg, Bernard, and White, David Manning, eds. **Mass Culture Revisited.** New York: Van Nostrand Reinhold Co., 1971.

Rucker, Bryce W. **The First Freedom.** Carbondale: Southern Illinois Univ. Press, 1968.

Twentieth Century Fund Task Force. **A Free and Responsive Press.** New York: Twentieth Century Fund, 1973.

15
Press responsibilities: accuracy and fairness

JAMES W. SCHWARTZ

When the news announcer reports the YMCA backpackers will leave on their four-year camporee next week, or the local newspaper quotes the mayor as telling his constituents they "need a fiend in city hall," nearly everyone dismisses the inaccuracies as unintentional. Obviously the announcer meant to say four-day, not four-year. And the newspaper, through a typesetting error that somehow escaped everyone's eye, dropped the "r" from the word friend.

Some members of the media audience, however, may not see things that way. They'll probably scoff at the announcer for his momentary mental lapse, counting it as just another example of reportorial ineptitude. And where the newspaper is concerned, they might even insist the word "fiend" was used deliberately as part of a campaign to discredit the mayor.

The foregoing examples may be unique and of little long-term consequence, but the situations they represent are familiar ones. No doubt you have detected errors of a like nature in newspapers or in other news media. Probably at times you have thought a particular account was biased in one direction or another. As a matter of fact, you've heard and read repeatedly over the past few years that the media are irresponsible, that they deliberately distort the news for purposes that range all the way from dark and treasonous conspiracy to the more mundane one of making the cash register ring.

What you may not have realized, though, is that those responsible for the tone and content of mass media are at least as deeply concerned over these questions as the public often claims to be. Professional journalists regard the twin problems of achieving **accuracy** and **fairness** as among the most important ones they face. They know the public will not accept without some form of protest an endless string of errors. And they are

JAMES SCHWARTZ is Professor and Head of the Department of Journalism and Mass Communication, Iowa State University. A former community newspaper editor and publisher and a former radio and television news editor and news director, he has been an Iowa State faculty member since 1945. He is a past president of the Association for Education in Journalism and has served on several AEJ committees. He has contributed chapters to several textbooks and was editor of **The Publicity Process**, first edition, as well as author of three of the book's chapters. In 1974, he was named a Master Editor-Publisher by the Iowa Press Association and is the first academician to be so honored.

mindful, too, of the many accusations of slanted reporting, justified or not, that are leveled at the press.

Conscientious journalists make sincere attempts to reflect accurately whatever circumstance or event they are called upon to report. In other words, they try to be objective. But errors, sometimes major ones capable of doing a great deal of harm, are bound to occur, and there is no such thing as an entirely objective report. This does not mean that inaccuracies are excusable. Far from it. The very nature of the profession makes journalists acutely aware that the mass communication system requires persons to work under heavy pressure to meet deadlines—to collect, verify, and process huge quantities of facts at great speed and to compress this information into less space or time than they would like. Under such drastic circumstances journalists know that on the smallest newspaper, the shortest news broadcast, or the most modest of magazines the opportunities for error can multiply enormously.

YOUR ROLE IN QUEST FOR ACCURACY

Journalists may be dismayed by error but they are not surprised by it. Certainly they are not complacent about it. They believe everyone connected with collecting and reporting information has an obligation to take all possible precautions to prevent inaccuracies. To them, that means responsibility rests upon reporters, editors, writers, proofreaders, and all others who make their livelihood in the mass communication industry. Further, it rests also upon those who supply information to the media, whether they are being interviewed as news sources or are voluntarily contributing material to the press. Perhaps journalists' responsibilities are the greater because they handle the material last, but neither journalists nor lay persons can in good conscience relax their vigilance.

On those occasions when you serve as an interview source or write for publication, your guiding rule for carrying out your share of the responsibility for accuracy should be this: Make no assumptions about facts. Never assume, for example, that you know how to spell a name; that you know without question the date, time, and place of an event; that you are quoting someone correctly; that because you were told something it must be so; that you are citing a statistic or any other fact accurately. Look it up in a reliable reference, ask the person or persons directly involved, or do whatever is necessary to establish beyound a reasonable doubt the accuracy of the information. Being certain has no real substitute, and the only sure way to be certain is to verify. Information that cannot be verified should not be used.

If you are being interviewed on a **sensitive matter** or one that involves many **intricate details,** a verification possibility may be open to you. Ask your interviewer if you might review the completed story or tape for accuracy before publication or broadcast. If you are allowed to do this, review the material promptly and adhere to your original pledge—that is, to **check for accuracy,** not for manner of expression. Never in this review stage should you try to "take back" your interview in an effort to stop publication of the story. A much better approach is to cooperate with the reporter in making the material as satisfactory as possible.

Not all representatives of the media will grant you this review privilege. When this happens, you might deal with the situation in several ways: (1) Refuse further interviews if the published material proves to be inaccurate through no fault of yours; (2) make the review privilege a condition to any interview, and

(3) require that questions be submitted in writing so you may answer in a like manner. None of these alternatives, however, is nearly as satisfactory as the freely conducted interview based on mutual confidence and respect. Whatever you can do to develop press relationships of this character will be to your advantage over the long run. Most press relations problems melt away automatically when that atmosphere prevails.

Once the material passes through your hands for the last time, there is little you can do to insure its accuracy. You are uneasily aware that an editor's alteration, a typesetter's lapse, an announcer's slip of the tongue, or whatever, can produce a published version marred by inaccuracy. But there is another way of looking at it. The many checkpoints the material must clear before it finally is approved for publication can serve as additional guarantees of accuracy. Editors and their assistants are trained to spot the inconsistency, the doubtful assertion, the questionable fact. As a consequence they can, and often do, head off embarrassment for the information source by correcting or rechecking with him what he may have overlooked.

THE MYTH OF "PURE OBJECTIVITY"

Much of what has been said thus far about the difficulty of achieving accuracy also applies to what is called objectivity. A long-standing (and often tiresome) controversy rages among journalists over whether reports should be interpretive, objective, or both. In recent years, the debate has concentrated on the "evils" and "virtues" of advocacy reporting. But the substance remains essentially the same. In the end, purely objective reporting must be considered an ideal, not an attainable goal. All true reporting is interpretation of a sort.

For centuries philosophers have been telling us that we are prisoners of our experience. We perceive selectively, remember selectively, report selectively. When we observe an objective fact (a thunderstorm), the information immediately becomes subjective (a Godsend, frightening, inconvenient, disastrous, beneficial, or any one of scores of other value judgments).

Journalists are no different from others in this respect, nor should anyone expect them to be. Although heavy stress ought to be and is placed on an **objective approach** to the reporting process, journalists still must select the facts they will use and discard the others, decide which facts to emphasize and which ones to play down, and determine what writing form will best lend itself to the information they intend to report. Similarly, editors are unable to use all that comes to their attention. They must therefore decide what stories to use, which ones to condense and which ones to expand, which stories are to receive major and minor emphasis, what manner of headline to use or what placement the story is to receive, and so on. All of this involves human judgment. The process amounts to a never-ending series of subjective decisions based on imprecise criteria journalists have developed through experience—criteria that they believe will best serve the public interest.

THE FAIR-MINDED APPROACH TO REPORTING

What the debate about objective reporting eventually gets down to is a firmly held judgment on all sides that the media should practice a high standard of **fairness**. Certainly no one would quarrel with that as an ideal. The trouble is that seldom can any two persons agree on what is fair and what is not. Journalists soon learn and accept this as a distressing and often frustrating circumstance, but it does not (or should not) deter them from adhering to what they regard as a fair-minded approach to the reporting process. In practice, the fair-minded approach means:

1. Offering all sides of controversy an opportunity to be heard.
2. Striving to report situations in perspective.
3. Discarding loaded words and labels in favor of facts.
4. Submerging personal biases and prejudices.
5. Paying careful attention to the context of events and situations.
6. Avoiding a participant's role.
7. Guarding against depicting the account with overly colorful expression.
8. Providing background information wherever it is needed.
9. Attributing opinions, judgments, and disputed "facts" to the appropriate source.
10. Reserving personal opinion for the page, section, or broadcast openly devoted to that purpose.

Where printed media such as newspapers and magazines are concerned, the level of fairness practiced depends largely upon the ethical standards of those responsible for what appears in those media—the reporters, editors, and publishers. In other words, there is no enforceable law that requires publishers of printed media to be fair. And the United States Supreme Court has said that's as it should be. In 1974, the Court declared unconstitutional a Florida law requiring newspapers to provide a "right of reply" privilege to political candidates who had been attacked in such publications. The Court said, in effect, that imposing a right of reply requirement on newspapers would be equivalent to dictating content, and that would be contrary to the provisions of the First Amendment. The journey of the challenge to the Florida law through the appeal process was watched with a great deal of interest by legal scholars and journalists as well. The argument in favor of the law had been that the trend toward monopoly ownership of newspapers tended to restrict public access to such media and to reduce the number of voices in the "marketplace of ideas." Therefore, it was claimed, right of reply statutes were needed. The Supreme Court ruled otherwise.

Broadcast media, on the other hand, are governed by a set of rules imposed by the Federal Communications Commission, the agency that licenses radio and television stations. (See also Chapter 11.) Those rules impose an **equal time** provision for political candidates and articulate what is known as the **"Fairness Doctrine"** on controversial issues of public importance. Stated simply, the FCC requires that:

1. When time is given or sold to a candidate for political office, all other bona fide candidates for that office must be offered equal time on the same basis.
2. When controversial matters of public importance are broadcast, the station or network must seek out and provide opportunity for all sides to be heard. In addition, if during the course of such a broadcast the integrity or character of a person or group is attacked, or if an editorial supports or opposes a political candidate, the person or group must be notified, furnished the content of the broadcast, and offered air time to respond.

The vigorous public debate on controversial issues that the FCC hoped would be stimulated by the equal time and fairness doctrine provisions has not materialized. In fact, many observers contend that the trend has been in the opposite direction. Broadcasters, fearful of the legal entanglements, have avoided any commitment of time to editorializing, controversial issues, or political candidates. They argue that it is unconstitutional for the FCC to compel "fairness" under threat of losing the license to broadcast. And they insist that the FCC's goal of encouraging a broad spectrum of opinion on issues of public importance would be better served by eliminating the equal time and fairness doctrine provisions altogether. To date, there is no indication that the FCC is considering such a step.

REPORTING OPINION AND JUDGMENT

You are certainly aware that the media publish a great deal of opinion in forms such as advertising, so-called comic strips or pages, editorial cartoons, letters to the editor, syndicated columns, political commentaries, editorial expressions, or lovelorn columns. Presumably, the public understands this and accepts the material for whatever it is worth. But the media also publish vast quantities of opinion as legitimate news and feature material. Examples are the remarks of politicians and of candidates for public office, the pleas for cooperation from charitable institutions and organizations, the evaluation of the season's prospects by the football coach, the propaganda issued by the myriad committees formed to support or oppose whatever may be currently at issue, the by-lined interpretations of the changing scene by journalistic specialists or other qualified persons, the efforts at persuasion by representatives of various governmental agencies, and the recommendations for applying scientific discoveries to the processes of everyday endeavor.

All of this involves expression of opinion and judgment. But it also qualifies as news—information that citizens want and need. Not only is the press obligated to carry out this phase of its overall reporting function as fully as circumstances will permit, but the fair-minded approach suggests that the media ought to make clear to the public **who or what agency is responsible for the observation being reported.** All such opinions and judgments should be credited to the source, clearly and unmistakably. Some examples should help to clarify the point:

Incorrect	Correct
This will be an extremely important meeting that everyone should plan to attend.	The Chamber of Commerce president urged interested persons to attend what he described as "an extremely important meeting."
Building a dam may create a lake, but it also will lower the value of adjoining farmland.	John Smith, chairman of the Natural Resources Council, asserted that "building a dam may create a lake, but it also will lower the value of adjoining farmland."
Vote a straight party ticket.	Representative Burns urged his listeners to vote a straight party ticket.

It's going to be the biggest and best fair in Center County history.

Blaine Evans, fair manager, predicted that this year's event will be "the biggest and best in Center County history."

The funds will be used for a good cause. The high school band is badly in need of new uniforms.

Mrs. Richard Wheaton, PTA president, explained the funds would be used to buy "badly needed uniforms for the high school band."

The foregoing examples illustrate the **attribution principle** for brief statements. But the same procedure should be used for longer accounts as well. The two versions of the story that follows illustrate why appropriate attribution is important:

No attribution

A large crowd was on hand Tuesday night to hear Rep. John Jessup speak at the Democratic rally for the Fourth Precinct. His remarks were enthusiastically received.

The meeting was larger than any held in this community this year and indicated the growing strength of the Democratic party in this area.

Republicans have been at fault in not being more concerned with the inadequate medical facilities of Johnson County.

Attribution

A crowd of approximately 350 persons attended a meeting Tuesday night to hear Rep. John Jessup speak at the Democratic rally for the Fourth Precinct.

John Heald, Democratic county chairman, said that the meeting was the most enthusiastic held this fall and indicated growing strength of the Democratic party in this area.

Representative Jessup charged that the Republican party had been negligent in not providing more adequate medical facilities in Johnson County.

If in any such situation none of the claims or assertions is credited to a source, the reader or listener is perfectly justified in concluding that the expressions are those of the reporter or of the medium carrying the story. But attribution can be carried to the point where it becomes ridiculous. Where facts are not in dispute (the time of a meeting, the location of an event, the details of a program, the date of an election, the name of a speaker, and so on), there is no need to attribute that information to a source.

There will be times when the working journalist comes to you for your opinions, or you may want to volunteer them for publication by calling in a reporter or scheduling a news conference. So far, so good. But don't be surprised or disturbed if the journalists you talk to also seek out the views of others on that particular subject. That is their job, and to be fair they ought to solicit all available information. If your remarks are reported accurately and in context—that is, fairly—you should have no complaint. The democratic process assumes the public must have access to the widest possible range of opinion if it is to make intelligent choices from among available alternatives. By functioning as a marketplace for ideas and opinions, the press and all those who contribute to this marketplace are supplying fundamental encouragement to the growth and development of the democratic ideal.

This latter consideration is one of the overriding reasons why mass media bear a heavy responsibility to present accurate and fair reports, insofar as that is humanly possible. The great problem, as has been indicated, is that most persons do not appreciate the difficulty of carrying out that responsibility, nor do they have a sufficient respect for its necessity.

READERS DEMAND ACCURACY

More than we may realize, modern society depends upon the mass media to satisfy a variety of wants and needs. Studies indicate typical adults spend from four to six hours each day with the mass communication devices at hand—newspapers, magazines, radio, television, books, movies. They rely upon them for countless pieces of information and for clues on which they base rather fundamental decisions, both consequential and inconsequential. They check the weather forecast, for example, to decide whether to go golfing, plan a picnic, cancel an out-of-town trip, stay inside for the day, or carry an umbrella. They study the financial pages to see how their investments are faring and to decide what their next moves will be. A citizen may seek the report of the city council meeting to find out how tax money is being spent and to discover whether projects he or she opposes or favors are being contemplated, For may of these same reasons citizens keep up with the latest publications serving their professions or businesses, the local school board news, the court report, statehouse developments, Washington news, the international scene, and so on. **They want to know.**

The only agency equipped to supply this information on a regular, continuing, and efficient basis is the press. Moreover, the average person realizes that in spite of its occasional inaccuracies and other shortcomings the press has an impressive overall record of reliability. Citizens demonstrate their confidence every day by accepting as fair and accurate the great bulk of the information they find in the press.

Another reason for the industry's great emphasis on fair and accurate reporting is a frankly selfish one—its own economic well-being. Although you undoubtedly can find numerous examples to the contrary, it is generally true that persistent inaccuracies and unprincipled exaggerations or distortions can contribute to a declining public confidence in the press. For a specific firm that can mean a drop in circulation or audience, less advertising, reduced income, and even the difference between a profit and a loss.

In addition, there is always the possibility that sloppy reporting can bring on a costly libel suit. Journalists who have spent a lifetime working in the media know that carelessness is the major cause of such suits. So much of the content of mass media deals with subject matter that is potentially libelous—reports of crime and wrongdoing of all descriptions—that accuracy and fairness become more than simple virtues; they are prime necessities. Material of this sort, inaccurately or unfairly reported, may hurt innocent persons. When that happens, even though the mistake or unfairness was not intentional, the consequences can be serious for the offending agency. It is not at all uncommon for persons who feel they have been defamed in the media to file libel actions seeking thousands, sometimes even millions, of dollars in damages. Journalists are uncomfortably aware that such a suit can be triggered by publication of a wrong name, initial, address, or other identifying information if the error is the consequence of carelessness and results in damage to someone's good name.

Although it is not likely that you will ever be involved in a libel action, understanding at least the fundamentals of libel law can broaden your appreciation for the rights and responsibilities of both the press and the news source. Under the law, **both** can be held liable for a published injury to a person's or a firm's reputation. The injured party may sue separately or jointly anyone who had a part in publishing the libel: the reporter, the editors, the publishing medium itself, and if he or she wishes, the source of that damaging piece of information when the source knew he or she was speaking for publication. For example, if Citizen A unjustly describes Citizen B as "a liar and a fraud," knowing that the remark is to be published in the local newspaper, Citizen B may sue the newspaper, Citizen A, or both.

Generally speaking, the media are legally responsible for any libels they may publish, whether those libels occur in advertising, letters to the editor, recordings, film, photographs, drawings, news stories, headlines, feature articles, reprinted material, contributed articles, or editorials. The reasoning is simply that the agency that gives circulation to the libel must also accept the responsibility for any damage that might result.

How do you recognize a libel? Three elements must be present before a libel can exist. They are:

1. **Defamation.** The words used must somehow injure a reputation or sully a good name. Many words are defamatory in themselves (crook, cheater, prostitute, Communist, racketeer, and hundreds more that indicate dishonesty, immorality, or impropriety). Others become defamatory because of special circumstances (the story falsely reporting that a clergyman attended what was widely known to have been a wild party). Any false statement which subjects the injured party to public ridicule, hatred, scorn, or contempt, or adversely affects the person in his or her job or professional capacity is defamatory
2. **Publication.** Where mass media are concerned, publication exists the moment the presses roll or the broadcast goes on the air. At that moment, distribution begins and publication has been accomplished. From a strictly legal point of view, however, publication exists the moment a third party hears or sees the defamatory statement.
3. **Identification.** The offending statement must refer to an ascertainable person or persons. The identification, however, need not be by name. It can be accomplished by means of a personality sketch, an address, a photograph, a drawing, by describing an occupation, or citing physical characteristics. Identification exists when any circumstances or details make it possible for the public to single out some specific person or persons as the object of the offending statement.

TRUTH IS BEST DEFENSE

If any of these three elements is absent, there is no libel. Where all three are present, however, the injured party can bring suit for damage to his or her reputation. Whether he or she will be successful depends upon how the jury sees the evidence—and this is when the chips are down. The best possible defense to any libel suit is **truth, when it can be established.** Unfortunately, it is one thing to know the truth (that John Doe is a crook) and quite another to prove it in court.

The principle also applies when the press is quoting news sources. It is not enough for the press to plead that it has quoted someone accurately, although that is important, too. There must also be proof that **what the person said is true**. Proving the truth is especially hard when facts have been exaggerated, when guilt by association is involved, or when damaging innuendo is inherent in the wording. Proving the truth is a somewhat easier proposition when the material in question is fair and accurate in all respects.

Although truth is a solid defense in any libel action, it is especially applicable in damage suits involving the private citizen and the person not previously in the limelight who suddenly comes into public prominence and is defamed. And if the defendant pleads truth as a defense he or she must establish it. Where public officials, public figures, and candidates for public office are concerned, however, the burden of proof shifts to the plaintiff. In a sweeping decision that has been elaborated upon in subsequent cases, the United States Supreme Court held in 1964 that, where public personages are involved, the injured party must prove that the offending material was published with what is known in legal terminology as **malice**. Said the Court:

The constitutional guarantees require, we think, a federal rule that prohibits every public official from recovering damages for a defamatory falsehood relating to his official conduct unless he proves that the statement was made with "actual malice"—that is, with knowledge that it was false or with reckless disregard of whether it was false or not.

In other words, if a defamatory statement published by the news media turns out to be false, persons in the public arena cannot collect libel damages unless they can prove the defendant either knew the statement was false at the time it was published or entertained serious doubts as to whether it was true and made no serious effort to check it out. The Court reasoned that the news media need such protection if free and robust debate on public issues is to be encouraged and if the media are to avoid continual harrassment in libel court.

OTHER LEGAL ASPECTS

Three other aspects of law deserve mention, two of them having implications for this chapter's central theme—fair and accurate reporting. They are the **right of privacy, shield laws**, and the **law of lottery**.

Right of Privacy

The right of privacy refers to the individual's right to be left alone—to go through life unnoticed. Most of us would be desperately unhappy if that actually turned out to be our fate, but the law's purpose is not to hamper the legitimate publicity that most people want and even seek. Its goal instead is to provide protection against **unreasonable publicity** on the one hand and against commercial exploitation of an individual's name or likeness on the other.

Some invasions of privacy occur when persons are unfairly identified with objectionable or embarrassing feature articles, feature pictures, or radio-television dramatizations. Examples might be: using a photograph of a person who was physically disfigured or, dramatizing a spectacular crime and identifying one of the principals even though he had led an exemplary life since paying his debt to society. In all likelihood, these would be regarded by the courts in most states as instances of unreasonable publicity.

Most privacy suits, however, arise because someone's name or picture has been used to advertise or promote a product without his or her permission. The safest and surest way to keep that from happening is to obtain a written release from the individual granting permission to use his or her name and likeness for advertising purposes and to pay whatever sum of money is agreed upon for that permission. It is a precaution that should be taken whether the individual happens to be your next door neighbor or a professional model. (See example in Chapter 7.)

The privacy right does not apply to coverage of news and of matters commanding great public interest. Again and again the courts have ruled that anyone who is involved voluntarily or involuntarily in a legitimate news event loses his or her right to privacy in connection with that event. Insofar as the courts are concerned, the public's interest in news events outweighs the individual's private interests. It is also true that persons who seek public attention or acclaim, or who have become public personages as a consequence of their accomplishments or even their peculiarities, thereby give up claims to privacy that the less well-known person has. The only limitation on such reporting and on the coverage of news events in general is that it be reasonable. Unhappily, the guidelines here are fuzzy, but court interpretations generally have been more liberal than restrictive.

Shield Laws

An area of law that has attracted a great deal of attention and led to extensive discussion in the 1970s is that covered by so-called shield laws. Historically, journalists have contended that they have the professional duty to protect the identity of their news sources. More recently they have maintained that they have an inherent constitutional right to do so as well.

Few persons will quarrel about the ethical principle. It's widely accepted that if journalists do not adhere steadfastly to the confidentiality standard, channels of information important to them and to the public's right to know will dry up. News sources in possession of sensitive information simply will not talk unless there is a promise of anonymity. As a consequence, the confidentiality principle has become an article of faith among journalists.

But the question of whether journalists have the inherent constitutional right to protect the identity of their news sources is another matter. The United States Supreme Court, while recognizing that the practice undoubtedly gives journalists and the public access to information that otherwise might not be available, nevertheless has ruled there is no inherent constitutional protection of the privilege. If such protection is to be provided, said the Court, it's up to Congress and the state legislatures to devise statutes that will grant journalists the right to shield the identity of their sources. By the mid-1970s, individual congressmen had proposed shield legislation but no such federal statute had been passed. Upwards of 20 states, however, have enacted shield laws that range from those purporting to offer absolute protection to those providing only limited protection. Whatever the language, however, all have provisions that will require journalists to reveal their sources under specified circumstances.

What this means, of course, is that where there are no provisions to the contrary journalists who have been ordered in a court of law to reveal their news sources or to testify about information gained in confidence must do so or face a contempt citation. Some journalists have gone to jail rather than testify, but such actions serve only as disturbing reminders that the larger issue remains unresolved.

From your point of view, two of society's purposes appear to be in conflict: Assuring that (a) the press can function as an effective watchdog on government, and (b) the courts have the authority to enforce their orders. Both are vital to the health of a democratic system.

Beware the Lottery

If one considers the sweeping and continuous condemnations of lottery schemes that have been a characteristic of this country's public debate, it could be concluded that such activities would not be tolerated. And indeed we've had systematic efforts in that direction throughout our history. Long ago, lotteries were declared to be contrary to public policy, and both courts and lawmakers have given ground grudgingly since then on what manner of schemes will be permitted. In most states, lotteries are illegal and promoters of them are subject to a fine and/or imprisonment. In those states where lotteries have been legalized, they are subject to strict regulation, with stern penalties prescribed for those who violate the regulations. In addition, federal laws prohibit the broadcasting of lottery information, deny mailing privileges for the circulation of such information, and provide penalties for those who promote such schemes in violation of federal restraints.

By common definition, a lottery is any scheme where **prizes** may be won by **chance for a consideration**. All three elements must be present for a lottery to exist. If skill is needed to win, there is no lottery. Similarly, there is no lottery if participants may compete without giving up money, substantial time or effort, or anything else of value. Because prizes are always offered in promotions of this sort, this is seldom at issue. But there is a great deal of confusion over the chance and consideration questions. Part of the confusion stems from differing state court interpretations, part of it from the differences between federal court rulings and those in the several states, and part of it from the fact that court decisions change with the times. The person who wants to know whether a particular scheme is a lottery may (1) check it with the local postmaster or the Post Office Department in Washington, D.C., (2) become familiar with the latest court decisions in his or her state, (3) get an opinion from a lawyer, or (4) discuss the scheme with an advertising representative of the local newspaper or broadcasting station.

The lottery question usually arises when local merchants or organizations are looking for quick ways to increase business or raise money. They may decide to stage a raffle, a bingo party, an automobile "giveaway" scheme, or any one of scores of other lotteries. Normally they will also want to advertise the affair in the local newspaper or over the community's broadcasting stations or both. No matter how good the cause, though, neither newspapers nor broadcasting stations are likely to accept such material until it has been modified to the point where it no longer is a lottery. That means eliminating either the chance or consideration requirement.

SHARPENING PROFESSIONALISM

No discussion of accuracy and fairness would be complete without at least some mention of recent developments, both internal and external to the news media, whose purpose is to encourage higher standards of professional practice.

Internally, news media are experimenting with a broad range of devices for improving accuracy and insuring fairness. They include regular and systematic checks with news sources inviting critical comment, establishing bureaus of fair play, appointing an ombudsman to accept complaints and arrange for corrections or adjustments where indicated, organizing community press councils to evaluate performance, and other variations. Studies indicate media in ever greater numbers are adopting approaches of this sort and indications are the trend will continue.

The essentially external developments have included the organization of a National News Council and a state press council (in Minnesota), and the founding of scores of journalism reviews throughout the country. The primary function of each of these agencies is, in one way or another, to evaluate the performance of news media and to publish their findings and criticisms. As you would expect, the quality of the critical output varies considerably, but it's reasonable to speculate that the observations are not being ignored.

SUMMARY

To summarize, accuracy and fairness in the news media are an ideal that should be of concern to everyone. Journalists work hard to eliminate error and to practice a high standard of fairness, but the nature of the news business is such that perfection in either accuracy or fairness will always be an elusive goal. As a citizen, you have a responsibility to serve as a constructive and informed critic of media performance. And when you become a news source or contribute to the media, you have a parallel responsibility to provide information that is both accurate and fair to all parties concerned.

SUGGESTED READING

Gilmore, Donald M., and Barron, Jerome A. **Mass Communication Law.** La Habra, Calif.: Foundation Press, 1969.

Graham, Fred P. **Press Freedoms under Pressure.** Twentieth Century Fund, 1972.

Nelson, Harold L., and Teeter, Dwight L., Jr. **Law of Mass Communications.** La Habra, Calif.: Foundation Press, 1969.

Nelson, Jerome L. **Libel: A Basic Program for Beginning Journalists.** Ames: Iowa State Univ. Press, 1973.

Holmgren, Rod, and Norton, William. **The Mass Media Book.** Englewood Cliffs, N.J.: Prentice-Hall, 1972.

Kreighbaum, Hillier. **Pressures on the Press.** New York: Thomas Y. Crowell Co., 1972.

Riley, David J. **Freedom of Dilemma.** Glenview, Ill.: Scott, Foresman and Co., 1971.

16

Advertising: it helps and it hurts

M. SUSAN MENNE

Michael T. Malloy, in a column written for **The National Observer**, described a "recurring nightmare" in which "There is this evil fiend, see, who wants to subvert, undermine, and generally destroy our society."

The fiend sets out to do his dirty work by eroding the Protestant ethic "which made capitalism and modern society possible. You know about the ethic, of course; work and save, plan ahead, don't let petty pleasures lead you off the straight and narrow."

Malloy's nightmare continues:

> Ten or 15 or 20 times an hour, the slogans pound home. For hours, every day. Extra messages-per-hour for kids; you want to hit them hardest while they're young, before the old ethic gets'em. Over and over again, until they've heard and seen the message a quarter of a million times before they're fully grown—**Now!** . . . **Don't worry about the future!**—more than they have heard any other moral message about anything.

The fiend pounds away incessantly and begins to see results of his efforts in divorce, debt, venereal disease in epidemic proportions, expediency in government, crime and social disorder, hatred between groups, and resentment

---

M. SUSAN MENNE is Associate Professor of Journalism and Mass Communication, Iowa State University, a former newspaper and magazine editor and reporter, and former advertising copy writer and copy director. She is a recipient of the Los Angeles Advertising Women's award for an Aerojet-General campaign in **Time** and **Newsweek** magazines, and she is the author of **How to Survive the Teaching of High School Journalism**.

of authority as everyone demands instant gratification. Malloy concludes:

> The nightmare ends in a sweat of fear and apprehension, always just short of revealing the utter and final collapse. A moment's nervous reflection and then, thank God, realization that it is just an overactive imagination at work. No rational society would ever let such a nightmare really happen.[1]

And so one reporter's nightmare dramatically poses the issues that impale the institution of advertising on the rusty nails of responsibilities that early advertising gurus could never have foreseen. Not the least among advertising's contemporary considerations is concern for children.

CHILDREN: A SPECIAL AUDIENCE

Who is a child? Consider Sam, the 43-year-old who suckles on beer; and Sally, the 38-year-old who married Sam and became his Mommy. When does the advertiser's responsibility to immaturity cease? If Bubble Gum Breakfast Flakos cannot be advertised to children because it has no nutritive value, why shouldn't Sam be protected from admonitions to grab all the gusto he can get?

But today the issue is **children**. Preschool children between the ages of 3 and 5 watch an average of 54 hours of television each week. That is more than nine full days out of every month. In 54 hours of children's television programming are more than 1,000 commercials, most selling cereals, toys, and candy.

Consumer groups believe that is too much too soon. Some would like to have television advertising to children stopped completely. Others demand more controls.

Revenues to television networks for airing children's advertising are estimated at more than $80 million a year; hence the networks' reluctance to abandon children's advertising.

Second to no commercials at all, say consumer activists, is stricter control over commercial content. The extent of that control fuels a seemingly nonstop train of controversy with government, the media, and advertisers tootling down the tracks. The train is so long you have difficulty counting the cars, but when the caboose finally passes and the clatter subsides, you find these areas of agreement about advertising to children:

1. Products advertised ought to look like they are going to look when Charlie Child gets them on his own living room rug. Charlie's not too knowledgeable about camera angles that make short rockets look long or about studio lighting that makes plain old paint look like shiny chrome.
2. Children often confuse fantasy and reality. They wouldn't be surprised to find the Jolly Green Giant in their neighborhood pea patch. Advertising should be careful not to pander to this confusion or try to sell products on its strength.
3. Keeping up with the little Joneses should be left to the little Smiths, without help from adult commercial makers. Children's commercials should not stress that owning a product will put them a step ahead of their playground peers.
4. Safety, if not first, remains right up there as a consideration in the making of commercials for **any** product, because there can be unexpected implications. An editorial in **Advertising**

---

1. Michael T. Malloy, "The Fiend and His Slogan-Projector," **National Observer**, May 25, 1974. Quoted with permission from **National Observer**, copyright Dow Jones & Company, Inc., 1974.

Age magazine described the plight of a four-year-old boy who decided to "get up and get away to McDonald's" all by himself. Maybe, the editorial proposed, the ad should insert the proviso—straight from the lips of Ronald McDonald himself—that children should wait for their parents to take them to those Golden Arches.
5. Violence is deplored.
6. Television commercials should not urge children to buy and should not suggest to them that they ask their parents to make purchases.
7. Everyone agrees that advertising to children should be truthful; that the advertiser should be able to substantiate all claims.

With all this agreement, what are the areas of contention?

1. **Premiums**—Should an advertiser be allowed to stimulate purchases by offering a Mister Marvelous invisible ink kit for a boxtop from Lollipop Puffs?
2. **Drugs**—Won't advertising for drugs and vitamins convince the child that health comes in a capsule?
3. **Sugared Cereals**—Doesn't advertising of these products dangerously increase the probability of an inadequate diet?
4. **Host Selling**—Is it cricket to allow Uncle Wiggly, who introduces the cartoons, to also introduce the commercials?

ADVERTISING CONTROLS

The kidvid (children's video) advertising controversy puts into a pint the gallons of conflict between "more control" and "less control" advocates.

A CBS executive has been quoted in **Variety**[2] as saying that advertising and program content of kidvid are issues that

2. June 12, 1974, p. 30.

are "inexorably intertwined (because) advertising pays for programs—not government funds, not donations from Action for Children's Television—but advertising."

It is true. Advertising pays for commercial television. Advertising pays for commercial radio. Advertising pays for approximately two-thirds of the costs of the print media. A subscription payment to **Playboy** isn't enough to pay for the magazine. The advertisers who address readers through its pages pay **Playboy** for the space they use, and that makes up the difference.

These economic facts of life assure us that the "more control-less control" prizefight has an infinite number of rounds to go. The advertiser wants to present the message he wants to present the way he wants to present it. The "presented-through" (radio, television, magazines, newspapers) don't want to offend the advertiser who buys time or space to make the presentation. The "presented-upon" (the rest of us) have at least 200 million continually changing American views on what constitutes acceptability in an advertising message.

The organizations that speak for the "presented-upons," such as Action for Children's Television, invariably have a protectionist cast. They want to protect us from harmful advertising rather than protect us from a narrowing of advertising message possibilities brought about by stifling legislative controls.

Individuals may be **credulous** or **reasonable**. In oversimplified terms, the credulous person is a believing one who accepts what he or she is told. The reasonable person is skeptical. He or she listens, evaluates conflicting messages, and makes a considered choice.

The Federal Trade Commission, if a speech by one of its former commissioners (Mary Gardiner Jones) conveys its attitude correctly, regards audiences as credulous and seeks to regulate advertising accordingly.[8]

On the other hand, a 1972 symposium of the Toronto School of Theology at the University of Toronto, in what may be the most thorough stirring of the ethics of advertising to date, chose to regard the audience for advertising as reasonable. It makes a difference.

The Canadian theologians rejected the credulous person because

> It involves the choice of the lowest common denominator; further it implies an unacceptable contempt for the intelligence and sophistication of the receiver or else amounts to an unacceptably romantic desire to protect even the tiniest minority. It smacks of paternalism. But the real and present moral danger it risks is that of an **excessive protectiveness which imperils freedom** . . . . We see the spectre of the protection offered by the lion to smaller animals who exclaim, in the fable, "but we really do not want to be protected that much."[4]

THE FEDERAL TRADE COMMISSION

For many years the Federal Trade Commission (FTC) appeared to be a particularly inept agency of government. It took 16 years to get the word "liver" out of Carter's Little Liver Pills. Investigation of Geritol's "tired blood" claims began soon after the product was first advertised. It took until 1967 for the FTC to bring down a "cease and desist" order against the Geritol commercials. Geritol allegedly neither ceased nor desisted. In 1969, the FTC turned the case over to the Justice Department for prosecution. In 1973, the judge handed down his decision fining the company and its advertising agency a total of $812,000. That decision was appealed. At this writing, it has been 15 years since the FTC questioned the Geritol "tired blood" commercials. Things, however, are speeding up. The whole over-the-counter drug scene, of which Geritol is a part, has come under the scrutiny of a revitalized FTC, enlivened by a Ralph Nader "raid" in 1968.

How does the FTC regulate? Section 5 of the Federal Trade Commission Act is the essential tool with which the FTC moves to regulate advertising. Simply put, Section 5 states that unfair methods of competition and unfair or deceptive acts or practices are unlawful.

Perhaps a real life case history can illustrate the operation of the FTC, as well as spotlight some of the current societal issues in advertising.

Nearly everyone remembers the commercials suggesting that Wonder Bread built strong bodies 12 ways. Girls and boys on television grew miraculously from preschool to high school size in 20 seconds. The FTC worried that youngsters might believe what they saw. In the Wonder Bread campaign lie these considerations:

● Children as a special advertising audience.
● Fantasy video, with the depiction of that zooming rate of growth.
● The unique or preemptive claim, which implies that an attribute claimed for a product is unique to that product, though it is shared by all similar products.
● Incomplete explanation of the nutritional value of a food.
● Exploitation of emotional concerns of children and of parents for healthy physical and mental growth.

---

3. American Academy of Advertisers, Phoenix, Ariz. March 11, 1973.

4. **Truth in Advertising: A symposium of the Toronto School of Theology.**

- The "halo effect" of advertising, which favorably influences consumers not so much by direct statements as by the overall psychological impact of the ads.
- Corrective advertising, an FTC alternative that can require that a product's future advertising include correction of earlier claims.

The Wonder Bread case provided advertising's critics with a veritable club sandwich of accusatory articles. One magazine wrap-up outlined the charges against International Telephone and Telegraph (ITT), the owner of Wonder Bread, then continued,

> ... ITT offered an astonishing defense—the Wonder Bread commercials weren't actually false or misleading because no one believed them. To add the proper note of bathos to this reasoning, ITT Continental Baking staged a heartrending public confession. It had all been a mistake, it told the judge; the 20 years of nutritional advertising was the biggest marketing blunder since the Edsel. Not mentioned were the continuing profits which made Wonder Bread so attractive an acquisition for ITT.[5]

Less flamboyant is the language of the **Journal of Marketing** in its regular report on the regulation of unfair competition. Its summation of the Wonder Bread litigation outlines the proceedings with objectivity:

> Chairman Engman disagreed with the dismissal of charges of unfairness against advertising claims directed primarily at children. He stated that the record evidence confirms that children under six years of age are highly vulnerable to the type of subtle psychological claim promising rapid growth contained in Wonder Bread advertisements, and that such advertising which is calculated to exploit "their known anxieties or capitalize upon their propensity to confuse reality and fantasy" is unfair within the meaning of Section 5 of the Federal Trade Commission Act.[6]

Unless or until the Congress establishes a national Consumer Protection Agency, the Federal Trade Commission remains the citizen's government contact on false and deceptive advertising. Complaints may be sent to the Bureau of Consumer Protection of the FTC, Washington, D.C. 20580. The questionable ad, if it appeared in a newspaper or magazine or came in the mail, should be included. For a television or radio commercial, the commission should be told the name of the product, the objectionable claim, and the station on which the advertisement was run. In addition to the FTC, complaints may be sent to the National Advertising Review Board, 850 Third Avenue, New York, N.Y. 10222.

SELF-REGULATION

The most serious attempt at self-regulation of advertising by the industry began in 1971 with the creation of the National Advertising Review Board (NARB). The purpose of the board remains that of "sustaining high standards of truth and accuracy in national advertising." The board consists of 30

---

5. James Rowen, "How to Keep Them Buying Even Though They Know You're Lying." **Washington Monthly**, Apr. 1973.

6. In re ITT Continental Baking Co., Inc. et al., CCH para. 20,464 FTC Dkt. 8860 (Oct. 1973); BNA ATRR No. 637 (Nov. 6, 1973), A-17 (D.C.). Quoted in **Journal of Marketing**, Apr. 1974.

advertiser members, 10 advertising agency members, 10 "public" (nonindustry) members, and 10 alternate advertising agency members.

The self-regulatory process begins with a complaint against national advertising brought by an individual, group, or company, or initiated by the NARB or the National Advertising Division (NAD) of the Council of Better Business Bureaus. NAD handles investigation of the complaint and requests that the advertiser complained against submit substantiation or proof of the claims made in the challenged ad.

The NAD can dismiss the complaint as unjustified or find that it is justified. It will then request that the advertising be modified or withdrawn. The advertiser can appeal the NAD decision if the complaint is found to be justified; or the complainant can appeal the decision if it is found not to be justified. In either case, an NARB panel gives the matter further consideration. If the findings of an NARB panel are in favor of the advertiser, the case is closed. If not, and the advertiser refuses to change or discontinue the challenged ad, the case is referred by NARB to an appropriate government agency.

A review of some cases encountered by NAD pinpoints fascinating ramifications of the truth-and-deception problem:

Easy-Off Oven Cleaner. The claim in question was, "33 percent more power cleaner than the other popular oven cleaner." NARB accepted as adequate the substantiation material proving this claim, which Easy-Off had earlier provided the FTC.

El Al Israel Airlines. The airline featured a "98-cent fare" in what the writer regarded as a humorous headline. NARB didn't laugh and the advertiser agreed to discontinue the ad.

Chuck Wagon Dog Food. The culprit here was a photograph of "tender, juicy chunks" that resembled meat but were actually soybean. The average consumer would tend to believe that "chunks" referred to meat and not to beans. (The average dog was not available for comment.) The complaint was dismissed chiefly because the advertising campaign was replaced.

Perhaps as many as one-fourth of the cases studied by the self-regulatory body were dropped because the offending ads were replaced by other campaigns after the months it took to process the complaint. This time factor has been a problem with Federal Trade Commission action as well.

Sunset House. This mail-order firm advertised an outdoor thermometer that "can be seen a block away." NAD members evidently felt, "Not without binoculars," and the complaint was upheld.

American Dairy Association. A cartoon commercial showed an airline stewardess getting an instant energy benefit from drinking a glass of milk. The NARB panel found that the ad "visually inferred" a short-term energy benefit that milk doesn't have. The American Dairy Association believed that obvious hyperbole and fantasy removed the possibility of the public taking the message literally. The commercial was, however, discontinued. As a result of this case, the NARB considered establishing guidelines for humor and fantasy—a ticklish business.

Schick. It took 300 pages of testimony for the NARB panel to conclude that the campaign for the Flexamatic electric shaver was "false in some details and misleading in its overall implications." The Flexamatic shaver was heavily promoted in direct comparison advertising against Norelco, Sunbeam, and

Remington shavers. When the NARB studied the testing procedures followed by Schick in establishing its claim for a closer shave, it found that the tests did not warrant the claim.

The kind of comparative or competitive advertising undertaken by Schick in this campaign had been earlier espoused by the FTC as an advertising practice that would benefit consumers by providing them with comparative buying information. Such advertising has now become routine.

Raid Yard Guard Insecticide. The television commercial said, "Raid Yard Guard. It's jungle tested." And it was. Right there in the jungles of Panama and Costa Rica.

Reader's Digest. A complainant felt that an ad was "confusingly similar" to editorial matter on the same page. That means the ad looked like a story. **Reader's Digest** pointed out that the use of a special border set the ad apart from editorial matter. The magazine agreed that in the future it would also put such ads at the bottoms of pages to further eliminate confusion.

Bold Detergent. A television commercial for Bold used what is called a "dangling comparative" in reference to Bold's capacity to get a wash "brighter." The reference is to the comparative case of the adjective—bright, **brighter,** brightest. The dangling comparative has been an advertising staple. Only the most conscientious advertiser has insisted that his or her advertising complete the comparative to read, "brighter than _____." The NARB panel reviewing the Bold case decided the complaint against the dangling comparative was not valid. Some panel members dissented, but the complaint was dropped.

Since then, the FTC has spoken against dangling comparatives. The Children's Television Advertising Guidelines of the Association of National Advertisers, Incorporated, included a policy against the danglers in 1972.

BACK TO THE FIEND

". . . There is this evil fiend, see, who wants to subvert, undermine, and generally destroy our society." And the name of the fiend is advertising. True or false?

It is first necessary to understand the nature of the fiend.

Advertising is not a system for providing comparative product information or for completely cataloging the physical attributes of a product.

Although many of advertising's critics flay the institution for failing to fulfill those functions, it is like criticizing an elm tree for not producing roses. An elm tree doesn't pretend to propagate the rose and advertising doesn't pretend to provide complete product information.

Advertising proposes to **persuade** persons to buy a product or to espouse an idea, not through a listing of objective facts, but through an appeal to a person's psychological needs and wants.

Most persons don't believe persuasion is evil. It is true that if I persuade you to pluck the wings from a butterfly, my goal could be considered evil. If, on the other hand, I persuade you to join the National Order for the Protection of the Butterfly, my goal could be considered good.

It is not persuasion that wears the black hat of the bad guy; it is the possible goal of persuasion and, some would say, the **techniques** used to reach the goal.

The next step, then, is to scrutinize the goal of advertising's persuasive message. If I persuade you to buy a tube of Glitter toothpaste, is that an evil goal?

Remember that you don't **have** to buy. I will do everything I can to find the right appeal that will make you **want** to buy. I might persuade you that Glitter, because of a new ingredient, whitens teeth beyond belief and therefore assures you of the acceptance and esteem of all yellow teeth haters. If the ingredient performs as promised, and if you crave acceptance and esteem, have I done you wrong?

There are other considerations.

First, we already have several satisfactory toothpastes on the market. Is another toothpaste really as important to the quality of life as, for example, the same amount of money invested in the development of new food sources from the seas?

Second, should you continually base your choices or considerations on how others view you, whether they will accept you, how much they can be made to love you? Or do you need to develop a stronger self image by which you might learn not to care about the opinions of the white teeth worshippers?

Advertising, because of what it is trying to do, is, in general, deliberately nonrational. It appeals to emotions, not intellect. At least one thinker is willing to state that "persuasive advertising, however, poses a real problem since some of the persuasive techniques used are intended to by-pass the intellect and reduce rationality, and may, if successful, lead to improvident actions." [7]

In the same essay the author concludes with a valuable checklist for judging the ethical level of advertising. Here is his list:

General Questions
1. What does the advertiser intend to do?
2. What are the actual effects of his advertising on the individual and on society as a whole?
3. Are these effects accidental, or do they result almost necessarily from the techniques used?

With Regard to Technique
1. Does the advertisement inform, or does it seek to persuade?
2. If persuasive, does the advertisement attempt to bypass the intellect?

With Regard to Content
1. Is the information truthful?
2. Are the motives presented valid reasons for acting?

With Regard to Psychological Effects
1. Does the advertising seriously disturb the psychic equilibrium of the individual without sufficient reason?
2. Does the advertising distort the hierarchy of values?

With Regard to Personal Consumption
1. Does it lead to a misuse of individual resources relative to the real needs of an individual?
2. Does it lead to an immoderate use of any particular product?

With Regard to Social Consumption
1. Does it lead to misuse of national resources in the actual economic situation of the nation?

Final Judgment
When the intent and technique are not evil in and of themselves, and where the harmful effects are not necessary, are there other effects which outweigh the harmful results?

Both the author's checklist and his fiat which condemns persuasive techniques that bypass the intellect would spark pithy discussion at a meeting of advertising practitioners, but the considerations are both valid and essential ones.

While advertising makes no secret of its use of emotional appeals and nonrational persuasive techniques, this honest admission of methods or means should not, by some shaky logic, be allowed to sanctify those means without more thoughtful debate. Advertising is

---

7. Thomas M. Garrett, S.J., "The Ethics of Persuasion," in John S. Wright and John E. Mertes, eds., **Advertising's Role in Society**.

big business and accounts for a substantial "cash flow" in the American economy. Annual expenditures for advertising total between $25 and $30 billion. (See Chapter 8 for further discussion of advertising expenditures.) The topic deserves continuing consideration and discussion because it is a pervasive one that affects virtually every consumer.

LET THEM EAT ADS

One area of advertising worthy of monitoring during the next several years might be food advertising. This is the arena wherein the next regulatory circus is billed for action.

The question of food advertising, as with advertising to children, encompasses some basic implications of advertising's relationship to society. All foods can be broken down into nutrients and caloric content can be determined. If the FTC or any other regulatory body requires that such information become a part of food advertisements, the shift from food advertising without content to content-loaded ads will put heavy burdens on those who create food sales messages.

It is simple to say that better nutrition information will promote better nutrition. The difficulty with saddling advertising with the task of delivering that better information lies with the very difficulty of communication.

Advertising penetrates the protective communication shield only when it appeals to the consumer in terms of his or her needs and desires; only when the product being sold can somehow be related to the very human aspirations and yearnings of the human being.

There is some doubt that good nutrition is a critically important human aspiration in American society, even though it is a worldwide dilemma that carries with it the seeds of worldwide disorder. An Industry Consumer Affairs Professional Conference sponsored by the Department of Agriculture in the summer of 1974 revealed several apt observations. "It's like trying to sell safety," said a government official, formerly in advertising, who felt there existed a "don't care" attitude among consumers. Marion Tripp, Vice-President for Consumer Affairs for J. Walter Thompson Company in Chicago, said, "I frankly think we're going to have to sell the consumer on nutrition.... All our food clients are interested in this: What we have to do is find out what motivates people about nutrition." She said "old" advertising research has shown that consumers are not generally interested in the nutritional aspects of most foods, "but this could be because of the way it was presented" in the ads. "What needs to be developed are some new creative approaches," she claimed.

What these persons are saying is that advertising may be called upon to effect a basic change in human aspirations. This has not been advertising's function in the past.

Some critics of advertising, however, have claimed for years that advertising does affect human aspirations and that its effects are to be deplored. The feminist points to the image of women portrayed by advertising and complains that the "ring-around-the-collar" image of woman is at least perpetuated and reinforced by advertising. The proponents of self-actualization psychology decry advertising's concern with "other-directed" (what other persons think) motivations. And the antimaterialists shudder at television's unending parade of products masquerading as the good life.

If advertising should now assume the obligation of changing human behavior by improving eating habits, it can at least be said that the end is a "better" one than that of depicting the good life as a succession of impulse purchases.

SUMMARY

Perhaps honest advertising should be allowed to continue to meet the public in its role as sales agent. Perhaps it should be free to appeal in meaningful terms to the needs and wants of consumers, without dictation by government of what those needs and wants should be.

Perhaps there should be developed a new form of communication, readily available to consumers and devoted to providing them with complete and factual product information.

It sets out a challenging assignment not to be attempted without deliberate consideration of these questions:

1. Who will pay for the information to be prepared?
2. How will it be channeled to the consumer?
3. How will we be assured that the consumer will read or hear the information?

In the answers to these three questions lies a whole new industry. In those answers, too, lie endless new questions, each turning to the light a new facet of advertising and its role in our society.

SUGGESTED READING

Howard, John A., and Hulbert, James. **Advertising and the Public Interest.** Chicago: Crain Communications, 1973.

Moskin, J. Robert, ed. **The Case for Advertising.** New York: American Association of Advertising Agencies, 1973.

Potter, David M. "The Institution of Abundance: Advertising." Ch. 7 in **People of Plenty.** Chicago: Phoenix, 1954.

University of Toronto. **Truth in Advertising: A Symposium of the Toronto School of Theology.** New York: Harper & Row, 1972.

Wright, John S., and Mertes, John E. **Advertising's Role in Society.** St. Paul: West Publishing Co., 1974.

Appendix

MASS MEDIA DIRECTORIES

Directories listing mass media outlets can be helpful to the publicist and to the consumer interested in knowing more, for example, about mass media costs and group ownership. The publicist is often called upon to create a mailing list to be used once or with regularity. In that situation, the mass media directories can be the publicist's best friends.

The following list of directories is not complete, nor is it intended to be. It is limited to national directories and omits all references to regional or area media guides, several of which are published. State press and broadcasting associations also publish directories of newspapers and stations within their respective states, as do some schools of journalism.

Even without the assistance of other guides, however, a reasonable mass media list can be created with the directories listed below.

Print Media

Ayer Directory of Publications (Philadelphia: Ayer Press, Annual). The **Ayer Directory**, published annually since 1869, is a household word in newspaper and public information offices across the land. It is a massive book full of detail concerning newspapers, magazines, consumer publications, business publications, technical and trade publications, and farm magazines and newspapers. The volume also includes detailed instructions for its most efficient use. The **Ayer Directory** also provides a special marketing service (for a price) whereby mailing lists of various groups of publications can be purchased, primarily for direct-mail advertising campaigns. Publications are listed by states, in alphabetical order. An alphabetized list of publications, by classification, is also provided as is a comprehensive index. The volume sells for more than $40 per copy, but the **Ayer Directory** can be found in most libraries and newspaper and public information offices.

Business Publication Rates and Data (Skokie, Ill.: Standard Rate and Data Service, Inc.). This is published by the Standard Rate and Data Service on a monthly basis. This hefty volume contains virtually every special interest publication that accepts advertising. Each business publication classification is assigned a number ranging from No. 1 (Advertising and Marketing) to No. 159 (Woodworking). In between are listed publications serving such diverse interests and businesses as plastics, tobacco, oil and gas, nursing, music, medicine, design, insurance, furniture, cosmetics, and air conditioning.

Consumer Magazine and Farm Magazine Rates and Data (Skokie, Ill.: Standard Rate and Data Service, Inc.). This is another of several special services published on a regular basis by Standard Rate and Data Service, primarily for the advertising industry. The SRDS publications are used extensively by the media specialists in advertising agencies and by the mass media interested in keeping a close eye on the competition. Although much of the information supplied by SRDS has to do with production techniques and restrictions, as well as advertising rates and deadlines, much of what is provided can be very helpful, indeed, to publicist or consumer.

Editor and Publisher International Year Book (New York: Editor and Publisher, Annual). This volume, subtitled, **The Encyclopedia of the Newspaper Industry**, is published by Editor and Publisher, an old and respected journal for newspaper personnel. The directory, which sells for approximately $15, is an excellent source of information concerning daily newspapers, although it does include a section devoted to the weekly press. Under alphabetically arranged state headings, the weekly newspapers published in each state are compactly listed with sets of mysterious abbreviations, which are clearly explained at the beginning of the section. The more expansive listings of daily newspapers are also arranged by the states (and the cities within states) where they are published. The volume provides other helpful information, including a chart for each state, listing numbers of papers and total daily and Sunday circulations within the state.

Politella, Dario. **Directory of the College Student Press in America** (3rd ed.) (New York: Oxbridge Publishing Company, Inc., 1974). This directory is listed because the field of college and university publications—newspapers in particular—is often overlooked by publicists and consumers alike. As is the case with the press in general, the performance of the college press varies from professional to pathetic. The campus newspaper, however, should not be ignored because it is an excellent medium for reaching students. It has been suggested that it is the **only** news medium most busy students use to "keep in touch" with developments.

Underground Press Directory (4th ed.) (Stevens Point, Wis.: William D. Lutz, 1970). This inexpensively reproduced directory makes an attempt to keep up with the "underground" press and the ceaseless changes in that fluid field of publishing. The existence of a directory highlights the fact that "underground" is a misnomer. The compiler of this directory, as a matter of preference, refers to it as a "guide to the alternative press." It has been available by writing Box 549, Stevens Point, Wis. 54481.

Electronic Media

Broadcasting Yearbook (Washington, D.C.: **Broadcasting, The Business-weekly of Television and Radio,** Annual). This publication is an excellent source of information concerning radio and television stations in the United States and Canada. Among other listings of interest, the publication reports, state by state, the broadcast stations, whether AM, FM, or TV, identified with newspaper or magazine ownership. In another section, it lists broadcast stations owned as parts of "groups." It includes a state-by-state listing by community of AM and FM stations in one section, and of TV stations in a separate section. The listings include some technical information of little or no interest to nonprofessionals. The compact listings do, however, provide any reader with much information of interest, including names of personnel, any connection with print media, the station's power and assigned frequency, its network affiliation (if any), its hourly advertising rate and whether it has facilities to show color, local slides, and local film (in the case of television). The **Yearbook** may be available in local radio and television stations, although most station managers would be hesitant to let the book leave their offices. It can also be found in many libraries.

APPENDIX

Spot Radio Rates and Data (Skokie, Ill.: Standard Rate and Data Service, Inc.). This is another monthly publication by the venerated SRDS, devoted solely to AM and FM radio stations. It provides a listing of stations, state by state, along with listings of regional networks and state, county, city, and metropolitan area market data and state media-and-market maps similar to those provided in **Spot Television Rates and Data**. (See listing below.) Of particular interest is the listing, alphabetically by state, of radio networks and groups. Often, by putting information "into the system" at a local radio station, it can be "passed around" the entire group or, at least, to those stations in the group whose audience may have an interest in the information. It can be a most efficient way of disseminating information on a broad scale. The listings also include power assignments and operating schedules. Each station's programming emphases are also noted.

Spot Television Rates and Data (Skokie, Ill.: Standard Rate and Data Service, Inc.). This monthly publication issued by SRDS lists television outlets according to the communities in which they are located, state by state. The publication includes state, county, city, and metropolitan area market data, primarily designed for use by advertising media specialists. For this reason, the guide also provides state media-and-market maps, TV market areas, and listings of cable television systems. The publication is excellent for the purpose for which it was designed. It includes much data of great interest to a publicist or consumer interested in potential audiences for various stations.

REVIEWERS OF PRESS PERFORMANCE

A healthy press relies upon a well-informed citizenry willing to provide intelligent assistance and criticism of the performance of the mass media. If the working press is the watchdog of government, the individual citizen is the "watchdog of the watchdog." Also playing that role are several publications, just three of which are listed here. No attempt has been made to list local press reviews, several of which do exist. In the mercurial field of local press reviewing, any such listing would probably be obsolete in a short time.

Columbia Journalism Review. A highly respected journal published bimonthly under the auspices of the faculty, alumni, and friends of the Graduate School of Journalism, Columbia University, 700 Journalism Building, Columbia University, New York, N.Y. 10027.

[MORE]. A relatively new publication (it made its appearance in 1970), [MORE] prides itself on "washing the media's dirty linen." It is a tabloid monthly, offering opinionated reviews of press performance. P.O. Box 576, Ansonia Station, New York, N.Y. 10023.

The Quill. Owned and published monthly by the Society of Professional Journalists, Sigma Delta Chi, this journal in recent years has been strengthened and improved. 35 East Wacker Drive, Chicago, Ill. 60601.

GENERAL AIDS

Two publications, both of which are outstanding handbooks for the publicist, are listed here because they are both inexpensive and readily available.

The Associated Press Stylebook (New York: The Associated Press, 1970). This slender booklet is a functional style guide for anyone writing for the mass media. It represents a cooperative effort between the Associated Press and United Press International wire services and is a recognized standard in most newsrooms throughout the nation. Traffic Department, The Associated Press, 50 Rockefeller Plaza, New York, N.Y. 10020.

Pocket Pal (New York: International Paper Company, 1973). This extremely helpful "graphic arts digest for printers and production managers" made its first appearance in 1934 and has gone through 10 editions and many revisions since that time. Printers and production managers aside, it is a fine introduction to the graphic arts for anyone. It covers history of printing, explains the different printing processes, discusses art and copy preparation, photography, platemaking, printing, binding, inks, and, predictably, printing papers. A compact gold mine of information. International Paper Company, 220 East 42nd Street, New York, N.Y. 10017.

INDEX

Absolutism, versus freedom, 141
Accuracy
  factual, 6
  grammatical, 6
  in press releases, 5, 6
  in reporting, 34, 159-61
Action for Children's Television, 173
Adams, Samuel, 142
Adjectives, avoidance, 5, 39
Advance man, 30
Advertiser pressure, on press, 151-52
Advertising
  artwork in, 82
  characteristics, 86, 178
  consumer, 86
  controls, 144, 173
  copy writing, 88-90
  costs, 99-100
  critics, 179
  direct mail, 91, 99
  ethical level of, 178
  of food, 179
  industrial, 86
  layout, 90-94
  local TV, 95
  magazine, 96-97, 100, 114
  media, 91, 95-99
  national expenditures, 85, 179
  newspaper, 95, 144
  personal insight in, 88
  radio, 97-98
  relationship to society, 179
  research, 87-88, 179
  retail, 89-90
  role, 85-86, 177-78
  spot, 95
  television, 95-96, 124, 130, 172-74
  trade, 86
Advertising Age, 85, 172-73
Advertising agency, compensation for, 100-101
Advocacy reporting, 161
Agate line, 99-100
Agence France-presse wire service, 134
Agnew, Spiro T., 149, 157
Alien and Sedition Acts, 143, 145
Almanacs, as reference, 29
American Book Publishers Council, 152
American Dairy Association, advertisements for, 176

American Home Products, advertising budget, 85
American Indian newspapers, 110
American Revolution, 141, 142
Anderson, Jack, 49
Angle, local, 22
Anti-Federalist party, 142
"Art Deco," 80
Artists
  style of, 79-80
  technique of, 81-82
"Art Nouveau," 80
Artwork. See also Illustration
  in advertising, 82
  color, 82
  media, 82
  selection, 82
  style, 79-81
  symbolism, 77
  uses, 77
Associated Press, 107, 123, 133, 134, 153
Association of National Advertisers, Inc., 177
Atlantic, The, 114
Atlases, as reference, 29
Attribution
  definition, 40
  importance, 40, 164-65
Attributive phrases, 45
Audiences
  analysis, 8
  children, 172
  consideration, 20
  knowledge, 43
  of newsletters, 49

Bache, Benjamin Franklin, 143
Backgrounding
  example, 27-28
  as research, 30-32
  sources, 29
Bagdikian, Ben H., 136, 137
Banzhaf, John, III, and "Fairness Doctrine," 130
Bartlett's Familiar Quotations, as reference, 28
Beats, news, 123
Bennett, James Gordon (editor, **N.Y. Herald**), 143

INDEX

Bennett, James Gordon, Jr. (editor, **N.Y. Herald**), 144
Berlo, David K., S-M-C-R model, 11-12
Better Homes and Gardens, slant of, 116
Bill of Rights, 155
Biographical sketch, as part of news story, 41
Black newspapers, 110
Bold detergent, advertisement, 177
Bombeck, Erma (columnist), 51
Boston Gazette, 142
Brevity
  in reporting, 34
  in speaking and writing, 37
Bristol-Myers Company, advertising budget of, 85
Broadcasting Yearbook, 125
Broadcast media. See Radio and television; Television
Broadcast news, sources, 123-24
"Broadcast wires," 123
Buchwald, Art, 51
Bureau of Consumer Protection, 175
Business Publication Rates and Data, 115
By-lines
  on columns, 50
  on interpretive reports, 34
  newspaper, 133

Cable television
  FCC limitations, 131
  growth of, 131
  local live programming, 131
  news operations, 131
  numbers of subscribers, 131
  use, 131-32
Caen, Herb, 49
Camera
  focusing of, 63
  quality required, 62
Capp, Al, 137
Cardozo, Benjamin (U.S. Supreme Court justice), 155
Carter's Little Liver Pills, advertisement of, 174
Causation. See Correlation
Chaldy, Bud (radio news director), 121-22
Channel, definition, in communication model, 12, 13
Checklist, publicity, 125-28
Chicago Daily News, 133, 135, 136
Chicago Sun-Times, 136
Chicago Tribune, 135
Children's Television Advertising Guidelines, 177
Children, viewing habits, 172
Christian Science Monitor, 107, 134
Chuck Wagon Dog Food, advertisement of, 176
Cinematographer, 122
Circulation, newspaper, 106, 109
City news wire associations, 137

Civil War, 143
Clarity, in journalism, 34
Clark, Frank (business manager, Register and Tribune Syndicate), 137
Coffee break, promotion of, 30
Cold War, and the press, 145
Colgate-Palmolive Company, advertising budget of, 85
Colliers, 144
Color
  negative, 65
  positive, 65
  print, 65
  slides, 124
  transparency, 65
Color story, 34
Columnists
  examples, 49
  relations with, 112
  semiprofessional, 52
Columns
  benefits, 51
  creation, 51
  defined, 49
  effectiveness, 50
  flourishing of, 49
  format, 54-56
  localizing, 53-54
  obligations associated with, 51
  personalizing, 53-54
  reader loyalty, 53, 112
  subjectivity in, 50
  suggestions for writing of, 51-54
  syndicated, 136-37
Comic strips, 137
Commission on Freedom of the Press, 150-51, 152, 155, 156
Commonweal, 114
Communication
  codes, 12
  flow of, 14
  Latin roots, 11
  model, 11-13
  process, 12
  in public relations process, 8
Communications Act of 1934, 129
Community Antenna Television (CATV). See Cable television
Congressional Directory, as reference, 29
Constitution, U.S., and press, 155
Consumer advertising, 86
Consumer concerns, 20
Consumer Magazine and Farm Publication Rates and Data, 115
Copperhead newspapers, 143
Copy, preparation of, 45-46
Correction notice, 6
Correlation, statistical, 31
Cosmopolitan, 144
Credulousness, in audiences, 174
Current Biography, as reference, 29
Current, differentiated from timely, 22

INDEX

Dana, Charles, A. (**N.Y. Sun** editor-publisher), 144
Data, distillation of, 32
Day, Benjamin (**N.Y. Sun** editor), 143
Deadlines, 5, 37, 135, 160
"Dear Abby" (newspaper column), 49
Declaration of Independence, 142
Democratic party, 22
Democratic process, operation in, 4
Department of Agriculture, 179
Depth report, 34
Des Moines
  Agnew speech, 149
  newspapers, 153
Des Moines Register and **Tribune,** 153
Dictionaries, unabridged, as reference, 29
Drawings. See also Artwork; Illustrations
  practicality of, 77
Dubuque Telegraph-Herald, 136

Easy-Off Oven Cleaner, advertisement of, 176
Editor and Publisher International Yearbook, 135, 136
Editorial
  as opinion, 34
  sources of, 133
Editorial writers, reading habits of, 114
Editors
  and accuracy, 160
  combat among, 143
  as "gatekeepers," 5
  magazine, 115-18
  New England, 142
  newspaper, 107-8, 111
El Al Israel Airlines, advertisement of, 176
Encoding, in Berlo S-M-C-R model, 12
Encyclopedias, as reference, 29
Errors
  correction, 6
  opportunities for, 160
"Establishment press," 153
Evaluation, in public relations process, 8, 13
Event, as base for story, 19

Fact-finding, in public relations process, 27
Facts on File, as reference, 29
Fair-minded approach, in reporting, 162
"Fairness Doctrine," 128-29, 130, 162-63
Farm Journal, 96
"Feature News and Picture Syndicate Directory," 136
Features
  definition, 40
  sources, 133
Feature stories
  advantages, 42
  on consumer difficulties, 19

distinguished from straight news, 34, 40
  editing, 40
  structure, 42
  uses, 40
Federal Communications Commission (FCC)
  and cable television, 131
  "Fairness Doctrine," 128-29, 130, 162-63
  limitations, 129-30
  regulatory functions, 125, 129, 162
Federalist party, 142
Federal Trade Commission (FTC), 173, 174-75, 177
Federal Trade Commission Act, 174, 175, 179
Feedback
  in advertising communications, 87
  in communication model, 12, 13, 14
Fenno, John (Federalist editor), 142
Film, motion picture, 65
First Amendment, 4, 130, 142, 150, 155, 156, 162
"Five W's and H," 35, 37, 42, 87
Flacks (press agents), 5
Ford Motor Company, advertising budget of, 85
Four Theories of the Press, 155-56
Frankfurter, Felix (U.S. Supreme Court Justice), 149
Franklin, Benjamin, 142, 144
Franklin, James (Benjamin's brother), 142
Freedom of press, 4, 141-42, 146-47, 155
Freedom of speech, 4
Free enterprise, 4
Freneau, Philip (anti-Federalist spokesman), 142

Garbage can, promotion of, 30
Garrison, William Lloyd (editor of **Liberator**), 143
"Gatekeepers"
  definition, 5, 16, 24
  values, 15
Gatekeeping, at source, 16
Gebbie House Magazine Directory, as reference, 115
General Foods Corporation, advertising budget, 85
General Motors Corporation, advertising budget, 85
Gerald, J. Edward (theorist on press freedom), 156
Geritol commercials, regulation, 174
Good Housekeeping, slant of, 116
Grammar, incorrect, 34
Graphic Artists Guild, 79
Great Depression, 145
Greeley, Horace, 143

Hacks, 5, 8
Hamilton, Alexander, 142

INDEX

Hamilton, Andrew (lawyer for John Peter Zenger), 142
Hand, Learned (judge), 149, 152
Harper's, influence of, 114
Harris, Benjamin (1690 publisher), 142
Harris, Sydney, 51, 52
Hearst Corporation, 136
Hearst, William Randolph, 135, 144
"Heloise" (newspaper column), 49
Hoover, Herbert (1920s Sec. of Agriculture), 129
Hoyt, James, 122
Human interest
  definition, 23
  examples, 24
  in feature story leads, 41

Illustration. **See also** Artwork
  decorative, 78
  descriptive, 77
  expense, 82
  expressive, 77
  in newsletters, 60
  production complexities, 82
Illustrators
  professional and free-lance, 78
  specialization of, 79
Image
  alteration, 30
  of political candidates, 31
Individuals, as gyroscopic organisms, 13
Industrial advertising, 86
Industry Consumer Affairs Professional Conference, 179
Information
  citizens' need, 35
  collection, 27, 42
  concise communication, 33
  major American source, 105
Institution, internal publics, 9
Interest, 21
International News Service, 135
International Telephone and Telegraph (ITT), 175
Inverted pyramid, 35, 37-38, 40
Iowa Daily Press Association, 137
Iowa Poll, 31
Iowa Radio Network, 121
ITT Continental Baking. **See** Wonder Bread

Jazz journalism, 145
Jefferson, Thomas, 142, 143, 157
Jones, Mary Gardiner (FTC commissioner), 173
Journalism
  jazz, 145
  reviews, 170
  style, 34
  yellow, 144
Journalists
  and accuracy, 160-61

  as "gatekeepers," 16
  writing characteristics, 34
Journal of Marketing, 175
Jungle, The, 144
J. Walter Thompson Company, 179

KASI Radio (Ames, Iowa), 121
Kaul, Donald (columnist), 49
Kelly, Walt ("Pogo" author), 137
King Features Syndicate, 136
Knight News Service, 134
KYUS-TV (Miles City, Montana), 124-25

Lacy, Dan (theorist, writer)
  on freedom of press, 156
  on news magazines, 152
Language, use, 43
Lasch, Robert (journalist), on monopolies, 152
Layout
  advertising, 90-94
  standard elements in, 90
  type selection, 91
Lead
  development, 36
  elements in, 35, 36, 37
  on feature story, 41
  human interest, 42
  summary, 35, 38
  types, 37
Levinstein, Morton, 89
Lewis, Boyd (former pres. Newspaper Enterprise Assoc.), 136
Libel
  causes, 165
  fundamentals, 166-67
Liberator (pre-Civil War protest paper), 143
Life, 145
"Lightning Rod Junior." **See** Bache, Benjamin Franklin
"Lil Abner" comic strip, 137
Lindstrom, Carl E., 153
Literacy, 5
Lithograph, 57
Logotype, 57
Look, 145
Los Angeles Times, 133
Los Angeles Times-Washington Post News Service, 134, 135
Lottery, 167, 169
Lovejoy, Elijah P. (pre-Civil War antislavery editor), 143
Luce, Henry R., 151

Magazine editors
  frustrations, 115-16
  multiple submissions to, 118
  queries to, 117
  relations with, 116
Magazines
  advertising rates, 100
  analysis, 114
  editors, 115

INDEX

growth of, 113
history, 144-45
as idea sources, 114
offices of, 114
as overlooked medium, 113
publicity opportunities in, 119
"slant" of, 116
study of content, 116
variety of, 113
writing rules for, 115
Mailer, Norman, 146
Malloy, Michael T., 171
Maps, 29
Marketing, advertising's role in, 86
Marketplace, of ideas, 6, 141, 155
Massachusetts Spy, 142
Mass media
 advertising, 28
 analyzing content of, 10
 columns, 49
 content, 19
 cooperation among, 47
 errors, 159
 feedback, 13
 "gatekeepers," 5
 monitoring, 10
 monopolistic ownership, 146, 156
 performance, 15, 170
 pictorial reports, 61
 and publicity, 4
 as reporters of government, 146
 reporting, 34
 responsibilities, 151, 165
 selection, 110
 societal dependence on, 165
 sophistication, 28
Max, Peter, 80
McCarthy, Joseph (senator), 145
McClure's, 144
McClure, Samuel Sydney, 136
Mean, statistical, 31
Media. **See** Mass media
Median, statistical, 31
Mediocrity, mass, 153
Merchandising, rules for, 27
Message
 alteration of, 15
 in communication model, 12
Midsummer Night's Dream (telecast), 154
Milline rate, 100
Minneapolis Star and **Tribune,** 153
Minority press cooperative bureaus, 137
Minow, Newton (former FCC chairman), 153
Mode, statistical, 31
Montgomery, Alabama, 149
Muckraking, 144

Nader, Ralph, 20, 174
National Advertising Division of Council on Better Business Bureaus, 176
National Advertising Review Board (NARB), 175-76
National Broadcasting Company (NBC), 122
National News Council, 170
National Observer, 107, 135, 171
National Press Council, 150
National Research Bureau, Inc., 115
Network, 95, 133
New-England Courant, 142
"New journalists," 146
News
 beats, 123
 composition, 27
 definition, 18
 recognition of, 24
 significance, 19, 20
 similarity of, 153
 situations, 34
Newsletters
 characteristics, 57, 58
 content, 60
 flexibility, 49
 illustrations in, 60
 nameplates, 57, 58
 popularity of, 57
 production, 57
 typography, 59
Newspaper Enterprise Association, 134, 136
Newspapers
 accessibility, 105
 advantages and disadvantages, 106-7
 as basic message vehicle, 105
 chain ownership, 111
 circulation, 105
 classification, 111
 content and capacity, 105-6
 copperhead, 143
 coverage, 106
 definition, 110-11
 market saturation of, 106
 monopolistic aspects, 106, 146
 nationally circulated, 107
 party, 142-43
 penny, 143-44
 publicity opportunities in, 111
 as sounding board, 111-12
 specialized, 110
 tabloid, 111
 technological improvements, 108-9, 111
 "underground," 110
 weekly and daily, 109-10
News peg, 19, 21
Newsperson, 27
News releases, 8, 17, 28, 105. **See also** News story; Press release; Publicity release
News services, 133-36. **See also** Wire services
News source
 radio and television, 123-24
 serving as, 15, 34

189

INDEX

News story. **See also** News release; Press release; Publicity release
  bases for arrangement, 38
  as communication model, 34
  conversation in, 44
  feature, 35
  interpretive, 34
  organization and structure, 37
  spot, 34, 35
  straight, 34, 35
  two forms of, 35
News value, 5, 18
Newsweek, 152, 155
Newswriting, 35
New York Daily News, 106, 107, 124, 135, 145
New Yorker, 78
New York Herald, 143, 144
New York Journal, 144
New York Sun, 143, 144
New York Times, 16, 107, 133, 134, 146, 149
New York Times Index, as reference, 29
New York Times News Service, 135
New York Tribune, 143, 144
New York Weekly Journal, 142
New York World, 144
Nixon, Richard M., resignation story of, 36
Nondaily newspapers, circulation, 109
Normal curve, 32
North American Newspaper Alliance, 134
N. W. Ayer and Son's Directory of Newspapers and Periodicals, 29, 30, 115

Objective approach, 161
Objectivity
  importance of, 39
  myth of pure, 161
  pride in, 5
  in reporting, 34, 161
  of wire services, 135
Offset printing, 57
Opinion polls, analysis of, 10
Outdoor advertising
  advantages and disadvantages, 98
  factors, 91

Paine, Thomas, 142, 143
Paragraph, length, 44
Paraphrases, 44
Party papers, 142-43
Patterson, Joseph Medill, 145
"Peanuts" comic strip, 137
Peg, news, 19, 21
Penny papers, 143-44
Percentile, 32
Peterson, Theodore, 155
Photographer, 62
Photographers' Association of America, 62

Photographs. **See also** Pictures
  contrast range of, 63
  mechanical and technical requirements, 63
  selection, 82
  subject matter, 62
  tonal separation, 63
Pica, 91
Pictures
  action and simplicity, 66
  background, 69-72
  clarity, 63
  composition, 63, 73-75
  costs, 62
  lighting, 72-73
  in mass communications, 61
  preparation for publication, 63-65
  reproduction, 63, 65
  "screening" of, 57
Picture wires, 124, 134
Planer, Ed (WMAQ-TV news director), 121-22
Playboy, and advertising, 173
"Pogo" comic strip, 137
Point, defined, 91
Policy establishment, in public relations process, 8, 11
Popular Mechanics, readers of, 115
Porcupine, Peter (William Cobbett), 143
Press
  criticism, 18, 20, 150
  duty, 19, 151
  excellence, 155
  in free society, 19
  as human institution, 141
  monopoly ownership, 152-53
  performance, 141, 146-47
  professionalism, 156
  as reflection of society, 150
  relations with, 161
  responsibilities, 159
  theories, 155-56
Press conference, arrangement, 28
Press councils, 150
Press release. **See also** News release; News story; Publicity release
  accuracy of, 5, 6
  definition, 4
  newspaper handling of, 108
  newsworthiness, 24
  requirements of, 5
  to syndicates, 137
Pressure group, 133
Pride and Prejudice, paperback copies of, 154
Prime time, advertising rates, 100
Privacy, right of, 167-68
Procter and Gamble, advertising budget, 85
Program planning, in public relations process, 8, 11
Prominence, in news stories, 23, 24
Promotional efforts, examples, 30

INDEX

Proofreaders, 160
Props, 66
Protestant ethic, 171
Proximity, in news stories, 22, 24
Publicists, 4, 5, 6, 27
Public image, 3
Publicity
  checklist for, 125-28
  definition, 3
  in democratic government, 3
  details of, 29
  free flow of, 4
  pictures, 62
  tools, 32
  training, 4
  uses, 30
Publicity release, 4, 38. See also News release; News story; Press release
Publick Occurrences, 142
Public opinion, measuring, 10
Public relations
  campaigns, 82
  counsel, 8
  definition, 3, 7
  ethical standards, 14
  management's role, 7
  model, 8
  policy, 11
  practitioner, 11
  process, 14, 27
  professionals, 7
  strategy, 13
  uses, 30
Publics
  attitudes, 10
  definition, 3, 8, 10
  diverse interests, 36
  internal and external, 9, 11, 57
  reactions, 7
Publishers Hall Syndicate, 136
Pulitzer, Joseph, 144
Pulitzer Prize, 134
Punched tape, 134, 153

Question-and-answer technique, story using, 34
Questionnaires, 32
Quotations, direct and indirect, 44

Radio Act of 1912, 129
Radio and television
  arrival of, 145
  general manger, 122
  governmental control, 128-30, 162-65
  job categories, 122-23, 126
  joint ownership and operation, 125
  licensing, 145
  news director, 122
  preparation of copy, 128
  publicity checklist for, 125-28
  sharing of news staffs, 125
  staff sizes, 122, 125
  stylebooks, 128
Radio stations, 124-25, 132

Radio-television networks, expenditures for news, 122
Raid Yard Guard Insecticide, advertisement of, 177
Random selection, 31
Rapid City (S.D.) **Journal,** 106
Reader's Digest, 96, 113, 114, 177
Reader's Guide to Periodical Literature, 28, 29
Receiver
  in communication model, 12, 13
  feedback, 14
  self-interest of, 13
"Red Lion" decision, 130
Ree Heights (S.D.) **Review,** 107
Regional wires, 134
Register and **Tribune** Syndicate, 137
Reid, Whitelaw (**N.Y. Tribune** editor-publisher), 144
Release form, photographic, 62
Reporters. See also Journalists
  cooperation with, 160
  wire service, 135
Reporting
  fair-minded approach to, 161-62
  of opinion and judgment, 163-65
Reporting forms, 43
Research, in public relations process, 8
Reuters wire service, 134
Review privilege, 160
Rewrite, 17
"Rip-and-read" stations, 123, 134
Rivers, William, 152
Rockwell, Norman, 80
Rolling Stone, 110
Roper Organization, Inc., The, 132
Royko, Mike, columnist, 49
"Rumor" game, 15, 16

Salespersons, 27
Sampling, for surveys, 10, 31
Saturday Evening Post, 145
Saturday Review, readers of, 115
Schick, advertisement for, 176
Schramm, Wilbur, 152, 155
Schulz, Charles M., 137
Scripps Company, 134
Scripps-Howard Newspaper Alliance, 134
Scripps-Howard Newspapers, 136
Sears Roebuck and Company, advertising budget of, 85
"Second day" stories, 22
Self-government, 6
Self-interest, in feature stories, 41, 42
Sentences, 43, 44
Shield laws, 167, 168-69
Shutter speeds, 63
Siebert, Fred, 155
Significance, 20, 24, 136
Sinclair, Upton, 144
"Sizzle," selling, 88
Slavery, abolition of, 143
S-M-C-R model, 12-13

Social Responsibility Theory, 156
Sounding boards, 10
Source
  for background information, 29, 32
  in communication model, 12
  of information for columnists, 52-53
  responsibilities of, 160-61
Spanish-American War, 144
Spelling, errors, 34
Standard deviation unit, 32
Standard Rate and Data, 29, 125
State press councils, 170
State wire, 136
Statistical Abstract of the United States, 29
Statistical scientific research, 31
Steffens, Lincoln, 144
Stone, Vernon, 122
"Stringers," 123
Successful Farming, 96, 115
Sunset House, advertisements for, 176
Surveys, instruments and uses, 32
Syndicates, 133, 136

Tabloid newspapers, 111
Tarbell, Ida M., 144
Teleprinters, 134
Telethons, 22
Teletype, 121, 133
Teletypesetter, 153
Television
  advertising, 95-96, 124, 130, 172-74
  news, 122-24, 132, 145
  stations, 124
Thomas, Isaiah (**Massachusetts Spy** editor), 142
Time, 30, 87, 96, 152
Time element
  in newsroom, 18
  in story preparation, 17
Timeliness
  definition, 21-22
  in story interest, 24
Times (London), 134
Toronto School of Theology, symposium site, 174
Trade advertising, 86
Tripp, Marion, 179
Truth, respect for, 34
Twentieth Century Fund, 150
Typesetters, 134
Type sizes, 91

"Underground" newspapers, 110
United Features Syndicate, 136
United Press, 135

United Press International, 107, 121, 123, 133, 134, 153
United States Supreme Court, 128, 130, 162, 167
University of Wisconsin-Madison, radio-TV survey, 122
Unusualness, 23, 24
Usage, in journalism, 34
U.S. News and World Report, 152
Ute (Iowa) **Independent,** 124

Van Buren, Abigail, 51. **See also** "Dear Abby"
Variablility, statistical, 31
Variety, 172
Video Display Terminal, 134, 135
Vietnam, 145

Wall Street Journal, 107
Wangchuck, Jigme Singhi (Dragon King of Bhutan), story about, 28
Warner-Lambert Pharmaceutical, advertising budget of, 85
Washingon, George, 142
Washington Post, 87, 133, 146, 149
Watergate, 134, 145
Watts, 18
WCBS-TV, 124-25
Webster, Noah, 143
Weekly newspapers, 109-10
White, Byron, 130
White, David Manning, 154
Who's Who in America, as reference, 28, 29
Wirephoto services, 134
Wire services
  bureaus, 133
  history, 135
  numbers of users, 135
  reduced numbers, 146
  speeds, 135
WMAQ-TV, 122
Wolfe, Tom, 146
Woman's Day, 96
Wonder Bread, ad campaign regulation, 174-75
Words, choice of, 43
World War I, 145
Writer, The, 115
Writer's Digest, 115
Writer's Handbook, The, 115
Writer's Market, The, 114, 115

Yearbooks, 29
Yellow journalism, 144

Zenger, John Peter, 142